Russia and America

We live in a wondrous time, in which the strong is weak because of his scruples and the weak grows strong because of his audacity.

Otto von Bismarck

Russia and America
The Asymmetric Rivalry

Andrei P. Tsygankov

polity

First published in 2019 by Polity Press

Polity Press
65 Bridge Street
Cambridge CB2 1UR, UK

Polity Press
101 Station Landing
Suite 300
Medford, MA 02155, USA

ISBN-13: 978-1-5095-3113-4
ISBN-13: 978-1-5095-3114-1(pb)

A catalogue record for this book is available from the British Library.

Library of Congress Cataloging-in-Publication Data
Names: Tsygankov, Andrei P., 1964- author.
Title: Russia and America : the asymmetric rivalry / Andrei P. Tsygankov.
Description: Medford, MA : Polity Press, [2019] | Includes bibliographical
   references and index. |
Identifiers: LCCN 2019007297 (print) | LCCN 2019020344 (ebook) | ISBN
   9781509531165 (Epub) | ISBN 9781509531134 (hardback) | ISBN 9781509531141
   (pbk.)
Subjects: LCSH: United States--Relations--Russia (Federation) | Russia
   (Federation)--Relations--United States. | Geopolitics--Russia (Federation)
   | Security, International.
Classification: LCC E183.8.R9 (ebook) | LCC E183.8.R9 T885 2019 (print) | DDC
   327.73047086--dc23
LC record available at https://lccn.loc.gov/2019007297

Typeset in 10 on 16.5 Utopia Std by Servis Filmsetting Ltd, Stockport, Cheshire
Printed and bound in Great Britain by TJ International Limited

For further information on Polity, visit our website:
politybooks.com

Contents

Preface

I began writing about US-Russia relations some fifteen years ago. When my book *Russophobia: Anti-Russian Lobby and American Foreign Policy* was published in 2009, I was hopeful that the two countries could overcome the divisive politics of the past and be guided by considerations of mutual national interest and global stability. Unfortunately, after a brief period of trying to engage in dialogue during 2009–10, relations between America and Russia entered an era of crisis from which they have not been able to find a path toward dialogue and cooperation. Both countries now frequently resort to accusations and ultimatums, eschewing diplomacy and honest discussion. The thin layer of trust that had existed in US-Russia relations has now all but evaporated.

As academics, the main thing we can do to contribute to the world's peace is to write good books and teach good students. I have been trying to do both and was happy to respond to Polity's invitation to write a book about Russia and America. When the publisher approached me, I had been teaching a course on Russia and the world order and thinking about the global changes that have affected Russia's relations with the United States. My courses and students remain a source of energy and inspiration. Most of my work is connected to or has grown out of the courses that I am privileged to teach at San Francisco State University.

My other source of ideas includes the scholars and intellectuals with whom I have been fortunate to interact and discuss some of my thoughts at various meetings, conferences, and forums. Many people in America, Europe, Russia, and China deserve credit for engaging me in stimulating conversations, inviting me to conferences, and helping me formulate the ideas expressed in this book.

Several reviewers of the book offered multiple suggestions on how it might be improved. Some of these – hopefully the best ones – I have utilized in producing the final draft.

My publisher Louise Knight has been very encouraging throughout the process, and provided excellent advice on softening my prose and improving the book's structure and content. I also thank Sophie Wright, Tim Clark, and everyone else at Polity responsible for the book's editing, production, design, and appearance. Matthew Tarver-Wahlquist provided editorial assistance and helped with proofreading the text. Needless to say none of the above-mentioned is responsible for the book's content or any errors it may contain.

Parts of several chapters draw on portions of my previously published works: *Russophobia* (Palgrave, 2009), *Russia and the West from Alexander to Putin* (Cambridge University Press, 2012), *The Strong State in Russia* (Oxford University Press, 2014), "Vladimir Putin's Last Stand," *Post-Soviet Affairs* 31:4 (2015); *Russia's Foreign Policy*, 4th edition (Rowman & Littlefield, 2016), "Relations with the United States," in Stephen Wegren, ed. *Putin's Russia* (Rowman & Littlefield, 2018), and *The Dark Double* (Oxford University Press, 2019). I would like to thank the publishers for permission to use these materials.

Finally, and as always, I wish to thank my family in Russia and America for their love and support and for simply being who they are. I dedicate this book to them, to my friends, and to all those open to dialogue whatever their political viewpoint. Even though this book is about power, it is also about ideas, the potential for dialogue, and the hope of a better future.

In transliterating names from the Russian, I have used "y" to denote "ы", ' to denote "ь" and "ъ", "yu" to denote "ю", "ya" to denote "я", "i" to denote "й" and "ий", "iyi" to denote double "и", "e" to denote "э", "kh" to denote "x", "zh" to denote "ж", "ts" to denote "ц", "ch" to denote "ч", "sh" to denote "ш", and "sch" to denote "щ". I have also used "Ye" to distinguish the sound of "e" (such as "Yevropa") at the beginning of a word from that in the middle of a word (such as "vnesh-nei"). I have not distinguished between "e" and "ё". Original spelling is retained in quotations.

1

Rivals, Not Enemies

Ever since Donald Trump's unexpected rise to power, the 2016 US presidential election has become the lens through which to view US-Russia relations. Many in the West believe that Russia interfered in the electoral process by hacking the Democratic National Convention's emails and promoting Trump on social media. Few have questioned the fact of Moscow's interference. While disputing its extent, politicians, experts, and journalists alike have overwhelmingly accepted it as reality. Even those who reject this consensus view agree that the election became a critically important event which continues to profoundly affect relations between the two countries.

This book seeks to understand how Russia's foreign policy has changed since Vladimir Putin's return to presidency in 2012, and how that change has contributed to a new conflict with America. I argue that Russia's goals and its means to achieve them should be understood in the context of an international transition toward a post-Western and multipolar world. The events of 2016 were crucial in making such transition irreversible. The West's lack of recognition of Russia's interests culminated in the conflict over Ukraine's 2014 Euromaidan revolution, and compelled the Kremlin to take unprecedented steps in defense of its perceived interests, including annexing Crimea, supporting Ukrainian separatists, and intervening in the political and media spaces of the United States and several other Western countries. Although historically the essential drivers of Russia's international actions had to do with the protection of its geographically limited national interests, Moscow was now prepared to defend those interests in an increasingly aggressive and global fashion. The United States' dismissiveness toward the Kremlin's complaints, Russia's preoccupation with security and great power status, and Vladimir Putin's character have all caused US-Russia relations to deteriorate to the point of what both sides acknowledge is an 'all-time low'.

Russia and America

Contemporary Russia and America are competitors rather than partners on most international issues. The Kremlin has challenged US hegemony both globally and in regional settings. Cooperation has become more difficult, while conflicts between the two countries have grown more intense, widened in scope, and taken on new dimensions. What in the 1990s was a disagreement over the nature of European security has developed into a rivalry over multiple regional and global issues, including the Middle East, Asia, nuclear and cyber security, energy, and values.

This progressive worsening of US-Russia relations has evolved through several cycles.[1] Following the early 1990s reforms in Russia, and attempts to establish cooperative international relations in Europe, the United States adopted the policy of expanding NATO eastward, excluding Russia from the process. Moscow responded by pursuing policies of integrating the former Soviet states under Russia's leadership, and strengthening ties with China, India, and other non-Western states.

The arrival of Vladimir Putin as Russia's new president in spring 2000 was the beginning of another cycle in the country's attempts to improve relations with the United States. Following the terrorist attacks on the US in September 2001, Russia sought to establish itself as a reliable partner in fighting terrorism globally, and, on that basis, to strengthen its economic and political ties with the West. However, already in the first half of 2003, the initially positive dynamics in US-Russia relations began to reverse as new tensions appeared, pushing the two sides toward conflict. In addition to the continued expansion of NATO, the United States declined negotiations over nuclear security by unilaterally withdrawing from the ABM Treaty. In May 2003, the US also invaded Iraq, over the opposition of Russia, France, Germany, and several other countries. In the meantime, Washington supported regime change in countries neighboring Russia, grew critical of the latter's political system as increasingly authoritarian, and supported energy projects that undermined Moscow's clout in Europe and Eurasia.

Responding to these moves, the Kremlin challenged US priorities in Europe, the Middle East, the nuclear arena, and democracy promotion. Russia launched a program of military modernization, sought to strengthen its position in global energy markets, and adopted policies to limit Western influence inside the country. In August 2008, following Georgia's military attack on South Ossetia and the deployment of Russian peacekeepers in the area, the Kremlin invaded Georgia. By defeating the army of a US ally in the region, Russia signaled that it was no longer prepared to accept the above-listed policies of the United States.

In 2009 the two countries made yet another attempt to establish cooperative relations. As with the two previous efforts, this one also failed. US president Barack Obama began his term in office by trying to "reset" relations with Russia, despite its intervention in Georgia, while Russia's new president Dmitry Medvedev demonstrated an openness to America's new approach. The two countries sought to leave behind their disagreements by signing a new START agreement and cooperating on several other issues. But the old concerns about European and Middle Eastern security, the US missile defense system, and democracy promotion continued to negatively affect relations. From the Kremlin's perspective, the United States, by refusing to negotiate over European security, meddling in Russia's domestic affairs, and intervening in the Middle East to preserve its global power, demonstrated that it still did not take Russia's concerns seriously.

These disagreements culminated in the Ukraine crisis that ended the third cycle and led to a new US-Russia conflict. Washington supported a regime change in Kiev that Moscow labelled as an "anticonstitutional coup." The subsequent Russian annexation of Crimea and support for Eastern Ukrainian separatists resulted in US-initiated Western sanctions against the Russian economy. The severity of the new crisis and the two sides' insistence on the legitimacy of their respective actions promised a prolonged period of rivalry, eliminating any prospect of another attempt at normalization or "reset."

The election of Donald Trump as US president in November 2016 served to consolidate these negative trends and became a lightning rod for fresh condemnations of Russia by Western leaders. The Kremlin's initially high hopes for normalizing relations with America soon evaporated, Trump's declared intention to strengthen ties with Moscow notwithstanding. The election caused a deterioration of the US-Russia relationship beyond expectations, adding the issue of Russian meddling in American domestic affairs to the already extensive list of disagreements. After US intelligence agencies concluded that Russia had indeed intervened in the US presidential election,[2] the issue became central to the new internal struggle between Trump and the Washington establishment. Russia's cyber activities, military strategy, and media role have come under particular scrutiny, with multiple investigations, hearings, and reports seeking to uncover the Kremlin's true intentions and capabilities.

In this climate, relations reached a new low during 2017. The US House of Representatives' approved a new package of sanctions against Russia, Iran and North Korea; both sides expelled diplomats and closed several diplomatic facilities; tensions erupted over Ukraine, the Middle East, North Korea, and the poisoning of British citizen Sergei Skripal and his daughter; and there were mutual accusations concerning nuclear treaty violations and the growing use of cyber weapons. In response to these developments, the United States and other Western governments imposed new sanctions against Russian officials and state-connected businesses, and sixty Russian diplomats were expelled from the United Kingdom and other European countries. The meetings between American and Russian leaders that took place in 2017 and 2018 were non-confrontational and business-like, yet did not result in agreements. Indeed, each such meeting generated a highly negative domestic reaction from the American political class and led to new US sanctions against Russia's officials and economy.

Is Russia launching a new Cold War?

Many observers describe the US-Russia conflict as a revived Cold War that is set to define the two sides' relations. The narrative of a new Cold War commands attention in political and scholarly circles. Critics of Russia tend to blame it for its non-democratic values and great power "revisionism." For instance, the former US Ambassador to Russia Michael McFaul presents the current relations with Russia as a new ideological struggle between democracy and autocracy.[3] Other observers, including Robert Legvold, document erroneous expectations and policies on both sides. While acknowledging that the contemporary era is different in many respects, Legvold points to similarities with the early stages of the Cold War (1948–1953), including a dangerous polarizing rhetoric and zero-sum perception on both sides, as well as potentially devastating global outcomes.[4] Even those sympathetic to Russia's position, such as Stephen Cohen, describe the new US-Russia relationship as a Cold War.[5] These analysts place responsibility for the conflict on the United States' insensitivity to Russia's interests and concerns, and not surprisingly Russian analysts frequently argue a similar case. Sergei Karaganov and Dmitri Suslov, for example, accuse the United States of attempting to impose the framework of a global Cold War on Russia and China for the purpose of weakening them as potential competitors.[6]

As compelling as it may seem to some observers, however, the Cold War framework is misleading. It fails to grasp the nature of the contemporary world and Russia's objectives in it. The current global context differs from that of the Cold War in several crucial ways. Most importantly, the Cold War narrative fails to address the global power shift and transitionary nature of the contemporary international system. In today's world, the old ideological dichotomy between communism and capitalism is no longer applicable. Rather, the competition now takes place in a global information space and is predominantly between liberal and nationalist ideas about how to regulate the economy and the political system. While in the eyes of many the West continues to represent liberalism, the realities of Brexit, Trump, and tightening migration regulations in the European Union demonstrate the global appeal of nationalist ideas.[7] The struggle between nationalism and liberal globalism is now intensifying within the West. Trump's proclaimed intention to reduce America's military obligations abroad and engage in economic protectionism signify major departures from both the Cold War and post-Cold War globalization. On the other hand, China, Russia, and other allegedly autocratic and nationalist polities continue to favor the preservation of a liberal global economy, opposing both regional autarchy and Trumpian protectionist policies.

As a result of this new global context, new expectations about the international system and state behavior within it are gradually being formed. The West initiated the post-Cold War globalization yet its rules of basic economic openness created the conditions for the rise of non-Western competitors. China, Russia, India, Turkey, Iran, and others are seeking to carve out a space for themselves in the newly emerging international system, just as the United States is struggling to redefine its place and identity in the new world. These changes have altered the position of the only superpower in the international system. Structurally, it is still the familiar world of American military, political, and economic domination. Yet dynamically the world is moving away from its US- and West-centeredness,[8] even though the exact direction and end point of this trajectory remains unclear.

In order to take advantage of the new opportunities, many non-Western countries are developing their own rules and arrangements in the world.[9] Russia and other non-Western countries increasingly have international options they never had before, as new global and regional institutions and areas of development outside the influence of the West gradually emerge. This does not always entail international confrontation. Most non-Western nations are not looking to challenge the superpower directly, and they continue to take advantage of ties with the West. A US-balancing coalition or a genuine alternative to the West-centered world has not yet emerged. Unlike in previous eras, the contemporary world lacks a rigid alliance structure. The so-called Russia-China-Iran axis is far from definitively formed, and exists largely in the minds of American neoconservatives and Russia-conspiracy-minded thinkers. International coalitions continue to overlap and are mostly formed on an ad hoc basis depending on issues of interest.

Under these global conditions, Russia's motives differ from those of the Soviet Union during the Cold War in significant ways. Although Russia is engaged in a rivalry with America, the Kremlin's main foreign policy aspiration is to benefit from the global shift of power and economic dynamism toward China and other non-Western nations. Unlike the USSR, contemporary Russia has no ideologically compelling reason to seek the destruction of the United States. Rather, as a number of observers pointed out, the Kremlin's objective has been to gain recognition and negotiate a larger space and great power status within the still largely Western-influenced global order.[10]

Following the Ukraine crisis in 2014, Russia's goals have also included the formation of non-Western international institutions and economic relations in response to the West's efforts to isolate Russia through sanctions and political pressure. But this was a second-best strategic option for gaining global recognition after it became clear that the preferred strategy of cooperation with America and other Western countries was no longer available. To a considerable extent, Russia's assertive behavior in Ukraine, Syria, and in cyber and information space can be explained by the Kremlin's desire to challenge its rival for the purpose of gaining respect and recognition as a great power with distinct interests in Eurasia and elsewhere. If achieving that goal entails a major revision of America's assumed role in the international system, then the Kremlin—in partnership with other powers—is prepared to lead the world to such an outcome. If anything, the situation may be reminiscent of the non-ideological great power rivalry in eighteenth- and nineteenth-century Europe. At that time, Britain, France, Russia, and other powers competed to preserve and enhance their respective influence in world politics. This time, however, the rivalry takes place in a global context with the participation of China, Russia, the United States, and others.

The drive to gain recognition as a great power explains what Russia wanted to accomplish by interfering in the 2016 US presidential campaign. Rather than aiming to get Trump elected, the Kremlin—to the extent that it was involved in coordinating various activities, from hacking the Democratic Party to posting pro-Trump ads on social media—wanted to gain some leverage in its dealings with the expected future president, Hillary Clinton. As I was conducting interviews with leading foreign policy experts in Moscow during the summer of 2016, the overwhelming majority of them shared two beliefs: Trump was going to lose and Hillary would be bad news for Russia. My interviewees saw Clinton as a hard-liner who was prepared to go beyond the sanctions policy initiated by Obama and escalate the conflict with Russia in several additional areas. Clinton had publicly compared Putin to Hitler, challenged the Eurasian Economic Union as a Russian neo-imperial project, proposed to establish a no-fly zone in Syria, and advocated providing Ukraine with lethal weapons and other forms of assistance. The Kremlin therefore concluded that there was little, if anything, to be gained from a Clinton presidency in terms of a balancing of distinct interests, and that the best tactic was therefore to demonstrate its power as a prelude to future bilateral negotiations.

Not only do Russia's motives differ from those of the USSR during the Cold War, but so do its power capabilities. It is in no position to challenge America and other Western nations globally, given the large—and in some areas widening—gap between Western and Russian power. Russia therefore does not seek to directly confront or defeat the other side; rather, its asymmetric capabilities are applied on a limited scale and for defensive purposes. When the Chief of the

Russian General Staff Valery Gerasimov first described the so-called hybrid war, some analysts understood this as a template for an offensive military strategy. His point, however, was that the West was already engaged in such a war against Russia and that Russia had to be better prepared for this new type of conflict.[11] Asymmetric power is selective and targets the competitor's most vulnerable areas. It is designed to put on alert and disorient, rather than achieve a decisive victory.[12]

Sensitive to this asymmetry, Dmitry Trenin has described Russia-West relations as a hybrid war characterized by "the huge inequality between the two principal antagonists, [and] the absence of a clear divide as there are no Berlin walls, no Iron Curtains," only the dynamism of competition in multiple areas on multiple issues.[13] Another analyst, Michael Kofman, defines the new Russian strategy in relations with the West as "raiding," or a series of operations to deny the stronger side a victory or "the opportunity to reinforce," followed by surprise attacks and withdrawal.[14]

Overlooking these differences between today's world and that of the Cold War era, the Cold War narrative misunderstands Russia's potential for both rivalry and cooperation with the United States and other Western countries. Their asymmetric rivalry does not exclude the possibility of Russia and the Western powers cooperating in some areas (such as nuclear non-proliferation, counter-terrorism, cyber issues) and regions (e.g. the Middle East and North Korea), while perceiving each other as competitors when it comes to the preferred rules and structure of the international system. In an increasingly fragmented world, Russia and the West may move beyond viewing each other predominantly as rivals if they can learn to focus on issues of common concern and find a way to reframe their values and interests in non-confrontational terms.

The rhetoric of the Cold War narrative, like any war rhetoric, has dangerous normative implications. By stressing conflict and escalation it has the potential to take on a discursive power that turns the US-Russia conflict into a self-fulfilling prophecy. Scholars and pundits are also citizens and have a responsibility to imagine a better world by researching the conditions for international cooperation and proposing joint solutions. A better world would be one in which America and Russia not only compete but also cooperate, and do so within the bounds of global rules.

World order transition

Rather than following the new Cold War narrative, this book develops an explanation of Russia's policy toward the United States that stresses changes in the balance of global power as well as national perceptions. The world order is undergoing a transition from the US-centered international system that emerged after the Cold War to a system in which the United States will have a diminished role and capacity. Any international order will be characterized by rules of behavior among major powers that reflect their ideas of justice and material capabilities.[15] Such rules typically concern these powers' perceived balance of forces, spheres of influence, and domestic political organization. World order transition begins when the power(s) responsible for enforcing international rules are challenged in their ability to do so by rising dissatisfied states. While remaining the most powerful nation, the United States is already in the process of retreating from the position of a superpower capable of unilaterally imposing international rules and principles. In order to preserve relative peace and stability in the world, Washington will increasingly come to depend on the support of other powers.

This change, however, is not currently accompanied by adequate perceptions on the part of Russian and US elites. Material capabilities, especially in times of transition, are rarely perceived accurately, with major powers more commonly tending to overestimate their abilities. In Russia, the idea of a great power that refuses to compromise on its sovereignty and independence has long historical roots, and it survived the end of the Cold War. Despite the breakup of the Soviet Union and the economic weakness that followed during the 1990s, Russia continued to believe in itself as a great power and desired to be recognized as such by the outside world. As the country's second Foreign Minister, Yevgeni Primakov, stated immediately following his appointment to the post, "Russia has been and remains a great power, and its policy toward the outside world should correspond to that status."[16]

Partly because of this obsession with status, Moscow failed to accurately assess the United States' role in the emerging international system, having assumed the appearance of a "multipolar" world since the late 1990s. Russia's foreign policy has frequently been based on an incorrect reading of US intentions; for example, the Kremlin assessed Trump's election victory as reflecting an irreversible decline of American power and expected the new president to reorient US foreign policy toward Russia by lifting sanctions and cooperating with Moscow on various international issues. In the event, however, Trump was rendered largely incapable of acting due to the internal opposition to his policy and the investigation into "collusion" with Russia launched against him by Congress and Special Investigator Robert Mueller. In addition, the US economy continued to grow and the United States maintained its capacity to strongly influence global and regional political developments. Finally, non-Western countries such as China, India, and others have not been as active in building the foundations for a multipolar international system, and remain eager to build economic and political relations with the United States.

The US political class has also succumbed to inaccurate perceptions of American and Russian power. American leaders and politicians often assumed that their country would remain an unchallenged global leader, and that without such leadership the world would be destabilized. They therefore expected Russia to accept the US role. As Angela Stent observes, Washington's aim was to position Russia as a junior partner supportive of America's global values and interests. Moscow, however, insisted on the legitimacy of its own interests and principles even from a position of weakness, but the White House failed to acknowledge this to the extent that Russia expected.[17] Each time, the US either didn't understand Russia's claims to equality and respect, or found them to be unreasonable.

Just as the Russians did not adjust their concept of power in the 1990s, the Americans failed to notice important changes in the world in the second half of the 2000s. While identifying themselves as "indispensable," "exceptional," and standing "taller than other nations," US officials frequently dismissed Russia as a major power, referring to it in condescending and disrespectful terms. Scholars and policy makers assumed that Russia's internal difficulties—such as corruption, slow economic growth, and ongoing demographic problems—would prevent it from acting as a great power and effectively protecting its national interests abroad. Reflecting the conventional wisdom, President Obama publicly referred to Russia as a "regional power that is threatening some of its immediate neighbors not out of strength but out of weakness."[18]

In the meantime, while hardly a match for the US in terms of overall material capabilities, Russia continued to develop its power and ability to challenge the United States. It has established multiple economic, political, and military relations with non-Western powers and strengthened its capacity to undermine US policy globally by engaging in asymmetrical rivalry. This has been made possible in part thanks to globalization, which allows for a mobility and a concentration of resources not previously possible. Russia's methods include the selective use of media and information technology, cyber power, hybrid military intervention, and targeted economic sanctions. The Kremlin has taken its assertive foreign policy to a new level by demonstrating its ability to project power across continents, as it did in Syria, effectively dispelling the common perception that as the weaker party it will have to accommodate the United States. Russia's Concept of Foreign Policy signed by Putin on November 30, 2016 stressed the importance of defending the country's priorities in the context of new international challenges and attempts by the United States to preserve its global dominance. The document announced that Russia "does not recognize the US policy of extraterritorial jurisdiction beyond the boundaries of international law" and reserves "the right to firmly respond to hostile actions, including the bolstering of national defense and taking retaliatory or asymmetrical measures."[19]

Globally speaking, Russia remains a defensive power aware of its responsibility for maintaining international stability. It wants to work with, not against, the other major powers. As such, Moscow's insistence on Western recognition of its own interests must not be construed as a drive to destroy the foundations of the international order, such as sovereignty, multilateralism, and arms control. At the same time, Russia is actively challenging what it views as a system of American domination at the expense of international law, an equitable distribution of power, and respect for cultural and civilizational diversity.

In the current world order transition, then, there is the potential for both rivalry and cooperation in US-Russian relations. During the

Cold War, the symmetric nature of the confrontation between the two nations often excluded any cooperation between them. Today's world is different and raises possibilities for both rivalry and cooperation depending on the issue. However difficult cooperation may be, it has taken place with respect to negotiations over START, counter-terrorism, and the non-proliferation of nuclear weapons. Russia and the United States have previously agreed on steps to prevent the development of a nuclear program in Iran. They have been able to coordinate some of their policies with respect to Syria and North Korea, even during very tense periods in the relationship. Such cooperation has been possible where the two sides have agreed on the source of a mutual threat posed to them and where their power potential was no longer sufficient for either to assert their favored approach unilaterally. While being defined by significant disagreements on status and the preferred world order, US-Russia power relations unfold in diverse geographic, material, and ideational settings. These relations differ depending on the issue, often pushing the two sides toward rivalry, but in some cases leaving room for their cooperation.

The book's organization

The book provides a detailed analysis of the themes and issues introduced above. Chapter 2 discusses the notion of world order transition as it affects US-Russia relations, reviewing the relevant historical cases in the terms of their post-war rules, power structures, and the degree to which the organizing states included the defeated powers. I argue that the post-Cold War Washington system defined by US hegemony is historically reminiscent of the post-Crimean War Paris system. The Washington system treated (Soviet) Russia as a defeated party even though Russia did not quite qualify as such. The Cold War differed from previous great power wars in multiple ways, and it ended not with the defeat and surrender of one side but as a result of mutually advantageous negotiations. Russia played a key role in ending the Cold War, yet the new international system did not seek to incorporate it in the way the Vienna system had incorporated post-Napoleonic France. At the same time, the Washington system differed from those of Versailles and Yalta by not imposing reparations on the "defeated" state, let alone dismemberment. The chapter places US-Russia developments and the contemporary world order transition up to the end of Obama's presidency in this theoretical and historical context.

Chapter 3 analyzes US-Russia relations following the election of Trump and explains these relations in terms of the two sides' worldviews, perceptions, power capabilities, and domestic politics. It argues that, while Putin's and Trump's worldviews are similar and guided by great power nationalism, their perceptions of status and domestic institutional settings are profoundly different. The United States continues to view itself as an "indispensable" and hegemonic power not dependent on cooperation with Russia. Due to Russia's severely damaged reputation within the US establishment, Trump, who initially expressed a preference for "getting along" with Russia, has lost the freedom of action in policy dealings with the Kremlin. In the meantime, Russia has developed a toolkit of asymmetric capabilities for challenging US policies across the world.

Chapters 4–6 then explore the US-Russia rivalry in regional settings. Chapter 4 argues that, while European power distribution is not in Russia's favor, the Kremlin possesses formidable asymmetric capabilities with respect to Ukraine and the Eastern/Central European region. By exploiting these capabilities and its geographic proximity, Russia has been able to undermine the Ukrainian state and prevent it from joining European institutions. Western sanctions have had the effect of discouraging an escalation of the Russia-Ukraine dispute, yet have failed to reverse the Kremlin's principal course of action. The US and Russia remain divided by their perception of the power balance and are not ready for a compromise in solving the crisis. Until such perceptions change, the room for cooperation will be limited.

The Middle East demonstrates a different power dynamic. Increasingly, Western powers including the United States are disengaging from the region, creating a vacuum to be filled by non-Western powers. Chapter 5 examines how Russia effectively exploited this advantage by intervening in Syria and strengthening its presence in the Middle East at the expense of the US. While prospects for stabilizing the region are remote, Russia's intervention has demonstrated its status as a major power and negotiations' broker. The more Washington comes to terms with the limitations of its power in the region, the more it will be prepared to engage in limited cooperation regarding a political settlement and reconstruction in Syria. In addition, the US and Russia have a mutual interest in reducing the capabilities of radical terrorist organizations in the broader region.

Chapter 6 considers the case of Asia and Central Asia. Here, Moscow has developed a strong partnership with China, which has weakened the US ability to influence economic and political developments in the region, hastening a decline that has been evident since the mid-2000s. If the US chooses to work toward reversing this trend, the potential for rivalry with Russia will only increase. This, however, is less likely as the region is increasingly defined by local powers including Russia, China, Turkey, and Iran.

Chapters 7–9 analyze global developments in US-Russia relations. Chapter 7 reviews the two countries' rivalry in the area of values and information. This rivalry is likely to remain intense because each side sees the other's values as threatening, and because both remain convinced of the power of their own media and information capabilities. Both engage in assertive propaganda and information manipulation, presenting the other as threatening, uncooperative, and lacking in moral values. The two countries' value systems are not fundamentally antagonistic in the way they were during the Cold War, yet they have come into conflict due to intensified interstate competition.

The rivalry in relation to nuclear and cyber issues documented in Chapter 8 also has its roots in the two sides' perceived power and deterrent capacity. However, as intense as it may be, this rivalry has the potential to subside due to both countries recognizing the potential for it to spin out of control. Unfortunately, for such recognition to be consolidated, additional crises in the relationship may need to occur.

Finally, Chapter 9 describes the United States' attempts to gain a greater share of control in energy markets and Russia's efforts to preserve its status as a major energy supplier to Europe and other regions. The countries remain divided by perceptions of energy security and the assessment of their own capabilities. This rivalry will continue as long as the US strives to gain the status of an energy power and seeks to limit that of Russia, while the Kremlin continues to rely on important levers and supporters of its energy policy in Europe and beyond.

The conclusion summarizes the analysis by bringing together its common themes and implications. In an increasingly fragmented and decentralized world, rivalry and cooperation are themselves becoming fragmented and issue-based. In this context, cooperation with Russia is more difficult but no less important; indeed it is highly desirable. Such cooperation also remains possible given that the United States in particular and Western nations in general continue to possess significant material and ideational influence. For such influence to be used effectively, however, American attempts to pressure Russia through containment and political confrontation must be replaced by selective engagement and a recognition of Russian concerns and interests. For not only does Russia have such concerns, it also possesses a wide range of asymmetric tools for protecting its interests in the world.

As difficult as it might be for the United States and Western nations to accept, there is no realistic alternative to engaging Russia in a joint effort to stabilize the situation globally as well as in various regions, including Ukraine and Europe more widely. Any new policy must be based on an understanding that the Kremlin's "revisionism" is in part a reaction to the West's refusal to recognize Russia as a potential partner. The alternative to a new cooperative engagement is not a compliant Russia, but a continued degradation of regional and global security.

2

The World Order Transition

The contemporary world order is in flux. Scholars disagree as to whether the global political system is in the process of collapse or restructuring. Politicians are also highly ambivalent about the future of world politics. Some expect a return of the "liberal" world order that emerged after the Cold War, while others view that order as historically contingent and unfit to meet the new challenges. For example, during his speech at the United Nations on September 25, 2018, Donald Trump took the opportunity to proclaim the end of the globalization era and announce the victory of his America First philosophy.[1] Even some of those opposed to Trump now recognize that his approach to world affairs has prevailed and that the future world order will never be the same. In Robert Kagan's analysis, the old consensus about America as the upholder of global security and free trade has collapsed in both US political parties.[2]

This chapter discusses the idea of a changing world order by reviewing relevant historical parallels and placing US-Russia relations in the context of international developments before and after the Cold War. Although Russia's foreign policy is frequently viewed as revisionist, the Kremlin has not challenged the global institutions and the UN-based decision-making mechanism established following World War Two. Nor did Moscow begin to seriously challenge the US-centered post-Cold War order until some fifteen years after it had emerged. For a considerable period of time, Russia tried to persuade the West of its importance through a series of cycles that moved from hope and cooperation to frustration and conflict.

The United States saw itself as the winner of the Cold War and wanted Russia to accept new international norms and principles that favored the US. Although Washington did not treat Moscow the way some previous victorious powers had treated defeated countries, it refused to accommodate Russia as a co-founder and full participant in the new international order. It was only a matter of time before a dissatisfied and increasingly resentful Moscow would claim what it viewed as its rightful place at the global table. The current world order transition began when Russia directly challenged American rules and the United States lost the ability to enforce them. This transition began years before Trump was elected, and can be traced to Russia's use of force against the US satellite state Georgia in August 2008.

Orders and transitions in world politics

World orders

World orders are based on norms and principles that regulate relations among major powers. These norms and principles typically reflect the ideas of justice and the material capabilities held by such powers. Although neither a consensus on legitimacy nor a balance of forces forecloses competition or confrontation, world orders regulate international relations and serve to reduce conflicts and uncertainty.[3] Norms and principles provide key actors with clarity and rules of behavior regarding at least three important dimensions—distribution of forces, sphere of influence, and freedom to organize domestic systems. More inclusive orders extend recognition to all major states, granting them sufficient power, influence, and internal sovereignty. Less inclusive orders deny such recognition to some prominent participants.

World orders rise and fall in response to the changing distribution of international power and the ambitions of some states to exceed the status granted to them by the system. Such orders are typically established following a major war in order to prevent the emergence of a new threat from a revisionist state.[4] A transition from one order to another begins when those responsible for enforcing international norms and principles no longer have the capacity to maintain order in response to challenges posed by revisionist states.[5]

In the centuries following the emergence of the Westphalia system that ended the Thirty Years' War in 1648, various world orders developed. Each time they began with a peace treaty between major powers.[6] Over the last 200 years, there have been five such orders, extending from the Vienna system to the current post-Cold War system.

The Vienna system was established by Russia and other European powers after the defeat of Napoleon in order to prevent another war on the continent. Russia formed a quadruple alliance with Austria, Britain, and Prussia. France was initially isolated, but several years later it was included in the arrangement at the Aachen conference in 1818. A new territorial settlement emerged: France's sphere of influence on the Rhine River was limited to the Alsatian zone but it was allowed to preserve its borders.[7] All the major powers honored Tsar Alexander's desire to dominate Poland as part of Russia's sphere of influence and as protection against another potential invasion from the west. Russia's commitment to its Orthodox allies in the Balkans was also not challenged. The Tsar proposed to form a Holy Alliance with Austria and Prussia based on principles of Christian and monarchical solidarity. The three countries even agreed to not recognize regimes brought to power by a revolution and to take necessary actions, including force, against any such regime.[8] The Vienna system therefore was relatively inclusive and ensured peace and stability in Europe for some forty years.

The system began to unravel and eventually broke down under pressure from the increased ambitions of its members, their perception of Russia's revisionism, and important changes in their internal political development. Britain, in particular, had growing ambitions in the East as the Ottoman Empire declined. In response to the Sultan granting additional rights to French Catholics, Russia wanted to negotiate similar rights for Orthodox Christians, but was perceived by Britain and France to be planning to partition the Ottoman Empire. In addition, Russia and the European powers were moving apart institutionally, the former consolidating autocracy and the latter moving toward liberalism. Even Russia's conservative allies had abolished serfdom—Prussia in 1806 and Austria in 1848. These contradictions resulted in the Crimean War, which formally ended the Vienna system. With both France and Britain involved, the war moved beyond being about Turkey or the Balkans and took on the status of a general European war. As A. J. P. Taylor wrote, "the real stake in the Crimean war was not Turkey ... The Crimean war was fought to remake the European system."[9]

Following Russia's defeat in the Crimean War, a new world order was established. At the Paris Congress in 1856, European powers removed Russia's right to keep a fleet in the Black Sea and to protect Orthodox Christians in the Ottoman Empire. In practice this meant that the Russian Empire lost the ability to participate in European affairs as a major power. The Paris system was therefore not as inclusive as that of Vienna, pushing Russia toward relative isolation and policies aimed to regather its strength and recover its losses. In 1870, Russia took the opportunity of closer relations with Prussia to refuse to be bound by the Paris Treaty. After the European conference in London in 1871 had cancelled the Paris conditions, Russia returned to the Balkans and defeated Turkey in 1877–8.[10] The newly unified Germany was a source of a massive loan for Russia, although at the Berlin Congress of 1878, Germany, along with other powers, did not recognize most of the Russian war gains.

The Versailles system established after the defeat of Germany and its allies in 1919 was another example of a punitive, non-inclusive system. Germany was excluded, as the victorious states imposed major reparations on the new Weimar Republic and occupied portions of the German Rhineland. Partly due to this lack of recognition, Germany was determined to remobilize and challenge the new international order, paving the way for World War Two.

At the end of that war, after the Soviet Union and its allies had defeated Nazi Germany, a new order was devised and largely agreed upon in Yalta in 1945. The new system was highly restrictive with respect to Germany, but inclusive with regard to the interests and claims of the USSR, Britain, and the United States. By the time the leaders of the three states met, the Soviet Union and Britain had already worked out an understanding on spheres of influence in the Balkans. In Yalta they finalized the future of Germany, insisting on its "complete disarmament, demilitarization, and dismemberment,"[11] and dividing it into occupation zones. They also agreed on new borders for Poland and to "consult" about affairs in the Eastern European countries, as well as founding global security institutions in the form of the United Nations and its Security Council.

World order transitions

World order transitions begin when rising or dissatisfied states claim a greater status within the existing system, while the dominant powers fail to enforce the established rules and distribution of forces.

The Vienna system was challenged from the mid-1840s onwards when its members revealed their ambition to take advantage of the declining Ottoman Empire. The most important opposition to Russia came from Britain, which was never comfortable with the Concert of Europe under Russia's leadership. Already in the 1830s influential British politicians, such as future Home Secretary Lord Henry Temple Palmerston and others, were devising schemes to strengthen their influence with the Ottoman Empire and to undermine Russia's position. In addition to its rising political influence, Britain's economic presence in the Near East had been steadily growing since 1829, whereas Russia's was declining.[12] The opposition of other European powers was also important, albeit less pronounced. Neither France nor Austria directly challenged the Concert, but they each wanted a greater share of power and each in its own way was uncomfortable with the dominant position of Russia in the system. France sought to renegotiate its relations with the Ottomans and increase its influence in the Near East, while Austria wanted greater influence in the Danubian principalities, which had been largely controlled by Russia. As one historian wrote, "Russia's strength or appearance of strength, proved to be a serious political liability, for it tended to make other countries even more fearful of Russia."[13]

The Paris system unraveled in 1870 when Russia announced to the European powers its rejection of the Black Sea clauses in the Paris Treaty. In his note to Russian ambassadors on October 31, 1870, Alexander Gorchakov explained that Russia could no longer be bound by the treaty, given that it constrained Russia's sovereign rights and that other European powers had already violated the agreement in the past. France and Austria were too weak to resist the move by Russia. Prussia was acting on the promise of support, and needed Russia to contain France. Britain was the only power that indicated its willingness to fight Russia, but it was marginalized by the lack of international support. In the meantime, a unified Germany appeared on the European political map as a major state with growing ambitions. Future international developments were accompanied not by the establishment of new rules, but by an increasingly bitter struggle for power and influence among major states. Russia's old ties with Germany collapsed as the two sides failed to renew what was known as the Reinsurance Treaty. By the early twentieth century, Nicholas II had formed the Triple Entente with France and Britain. Germany and Austria remained allies, and both sought to dominate the Balkans while Russia preserved its obligations to the Orthodox people in the peninsula. Only an informal balance of power emerged, with each state working to challenge it. It was over the Balkans that the two sides came into a conflict that led to the outbreak of World War One.

The Versailles system began to decline due to internal changes in Germany, and the system had become largely obsolete by the time of Adolf Hitler's election as the country's Chancellor in 1933. During that same year Germany withdrew from the League of Nations. In 1935 Hitler restored compulsory military service and embarked on a military modernization program. In 1936 he reoccupied the Rhineland, denied to Germany by the Versailles conditions. The Soviet Union worked to build a collective security system to stop Hitler but failed to muster sufficient support from France and Britain, each highly mistrustful of Moscow's intentions.[14] The two powers failed to act even after Germany's annexation of Czechoslovakia. In response, the Soviet leader Josef Stalin ceased his efforts to engage with the West and signed a non-aggression treaty with Germany. That treaty, however, failed to prevent the Nazis' provocation of world war and invasion of the USSR.

The challenge to the Yalta system came soon after its establishment and resulted in what came to be known as the Cold War. Some norms and principles agreed upon in Yalta survived until the late 1980s. The two sides continued to recognize established spheres of influence in Eastern Europe and respected the United Nations as the place for debating the most fundamental issues of international security. This made a limited cooperation among major powers possible, leading to periods of intense dialogue and a relaxation of tensions. Nevertheless, both the Soviet Union and the West challenged the post-war balance of power, neither formally recognized each other's spheres of influence outside of Eastern Europe, and both worked to undermine each other's political system and ideology.

As a result, two mutually threatening international orders emerged: socialist/communist versus liberal/democratic. Multiple crises from Berlin to Cuba to Afghanistan extended across much of the Cold War era. State propaganda on both sides was reinforced by an intense ideological confrontation accompanied by military maneuvers and preparations for a nuclear war. The Oscar-nominated film *Bridge of Spies*, directed by Steven Spielberg, reproduces some of the hysterical atmosphere in the United States, where the public was mobilized for any action, including military, in support of the government. In the Soviet Union it was no different. For the world outside the West and the USSR, this was not peace but an increasingly chaotic and violent time—a conclusion well documented by scholars of the Third World. The Cold War did not result in a major war—unlike previous world order transitions—largely because of the nuclear deterrent and the established balance of threat between the two sides. The transition from the system began in the second half of the 1970s, reflecting the Soviet Union's decline and its growing inability to compete with the United States.

The Washington system

Rules of the post-Cold War order

The post-Cold War Washington system was not as restrictive with respect to the "defeated" Russia as those of Versailles and Yalta were vis-à-vis Germany. The Western nations did not aim to disarm Russia or punish it by dismembering it or imposing reparations, and indeed they wanted to keep the appearance of accommodating Russia's needs in the new system. For example, Russia was included in the G7 and offered ways in which to cooperate with NATO. In fact, the United States was instrumental in making Russia a G7 member in July 1992 against the opposition of both Britain and Germany. In addition to boosting its status, G7 membership offered Russia programs of financial assistance. Following the decision to expand NATO, Washington also offered Moscow membership of the Partnership for Peace program in 1994, in order to develop Russia's relations with the Euro-Atlantic alliance.

At the same time, the Washington system was not as inclusive as that of Vienna and was rather reminiscent of the Paris system. An important distinction is that the Washington rules were introduced informally, without being announced to Russia at an official gathering marking the end of the Cold War. Washington did not want to insult the Kremlin, and its treatment of Russia as a defeated state remained mostly implicit. Still, from the US perspective, the fact that the Warsaw

Pact was disbanded while NATO persisted signified the West's victory in the Cold War. The dissolution of the Soviet Union in 1991, following the fall of the Berlin Wall in 1989, served to strengthen this triumphalist perception among American elites. Acting on that perception, President George Bush proclaimed victory in his 1992 State of the Union address. The Clinton administration then entrenched the rhetoric of victory by drawing an analogy between Russia and the defeat of Germany and Japan in World War Two. In Stephen Cohen's account, US officials and members of the political class assumed that America was the victor, Russia was the defeated nation, and that therefore it should be supplicant and subordinate to the United States.[15] Few Americans believed that the end of the Cold War was a victory for both sides.

This perception was reflected in policy. While Washington did not impose reparations on Russia for "occupying" Eastern Europe, it denied it recognition as a major power and deprived it of the opportunity to act as an equal in shaping a new world order. Instead of participating in rebuilding European security, Moscow had to watch as, one by one, its former satellite states and even parts of the Soviet Union adopted NATO standards and applied for membership in the alliance. Although Russian politicians had expected a grand bargain with the West comparable to the Marshall Plan, European and American leaders treated Russia more like a subordinate country that deserved assistance but was not worthy of integration within the Western economy. Western aid to Russia, while considerable, was never comparable with that given to Eastern Europe.[16] Russia also had to swallow the United States' military interventions against Moscow's traditional allies from Serbia to Iraq. Finally, after going through an extremely chaotic period of economic collapse and state disintegration, Russia rediscovered the importance of state governance and order. However, as first Boris Yeltsin and then

President Putin attempted to restore the state's ability to govern in economic and security affairs, American and European leaders frequently criticized them for their "heavy handed" approach and lack of respect for human rights. The latter amounted to limiting Russia's freedom to organize its domestic institutions according to its own understanding of the country's economic and political challenges.

The Washington system therefore deprived Russia of great power status by imposing a new balance of forces and denying Moscow a sphere of influence and sovereignty over its domestic affairs. Rather than renegotiating the issue of Russia's participation in the European security system, the United States unilaterally moved into the area formerly controlled by the Soviets with the expansion of NATO. Eastern European nations were invited to join—a decision which they welcomed as heralding the end of the Soviet "occupation." Even though the spheres of influence established at Yalta had been negotiated jointly with the United States and Britain, Russia alone was viewed as responsible for having deprived Eastern Europeans of their freedom. Many in Russia perceived the decision to expand the Western alliance largely as an attempt to fill the existing security vacuum by taking advantage of Russia's weakness. Even the country's most liberal-minded Foreign Minister, Andrei Kozyrev, saw it as a "continuation, though by inertia, of a policy aimed at containment of Russia."[17] The global balance of power was now to be centered on the United States' primacy and decision-making monopoly.

As a "defeated" power, Russia was also widely expected not to challenge the West's international priorities and to accept the Western liberal narrative of "universal" values. After all, the West had proved to be morally superior and was now in a position to teach Russia and the rest of the world all about the "right" economic and political institutions. In the words of the *Wall Street Journal* and *Foreign Affairs*, there was now only "one dominant principle of legitimacy, democracy," and only one dominant power to uphold this principle due to the superiority of its military, economic, and ideological capacities.[18] That Russia's post-Gorbachev reformers were prepared to follow Western recommendations only served to strengthen the victorious perception in the United States. As American commentators were proclaiming the global spread of market democracy, Russia was viewed as an object, not a subject, of the transformation.

Table 2.1 summarizes the Washington order and its treatment of the "defeated" power relative to other international orders.

Table 2.1 World Orders and Defeated Powers

	Balance of power	Sphere of influence	Internal sovereignty
Vienna, 1815	• Russia-ruled • France included	Limited to Alsatian zone	Respected
Paris, 1856	• France and Britain-led • Russia subordinated (no Black Sea fleet)	Denied to Russia (no right to protect Orthodox subjects)	Respected
Versailles, 1919	• France and Britain-led • Germany subordinated (reparations imposed)	Denied to Germany (Rhineland occupied)	Respected
Yalta, 1945	• US-USSR-Britain-led • Germany subordinated (reparations imposed)	Denied to Germany (division of the country into sectors)	• Denied to Germany; • Split into two systems
Washington, 1993	• US-led • Russia subordinated (not included in US alliances)	Denied Russia's influence in Eurasia	• Denied to Russia; • Liberal democracy standard

Russia's opposition

Russia could not agree with the role assigned to it by the Washington system. Moscow did not see itself as defeated in the Cold War. In Russia's perspective, the end of that war was a result of mutually beneficial negotiations without which the West-Soviet confrontation would not have ended.[19] The new Russia wanted to become a full participant in the post-Cold War order, but gradually developed a resentment toward what the Kremlin saw as a disregard for its concerns and interests by the United States and other Western states.

During the 1990s, before the restrictions of the new international system became apparent, the Kremlin pursued the idea of integration and strategic partnership with the West. Russia's initial path included radical economic reform (the so-called "shock therapy"), attempting to secure full status in transatlantic economic and security institutions such as the European Union, NATO, the International Monetary Fund, and the G7, and separating the new Russia from the former Soviet republics economically, politically, and culturally. This vision of integration with the West shaped the new foreign policy concept prepared in late 1992 and signed into law in April 1993.

The vision collapsed because the West was not willing to treat Russia as an equal partner and contributor to the post-Cold War rules. Not only was Russia viewed as "defeated," it was also seen as economically weak and dependent on Western financial assistance. Rather than trying to integrate Russia economically, including by providing the rapid and massive assistance which was expected by Moscow, the US had the more limited goal of turning Russia into a market economy and achieving macroeconomic stabilization. Instead of political and military integration, the US decided to expand NATO eastward while excluding Russia from the process. This decision strengthened the sense of Russia not being accepted by the West as an equal and one of its own, and was the beginning of Moscow's growing frustration with Western policies.

Gradually, Russia began to register its disagreement with the Washington system and the West's actions. As a result of the US denying Russia recognition of its status, sphere of influence, and sovereignty, the two countries' relations did not progress toward strategic partnership, instead moving from misunderstanding to mistrust and mutual fear. Cooperation was limited to individual issues on which agreement could still be reached.

In the second half of the 1990s, the Kremlin adopted new policies in response to NATO's expansion and the restrictions it placed on Russia's participation in securing Europe and the former Soviet space. Under the country's second Foreign Minister, Primakov, Russia attempted to integrate its neighboring states under tighter control from Moscow, and to counter-balance the West by building strong relations with non-Western countries. Its National Security Concept of 1997 recommended that Russia maintain an equal distancing in relations to the "global European and Asian economic and political actors," and presented a positive program for the integration of a Commonwealth of Independent States in the post-Soviet region.[20]

Vladimir Putin's vision of Russia's role in international relations also contradicted that of Washington. While initially embracing the vision of a strategic partnership with the West, he made it clear that his priority was one of restoring Russia's great power status. After September 11, 2001, Putin was among the first to call President George W. Bush to express his support and pledge significant resources to help America in its fight against terrorism. Putin also promoted Russia as a reliable alternative to traditional Middle Eastern sources of energy, and proposed a new framework for strategic interaction with the United States.

Putin's vision soon came up against the rules of the Washington system. Not long after the invasion of Iraq, the United States was encouraging the entire former Soviet region to transform its political institutions and was working on extending NATO into former Soviet states such as Azerbaijan, Georgia and Ukraine. In addition, President Bush chose to withdraw from the ABM Treaty and to unilaterally develop a new global system of missile defense.

While Bush's successor Barack Obama proposed to "reset" US-Russia relations, he failed to address the roots of the mutual mistrust. Russia remained critical of the US proposal to develop its missile defense system jointly with the Europeans but separately from Russia. At the end of 2010, Moscow shelved its initiative to negotiate a new security treaty with European nations after getting no support from NATO officials and the United States. The Western nations remained rhetorically supportive of the former Soviet states' bid for NATO membership, whereas Russia maintained its right to protect its interests in Georgia and elsewhere in the former Soviet region. The Kremlin was also not happy with the West's handling of the Middle Eastern crisis and its involvement in fostering regime change in Libya and Syria, as well as Western criticisms of Russia's own centralized political system. On Afghanistan, Moscow's call for a joint strategy did not elicit a serious response from Western countries, despite their appreciation for Russia's cooperation.

During the mid-2000s, the Kremlin moved from rhetorical disagreement with the Washington rules to an assertive promotion of its interests. In response to Washington's decision to deploy elements of its missile defense system in Europe, Putin declared a Russian moratorium on implementing the Conventional Forces in Europe Treaty, which would allow Russia to freely move its conventional forces within its territory. Responding to the NATO expansion, the Kremlin used force against Georgia in August 2008. It also sought to strengthen its energy position in world markets by building pipelines in all geographic directions, purchasing shares abroad, raising energy prices for its oil and gas, moving to control transportation networks in the former USSR, and coordinating its activities with other energy producers. There emerged a new foreign policy consensus that this assertive style of achieving the objectives of development, stability and security suited Russia well.

The Kremlin also criticized the United States' global policy of regime change as "unilateral" and disrespectful of international law, and disagreed with the West's critique of Russia's political system. Following the Kremlin's use of force in Chechnya and Putin's attempts to centralize the state, Russia was systematically presented by Western media and officials as an authoritarian regime that was failing to comply with the "universal" standards of human rights and democracy. The Russian leadership, however, aimed to preserve the country's traditionally strong executive branch. Even Yeltsin, who in the West is frequently viewed as the father of Russian democracy, proposed a new constitution in which there were few checks and balances on presidential power; he also used force in Chechnya and even attempted to discipline the Russian oligarchs by unleashing the security services on them. Although Yelstin did not (and could not) go as far as Putin in strengthening his political power, he too understood the importance of state centralization for effective governance. It was symbolic that Yeltsin himself selected Putin as his successor. Putin's acceptance of democracy was conditional on the restoration of a strong Russian state. Answering a question about Chechnya and human rights, for example, he stressed that "if by democracy one means the dissolution of the state, then we do not need such democracy."[21]

The new world order transition

New opportunities for Russia to challenge the Washington system were presented by the relative decline of American power and by US foreign policy errors. This decline became evident from the second half of the 2000s, thereby setting the stage for a new world order transition away from the system established at the end of the Cold War.

Decline of US power

The debate on the decline of American power concerns its timing, causes, and implications for international order. Some scholars argue that the decline is set to continue, since it is caused by major changes and material power shifts in the system. Others attribute it to the "crisis of authority" and Washington's foreign policy errors, implying a possible revival of US global leadership.[22] There is also disagreement as to whether the US decline means the end of liberal globalization or whether the liberal regime will survive.[23] These disputes notwithstanding, many scholars share the view that the United States has been gradually retreating from acting as the sole superpower capable of unilaterally setting and enforcing rules of behavior for other powers. This retreat has material and symbolic dimensions and has resulted from the rise of other powers as well as the US's own errors and unwillingness to adjust its international rules.

The United States' relative decline began soon after its military intervention in Iraq in 2003. Both the unilateral decision and its destabilizing consequences damaged the United States' reputation in the world and undermined its own confidence, placing its ability to serve as the world's moral leader in question. According to sociologists, 2004 was the last year in which public confidence in most American institutions averaged better than 40 percent.[24]

The US decline is evident in various dimensions. Its military standing has been challenged by the growing proliferation of nuclear weapons and by incidents of the unsanctioned use of conventional weapons in non-Western regions. Signs of its military decline include its failure to successfully complete its military operations in Afghanistan and Iraq, to stabilize the Middle East, to impose its rules on Russia in Eurasia, to facilitate stabilization in Ukraine, and to prevent North Korea from developing its nuclear program. Russia's military conflict with Georgia in 2008 undermined the US monopoly on the use of force in world politics, while the Kremlin's subsequent annexation of Crimea—not explicitly condemned by non-Western powers—challenged US global legitimacy. By using force in the Caucasus in 2008 and then, covertly, in 2014 in eastern Ukraine, Russia decentralized hard power usage, largely ending the Western aspiration to further extend NATO's geopolitical influence at the expense of non-Western political arrangements such as the Shanghai Cooperation Organization (SCO) and the Collective Security Treaty Organization. Russia's intervention in Syria since October 2015 has placed additional limits on American power in this critically important part of the world.

While US economic and financial power remains dominant, other nations are increasingly reformulating their interests to better protect their societies, and redirecting attention to their regional environments instead of relying on the protection and welfare of Western hegemony. The financial crisis of 2008 revealed the United States' vulnerability. The rise of China in particular has led to the Asia-Pacific region becoming a new global center of gravity. A new coalition of non-Western powers has emerged, seeking to diversify global commercial and monetary transactions. The rising economies of China,

India, Brazil, and others have challenged the dominant position of the West by establishing cooperative institutional arrangements, including annual meetings of BRICS (Brazil, Russia, India, China, and South Africa) and the SCO, the pooling of financial resources, and producing around 30 percent of global GDP.[25] The BRICS members have agreed to establish a new development bank, a pool of reserve currency, and an alternative energy association.[26] The G20, rather than the G8, has been increasingly successful in representing and articulating positions required for stabilizing the international order.

Finally, the US-promoted idea of liberal democracy, while still attractive, no longer commands the same attention. Observers have noted the intensification of processes of cultural reformulation and the rise of alternative soft power projects both within and outside the legitimizing language of democracy. For example, despite their differences with the West, both Russia and China present their grand visions as consistent with the idea of democracy. Islamists promoting a caliphate, however, do not hide their contempt for secular democratic ideals. In part, the decline of liberal democracy's attractiveness has resulted from the United States' abuse of power and its attempts to impose democracy on other parts of the world, including by force. Not infrequently this has led to state failure, lawlessness and ethnic violence.

The new US-Russia rivalry

The US decline and its multiple policy errors have resulted in new international crises and exacerbated tensions in its relations with Russia. Rather than adjusting its international rules and changing its policies, the US has continued on the established course. In response, the Kremlin has continued to act assertively in promoting Russia's sovereignty and interests. Its Foreign Policy Concept released in February 2013 stated that "[t]he capabilities of the historically established West to dominate the global economy and politics continue to decline," and that the "global potential of strength and growth is dispersing and shifting eastwards, particularly towards the Asia Pacific region."[27] The document also emphasized global economic competition, in which different "values and development models" would be tested and "civilization identity" would take on a new importance. Russia was now seeing itself as culturally and politically independent from the West.

The US and Russia have continued to clash with respect to the balance of power and influence in both Europe and the Middle East. The US supported the armed opposition to Bashar al-Assad in Syria, while the Kremlin expressed concerns about instability in the country and the wider region, and blamed Western leaders for exacerbating this.[28] When the US accused Assad's regime of using chemical weapons against the rebel forces, Russian officials responded by rejecting the accusation, characterizing it as an effort to derail a planned peace conference on Syria.[29] While Washington refused to recognize Assad, Moscow insisted on the necessity for negotiations between Syria's existing government and the rebel opposition.

A major example of Russia-West disagreement concerns the situation in Ukraine, where the Kremlin intervened in February 2014. According to Putin, Western nations had been behind the revolution in Ukraine without understanding its destabilizing consequences. When Putin intervened in Crimea by sending additional troops to the region, the United States threatened to apply a broad range of sanctions against Russia and to expel it from the G8. President Obama described Russia's intervention as a clear violation of the independence and sovereignty of Ukraine that was "deeply destabilizing" and would incur "costs."[30] European governments soon joined the US in imposing sanctions.

The Western nations, however, did not see themselves as meddling in Ukraine. Instead, they condemned what they saw as Russia's "imperialism" and its violation of a neighbor's sovereignty. In response to Putin's initiative to build a new union among the post-Soviet Commonwealth of Independent States (CIS), US Secretary of State Hillary Clinton referred to it as a "re-Sovietization" and promised to find "effective ways to slow down or prevent it."[31] Speaking for many in the US political class, Republican Senator John McCain called the proposed Eurasian Union "an old idea that the Russians have had dating back to the days of the tsars."[32] European leaders too were worried that Russia was aiming to pull Ukraine into a Russia-centered Eurasian Union and away from the EU and its values. EU officials characterized the proposed arrangement as anti-European and offered Kiev an opportunity to sign an Association Agreement with the European Union.

There was no progress either on nuclear issues. Immediately after being re-elected as president in 2012, Putin indicated his displeasure at the US missile defense system (MDS) program by cancelling his trip to a NATO summit in Chicago.[33] Emphasizing Russia's insecurity as a result of the West's nuclear policies, he refused to renew the Nunn-Lugar Cooperative Threat Reduction Program. The United States indicated that it was interested in further nuclear reductions, but not in establishing the joint MDS preferred by Russia. Russia, however, did not want to consider further cuts, viewing nuclear force as the basis of national defense and international stability.

The two countries also continued to clash over democracy and human rights. In particular, Putin's return to the presidency generated growing criticism in the United States. Rhetoric about an "aggressive" and "authoritarian" Russia was powerfully present during the 2012 US presidential election, when several prominent politicians called for a severing of ties with Russia, now viewed as "without question our number one geopolitical foe."[34] Obama's administration had rarely engaged in criticism of Russia under Medvedev during 2009–2011, and they had not expected Putin to return as president. During his trip to Moscow in spring 2011, Vice-President Joe Biden even went as far as to advise Putin against running.[35]

Washington and other Western governments expressed strong criticism of the Kremlin's handling of protesters against fraudulent elections to the State Duma, and of the Russian court's decision to sentence members of the punk band Pussy Riot to two years in jail for a protest performance in Russia's main cathedral. In December 2012, the US Congress passed a bill named after the Russian tax accountant Sergei Magnitsky, who had died in prison. The bill imposed visa bans and asset freezes on human rights violators in Russia. The United States expressed further disappointment at Russia's new law against "propaganda of non-traditional sexual relations among minors" (that is, homosexual relations), passed in June 2013 and supported by 88 percent of Russians.[36]

In the summer of 2013 yet another problem arose with the defection of the former CIA employee Edward Snowden to Russia. Washington viewed Snowden as a traitor for making public the surveillance activities of the US security services, and expected Moscow to extradite him. Instead, the Kremlin granted him political asylum.[37] In response, President Obama cancelled a bilateral summit with Putin scheduled for September in Moscow.

Despite these clashes, there remained some areas of Russia-US cooperation. In September 2013, the two sides agreed on a phased elimination of Syria's chemical weapons. Russia proposed an international process of monitoring and eliminating such weapons after the US threatened to use force in Syria in response to claims that the Assad government had used chemical weapons against its own people on a mass scale. The two countries also cooperated on preventing Iran's development of its nuclear program. In July 2015, following extensive multilateral negotiations, the United States, Russia, the United Kingdom, France, China, and Iran reached an agreement on limiting the Iranian nuclear program in exchange for the lifting of international sanctions.

At the same time, Russia and America also shared a concern about the growing instability in Afghanistan. The Kremlin was worried that the US military withdrawal from the country could jeopardize security both internally and in the broader region. Russia helped to stabilize Afghanistan by providing economic assistance and by training police, military, and anti-drug specialists. It also provided the US with intelligence on counter-terrorism. For example, Russian intelligence services warned the FBI and the CIA about the radicalization of Tamerlan Tsarnaev, who was involved in the Boston Marathon bombing in April 2013. Tsarnaev had travelled to Russia in order to establish ties with radical Islamists in the North Caucasus.[38]

The two countries also displayed a desire to cooperate in several other areas, including economic development and space exploration. For instance, Russia continued to build relations with American and European energy companies and signed a number of agreements with ExxonMobil and British Petroleum, including on a proposed joint exploration of the Arctic. In regard to space exploration, following President Obama's cancellation of the new Space Shuttle program, the United States became dependent on Russia to fly NASA astronauts to the International Space Station.

The next chapter describes a new context in which US-Russia disagreements developed.

3

Putin and Trump

To a large extent, Putin's and Trump's worldviews are compatible. Both leaders can be described as pragmatic great power nationalists. Both prioritize national greatness, defined less in ethnic than in economic, political, and military terms. Politically, both have demonstrated a willingness to compromise under domestic and international pressures. This chapter takes a closer look at Russia's and America's international visions and interests by focusing on the perspectives of the two presidents.

In his United Nations speech of September 2018, Trump stressed "America First" as the guiding principle of his foreign policy: "We will never surrender America's sovereignty to an unelected, unaccountable, global bureaucracy. America is governed by Americans. We reject the ideology of globalism and we embrace the doctrine of patriotism."[1] Long before Trump's arrival on the scene, however, Putin had formulated the Russian idea of patriotism as that of a great power building relations with others on the basis of equality and mutual recognition.

This ideological similarity notwithstanding, Putin and Trump are nevertheless predominantly rivals rather than partners. Although the language of nationalism and great power interests assists them in understanding each other's perspective, this does not make it easier to come to international agreement. Trump is a believer in the effectiveness of negotiating from strength, and has tried coercive negotiation tactics on various global issues from North Korea to Iran, Mexico, and Venezuela. In his turn, Putin, while being the weaker party, remains highly sensitive about Russia's great power status and is unlikely to yield to Trump's demands.

These mutually incompatible perceptions are accompanied by complicated domestic politics and formidable, if different, power capabilities, all of which are prone to producing tensions and crises in bilateral relations. This chapter documents the evolution in Putin's and Trump's misperceptions and the conflicts that have resulted since Trump's inauguration in January 2017. After initial attempts to put relations with Washington on a cooperative footing, the Kremlin resorted to promoting its interests unilaterally by relying on Russia's considerable if asymmetric power. The concept of an asymmetry in power relations assumes that, even when the weaker actor lacks comparable material resources, its resources are sufficient to make it impossible for the stronger actor conclusively to defeat the weaker.

Compatible worldviews

Putin's vision of Russia is that of a strong state capable of exploiting liberal globalization for its own national interests. In economic affairs, the Kremlin has insisted on protecting a national path of development relying heavily on its own natural resources. According to this perspective, reliance on market forces is necessary but insufficient. In his 1999 PhD thesis entitled "Mineral Raw Materials in the Strategy for Development of the Russian Economy," Putin had already stated his reasons for embracing state intervention in the economy: "Even in developed countries, market mechanisms do not provide solutions to strategic tasks of resource use, protecting nature, and sustainable economic security."[2] In political affairs, Russia has sought to shield itself from what it views as the harmful influence of the West's global democratization program. Russian officials have been among the most vocal critics of Western military interventions in Yugoslavia, Iraq and Libya, justified by the West on humanitarian grounds. In response to the political instability of the 1990s and the "color revolutions" of the early 2000s, the Kremlin insisted on Russia's right to "decide for itself the pace, terms and conditions of moving towards democracy," and warned against any attempt to destabilize its political system by "unlawful methods of struggle."[3]

This forceful rejection of any external interference in Russia's domestic development has only grown stronger over time. Theorists sympathetic to the official agenda have developed the concept of "sovereign democracy," justifying it by the need to defend an internally determined path to political development and to protect the values of economic prosperity, individual freedom and social justice from potential threats. These include "international terrorism, military conflict, lack of economic competitiveness, and soft takeovers by 'orange technologies' in a time of decreased national immunity to foreign influence."[4] The Kremlin has also trained its own youth organizations to protect the regime's stability, restricted the activities of Western NGOs and radical opposition groups inside the country, and warned the United States against interference in Russia's domestic politics.

Since Putin's return to the presidency in March 2012 the official emphasis has been on Russia as a culturally distinct power committed to defending particular values relative to those of the West and other civilizations. In multiple statements Putin has criticized what he sees as Europe's departure from traditional religious and family values. He has quoted Russian traditionalist thinkers and declared that "the desire for independence and sovereignty in spiritual, ideological and foreign policy spheres" is an "integral part of our national character."[5] He has further positioned Russia as a "conservative" power and a defender of traditional values worldwide.[6] In addition to stressing such values, Putin has articulated a new idea uniting ethnic and non-ethnic Russians in domestic affairs. The Kremlin presented this as the idea of a state-civilization in which, historically, a special role has been played by ethnic Russians, who are identified as "the core (*sterzhen'*) that binds the fabric" of the country's culture.[7] Along these lines, the new official nationalities strategy signed by Putin reintroduces Russia as a "unique socio-cultural civilization formed of the multi-ethnic Russian nation," and, under pressure from Muslim constituencies, removes the reference to ethnic Russians as the core of the state.[8]

The discourse of distinctiveness was intensified in the context of the Ukraine crisis and the Western sanctions that followed Russia's annexation of Crimea. Stressing Russia's civilizational difference, Putin sought to justify the annexation by presenting Crimea as "an inseparable part of Russia" and a foundation of its civilizational values, a place in which Prince Vladimir, who christened Rus' people in the Orthodox faith, had been christened himself.[9]

Putin's commitment to great power nationalism does not mean that his regime is dependent on ethno-nationalist groups. Politically, it seeks to maintain an equal distance from both pro-Western liberals and Russian ethno-nationalists. Russian liberals frequently advocate prioritizing relations with the West. The Kremlin remains interested in economic cooperation with the West, especially Western European nations, and the sanctions imposed following the Ukraine crisis did not fundamentally change the reality of Russia's considerable economic dependence on Europe. Although Putin feels threatened by the West's human rights rhetoric, and is often at odds with EU and US foreign policies, he continues to recognize the economic reality. The Kremlin is also pragmatic in its relations with ethno-nationalists. The state has sufficient resources to be ideologically flexible and noncommittal on the ethno-nationalist agenda—partly due to the latter's lack of organizational cohesiveness and domestic influence.

Putin's view of Trump has likewise proved flexible and non-committal. Although he has described Trump as a "brilliant" (*yarkiy*) politician, he refuses to be perceived as Trump's unequivocal supporter, stressing that both presidents are motivated by their respective countries' interests, rather than any personal "chemistry."[10] During a press conference at the BRICS summit in China in September 2017, the Russian president famously quipped that Trump "is not my bride. I am not his bride, nor his groom. We are running our governments."[11] During his meeting with Trump in Helsinki in July 2018, Putin said it was normal for the US and Russia to not trust each other because of their commitments to their own national interests.[12]

Putin's flexible perspective on Trump reflects Russia's complex internal perception of the declining US-centered world order. The Russian foreign policy community has been divided between those favoring an increase in Russia's assertiveness and those cautioning against a fundamental disruption of the international system. The latter point to the limitations of Russia's power and to the uncertainty inherent in the contemporary world order transition. Unlike those pushing for change, the more pragmatic voices are skeptical that such change will result in a stable and secure global order.

For example, Russia's most influential think tank, the Council of Foreign and Defense Policy, concluded a 2016 report with the prediction that "the old West will not remain the leader," yet "the rapid shift of influence toward the 'new' centers of power observable over the last fifteen years will most likely slow down, while competition for power will increase."[13] Some Russian analysts propose to draw lessons from the late nineteenth-century rivalry between the great powers that led to World War One. As Timofei Bordachev argues, economic interdependence and nuclear deterrence notwithstanding, great power relations are likely to descend further toward military confrontation if the right conclusions are not drawn from the precedent of 1871–1914.[14] Members of this group warn that during a period of international uncertainty Russia should be wary of overextension and concentrate on domestic issues and reform.[15] Still others, such as Andrei Kortunov, argue that any viable alternative to US hegemony will still be a Western liberal order because it remains the one that is "based on rationality, openness, and institutional norms."[16]

This divide is also evident in the Russian foreign policy community's assessment of Trump. During the 2016 US presidential election, those favoring the decline of the US-centered order did not hide their preference for Trump's presidency and celebrated his victory in the hope of securing a grand bargain with America.[17] Others either expressed no preference or supported Hillary Clinton as a more predictable candidate than the highly impulsive Trump.[18]

Subsequent developments in the United States have complicated the world order debate inside Russia. The investigation into Trump's possible "collusion" with the Kremlin has made it difficult for him to act on his promises to normalize relations with Russia. His supporters in Moscow no longer advise the Russian leadership to reach out to Trump in order to jointly negotiate a new global order. Instead, they advise continuing with the assertive foreign policy, thereby strengthening Russia's bargaining power in future negotiations with the West. Others have felt vindicated in their initial skepticism with respect to Trump and the United States as a potential partner, and call for strategic restraint, patience, and a focus on domestic affairs.[19]

As noted at the beginning of this chapter, Trump's perspective is also that of great power nationalism. Although his views are not systematically developed, the US president instinctively takes the side of those defending the values of national greatness, economic self-sufficiency, sovereignty, and cultural cohesiveness.[20] While campaigning for the presidency, Trump advocated scaling down America's commitments to its allies in Europe and Asia. He promised to put America first by withdrawing from expensive military engagements abroad and by leaving the World Trade Organization. Like all populists, he had simple messages for his main audiences at home—workers who fear losing their jobs to global markets, segments within the middle class who see their pay shrinking as the rich get richer, and military personnel tired of fighting wars to preserve the United States' global leadership. For the first time since the post-World War Two era, the old internationalist consensus was being questioned by an American president advocating different rules of military, political, and commercial engagement.

This commitment to reducing America's international obligations was also on display in Trump's inaugural address, in which he promised to be guided by the America First principle. In particular, the president pledged to revive America's industry, military, infrastructure, and middle class by "transferring power from Washington, D.C. [to] ... the American People" and by ensuring that "every decision on trade, on taxes, on immigration, on foreign affairs [would be] made to benefit American workers and American families."[21] Trump claimed that "for many decades, we've enriched foreign industry ... subsidized the armies of other countries ... defended other nation's borders ... spent trillions of dollars overseas ... We've made other countries rich while the wealth, strength, and confidence of our country has disappeared over the horizon."[22]

Trump's subsequent actions while in office have continued to reflect his great power nationalism, attempting to curb what he sees as America's excessive international commitments in the face of resistance from many within the political class. The United States has withdrawn from the Trans-Pacific Partnership agreement negotiated by the previous administration, from UNESCO, and from the Paris Climate Accord. It also cut the country's contribution to the United Nations' budget for 2018–2019 by 5 percent. Furthermore, Trump has proclaimed his intent to renegotiate the nuclear deal with Iran, and announced an expensive program of nuclear rearmament. The Draft Nuclear Posture Review revealed what some observers viewed as an American drive for global hegemony that could potentially lead to a nuclear arms race with Russia.[23] Finally, Trump has insisted on US allies increasing their share of military spending and threatened the EU and China with high trade tariffs where they do not open their markets for American goods.

On Russia, Trump's views have departed significantly from those of the US establishment. The American political class has been largely in agreement in its view of Russia as pursuing an aggressive foreign policy intended to destroy the US-centered international order. Influential politicians, both Republicans and Democrats, have commonly referred to President Putin as an extremely dangerous KGB spy with no soul. Trump, in sharp contrast, focused on interests and saw Russia's international concerns as not being fundamentally different from those of America. In particular, he advocated for the US to find a way to align its policies and priorities with those of the Kremlin on defeating terrorism in the Middle East—a goal indeed shared by Russia. He promised to form new alliances to "unite the civilized world against Radical Islamic Terrorism" and to eradicate it "completely from the face of the Earth."[24] He further hinted that he was prepared to revisit the thorny issues of Western sanctions against the Russian economy and the recognition of Crimea as a part of Russia. Trump has not commented directly on Russia's political system but he has expressed his admiration for Putin's leadership and high level of domestic support: "[Putin] is really very much of a leader. I mean, you can say, oh, isn't that a terrible thing—the man has very strong control over a country. Now, it's a very different system, and I don't happen to like the system. But certainly, in that system, he's been a leader, far more than our president has been a leader."[25]

Subsequent developments forced Trump to accept the dominant view of Russia advocated by his advisors and the political establishment. The US National Security Strategy and new Defense Strategy reflected the consensus view that Russia, alongside China, Iran, and North Korea, topped the list of security threats for the United States. Trump demonstrated that he was prepared to be politically flexible under powerful domestic pressures. He fired several loyal supporters, including his main ideologist Steve Bannon, and reversed his views on important international issues. Investigations, intelligence leaks, and critical media commentaries concerning Trump's possible "collusion" with the Kremlin made it difficult for him to act on his promise to work on strengthening ties with Russia.

Overall, Trump's principal beliefs have remained those of an American nationalist guided not by a universal mission but by a commitment to the nation-state of the American people.[26] As the president stated in his inaugural address, "We do not seek to impose our way of life on anyone, but rather to let it shine as an example for everyone to follow." In his January 2018 State of the Union address, Trump stressed "a clear vision and a righteous mission—to make America great again for all Americans."[27]

Competing Claims of Status

The similarity between Putin's and Trump's worldviews is not a sufficient condition for their developing cooperation. It may make it easier for each to understand the other's position, but nationalism and the propensity to think in terms of the balance of power introduce a potentially misleading lens when it comes to each side assessing the other's capabilities and intentions, a difficulty which may only be exacerbated further by domestic politics. This has driven the two leaders into an attempt to bargain from a position of strength.

Russia's foreign policy consensus is that the country remains an independent great power with global capabilities and a major voice in international institutions. Ever since the 2000 Foreign Policy Concept warned of the threat of "a unipolar structure of the world under the economic and military domination of the United States,"[28] the Kremlin has insisted on an alternative organization of the world order. It has been committed to a multipolar and multilateral world of great powers, and under no circumstances has it been prepared to settle for the status of a follower in a US-led coalition.

Multilateralism is of special significance to Russia insofar as it seeks to compensate for the relative weakness of its power capabilities with active diplomacy. In his speech at the Munich Conference on Security Policy in February 2007, Putin was extremely critical of US "unilateralism," accusing the United States of "disdain for the basic principles of international law" and of having "overstepped its national borders in … the economic, political, cultural and educational policies it imposes on other nations."[29] In another landmark speech, in 2012, Putin called for collective solutions to the world's problems but also made it clear that "the foreign policy of Russia was, is and will remain independent [which] reflects the unique role that … this country plays in world affairs."[30]

This view of Russia as an upholder of international law and the balance of power has encompassed both material and institutional dimensions in the emerging world order, reflecting the Kremlin's belief in strengthening its relations with non-Western nations. Since his return to the presidency in 2012, Putin has advocated for a world order respectful of cultural and political diversity. In a speech to the Valdai International Discussion Club in September 2013, he defended the notion of "the God-given diversity of the world" and the principles of collective leadership and decision-making, contrasting the post-Cold War order with those established following the Napoleonic Wars and World War Two:

> Russia agrees with those who believe that key decisions should be worked out on a collective basis, rather than at the discretion of and in the interests of certain countries or groups of countries. Russia believes that international law, not the right of the strong, must apply. And we believe that every country, every nation is not exceptional, but unique, original and benefits from equal rights, including the right to independently choose their own development path ... I want to remind you that the Congress of Vienna of 1815 and the agreements made at Yalta in 1945, taken with Russia's very active participation, secured a lasting peace.[31]

Putin further stressed the importance of multilateralism and international law while speaking at the plenary meeting of the 70th session of the UN General Assembly in September 2015, describing "any attempts to undermine the legitimacy of the United Nations as extremely dangerous," and again drawing a positive comparison with the Yalta agreement.[32]

Russia's intervention in Syria and Ukraine reflected the Kremlin's interpretation of sovereignty, cultural/civilizational diversity, and the multipolar balance of power in international relations. In attempting to build Russia's influence in Eurasia, Putin continued to put pressure on Ukraine and other former Soviet states. The Kremlin also worked to strengthen its relations with China, Iran, India, and to exploit non-Western institutional vehicles, such as the BRICS and the Shanghai Cooperation Organization.

In seeking to uphold the principle of a multipolar and culturally diverse world, Moscow has sought to demonstrate both its military capabilities and what Putin describes as its "geopolitical relevance."[33] The Kremlin's insistence on the status of Russia as a fully-fledged member of a multilateral, multipolar world is strongly shared by the country's foreign policy community. The above-described differences notwithstanding, its members agree that, when pressured by the West, Russia must defend its status and core interests. The widely shared opinion across political and expert circles is that, since the Cold War, the West, and the United States especially, has gone too far in ignoring Russia, and that such a state of affairs can no longer be tolerated. According to the influential Council on Foreign and Defense Policy, the Ukraine crisis made it clear that the West aimed either to restore the military and political divisions of the Cold War or to preserve the global dominance it had enjoyed in the 1990s.[34] In particular, the overwhelming majority of Russia's political establishment accepts the annexation of Crimea as a strategic necessity. The country's political class is in favor of engaging the West in meaningful cooperation, but not at the expense of recognizing Russia's right to protect its interests and act as a great power.

The position of the United States, however, has been radically different. Washington's consensus is centered on the idea of US global leadership and the preservation of its status as the dominant power.[35] With respect to Russia, the conventional wisdom has been that it is a declining autocratic power in no position to compete with the US on the global scene. Moscow's assertive foreign policy is therefore seen as a mask for the country's internal weaknesses, for which it is attempting to compensate with aggressive revisionist behavior abroad. On this view, the United States and other Western nations are better off trying to contain or transform an autocratic Moscow, rather than engaging with it as a partner in shaping the global system.

Official statements from Washington reflect this perspective. Following President Obama's reference to Russia as a "regional power" that threatens others "out of weakness,"[36] other US officials expressed similar convictions, even while recognizing Russia as a high-level national security threat. Acting on the assumption of Russia's weakness, they often dismissed the Kremlin's opposition to US foreign policy and expected it to concede under pressure. Following the imposition of sanctions, Obama claimed in January 2015 that the Russian economy was "in tatters," while Anders Aslund of the Peterson Institute for International Economics predicted a 10 percent drop in Russia's GDP during the year.[37] In fact, Russia's economy contracted by 3.7 percent. Many American observers viewed Russia's military intervention in Syria as indicative of Putin's "autocratic" instincts and "adventurist" foreign policy, which, they warned, was likely to result in failure. Obama even stated that "an attempt by Russia to prop up Assad and try to pacify the population is just going to get them stuck in a quagmire."[38] The quagmire scenario never materialized, and by early 2017 the coalition of Russia, Syria, Iran, and Turkey had defeated ISIS in Aleppo and Palmyra, achieved a ceasefire, and initiated the process of political negotiation between Damascus and the Syrian rebel factions.

The arrival of Donald Trump and his initial statements on Russia were perceived by many in Washington's establishment as indicating his readiness to engage with Putin on the latter's terms. To many Democrats and liberal observers, Trump's disinterest in promoting global institutions and his publicly expressed doubt that the Kremlin was behind the cyber attacks on the Democratic National Committee served to exacerbate the problem. Several intelligence leaks to the press and Congressional investigations further contributed to the image of a president who was not motivated by US interests. The intelligence report on Russia's alleged hacking of the US electoral system released on January 8, 2017 served to consolidate the Russia-as-enemy image. After losing the presidential election, Hillary Clinton partly attributed Trump's victory to the role played by Russia. Overall, domestic politics have served to complicate Trump's relations with Russia. The Washington establishment sought to exploit the issue of status and secure the US position within the international system by attacking Trump for being "soft" on Russia. However, the president soon made it clear that he was not willing to concede on power grounds and instead wanted to engage in tough bargaining with Russia by insisting on American terms. As one commentator observed, "President Trump may be looking for 'good deals' for the United States in working with Russia—meaning deals in which he believes that America gets what it wants and needs from Moscow at the lowest reasonable cost to Washington."[39]

This belief in engagement on American terms reflected the position of others in the Trump administration. For example, speaking with NATO countries in February 2017, US Defense Secretary James Mattis expressed an openness to "opportunities to restore a cooperative relationship with Moscow, while being realistic in our expectations and ensuring our diplomats negotiate from a position of strength."[40] This view was later incorporated into Trump's new Defense Strategy, which stated that, "More than any other nation, America can expand the competitive space, seizing the initiative to challenge our competitors where we possess advantages and they lack strength ... As we expand the competitive space, we continue to offer competitors and adversaries an outstretched hand, open to opportunities for cooperation but from a position of strength and based on our national interests."[41] The belief in power superiority remains firmly rooted within the US political class, making it difficult for America to engage with Russia on mutually acceptable terms.

Russia's asymmetric capabilities

The limits of Russia's power

Since the end of the Cold War Russia has been acutely aware of its considerably reduced power capabilities. As the United States and other Western nations strengthened their position in the international system, Russia suffered a loss of territory, a major economic depression, and a decline in governance. As one observer wrote in 2001, Russia was becoming irrelevant and unable to "make it," with or without Western help.[42] The country began to recover only in the second half of the 2000s, surpassing its 1990 GDP and reducing its poverty rate to 10 percent in late 2006.[43] Putin's leadership helped to revive the economy and a good measure of political viability. Soon after coming to power, he concentrated on integrating the previously excluded security elites into the ruling class and rebuilding Russia as a "normal great power" by reforming the economy, offering competitive energy prices on the global market, and ensuring political stability.[44] In

2007 Putin delivered a sharply phrased speech at the Munich Security Conference in which he indicated Russia's readiness to defend its interests, values, and status.

Even after having recovered from its crisis, however, Russia was in no position to directly challenge the United States and the US-centered international order. From an economic, military, and reputational standpoint Russia's power was of a regional rather than global caliber. Its capacity to defend its interests and project influence—whether by means of soft or hard power—was limited even in Eurasia. For example, Russia's conflict with Georgia in August 2008 demonstrated the need for military reform and a strategy for strengthening its reputation among its neighbors. When Moscow recognized South Ossetia and Abkhazia's independence from Tbilisi following the war with Georgia, not even Russia's closest allies such as Belarus and the Central Asian republics supported the Kremlin.

Moscow has been also mindful of the Cold War experience, which taught it that Western pressures cannot be withstood by attempting to match the West's resources and defense expenditures or replicating its methods of competition. Such an approach was partly responsible for the breakup of the Soviet system, which collapsed due to Mikhail Gorbachev's flawed policies as well as the misguided decision to maintain defense expenditures at the level required to sustain an arms race with the United States. The policy of preserving strategic parity had undermined the Soviet's energy-dependent economy and had to be avoided in the future. During the Cold War, the Soviet military budget had accounted for 15–20 percent of GDP, rising to roughly 40 percent in the 1980s.[45]

While the post-Cold War order placed the United States in the position of unipolar leader, it did not eliminate the space for competition among states.[46] Realist scholars of international relations tend to measure power in aggregate terms, thereby missing its more subtle dimensions.[47] Still, even those realists who insist on the durability of the unipolar system acknowledge that a unipolar world is consistent with almost any distribution of non-military power.[48] In addition, many scholars challenge the notion of unipolarity, arguing that a transition is now underway toward a different kind of system.[49]

Russia's strategy of defending its national objectives in a US-centered world took Western superiority as a given. However, the Kremlin also assumed that the West's power was in gradual decline and that this could be exploited in the Russian interest. The goal was not to force a defeat or surrender of the other side. Rather than aiming for conflict, Russia wanted to secure the West's cooperation and its recognition of what Moscow views as its proper status in the international order. The goal has been to make the Western nations recognize that status by demonstrating the limitations of their power and revealing their vulnerabilities in military, economic, political, and cultural dimensions.

Russia's policy makers have sounded in unison by stressing pragmatic ("*nezatratnyi*") means for achieving the country's objectives. Ever since Putin's rise to power, the definition of Russia's international objectives in official documents has shifted from that of attempting to balance the West toward one of exploiting it to Russia's advantage. For instance, in his Annual Address of 2012, Putin stressed the importance of Russia filling the geopolitical vacuum:

> Russia must not only preserve its geopolitical relevance—it must multiply it, it must generate demand among our neighbors and partners. I emphasize that this is in our own interest. This applies to our economy, culture, science and education, as well as our diplomacy, particularly the ability to mobilize collective actions

at the international level. Last but not least it applies to our military might that guarantees Russia's security and independence.[50]

Putin further insisted on the preservation of a "new balance of economic, civilizational and military forces" and instructed the government to pay more attention to the development of patriotic and military education. In the meantime, the Russian military has been debating the notion of winning wars without direct military contact with stronger adversaries by relying on technologically sophisticated covert tactics and non-state actors.[51] Finally, Russian diplomats have long appreciated the importance of flexible coalitions. In Foreign Minister Sergei Lavrov's words: "contemporary international life with its increased complexity and dynamics requires creative solutions that are easier to find through network diplomacy rather than entangling military-political alliances with their burdensome rigid commitments."[52] Russia's diplomatic pragmatism assumes the growing importance of multiple models of economic and political development that are increasingly replacing the dominant Western model.[53]

The asymmetric rivalry

Russia therefore seeks to defend its interests, values, and status by avoiding unnecessary antagonisms with the West and relying on low-cost methods. In principle, as recognized by the Chairman of NATO's Military Committee, General Petr Pavel, the new relationship with Russia is no longer binary or mutually exclusive and can involve elements of deterrence, competition, and engagement, depending on the issue.[54] However, because the Western nations view Moscow's assertion of its international priorities as a threat to the US-centered order, Russia's actions often take the form of asymmetric rivalry.

Asymmetric international relationships, as defined by Brantly Womack, are those "in which the smaller side cannot threaten the larger, and yet the larger cannot force its preferences on the smaller at a cost acceptable to itself."[55] In this sense, "asymmetric relationships remain problematic for the stronger side," and "sustainable leadership, even by a great power, is not simply a question of maintaining relative power."[56] As summarized by David Baldwin, whereas Thucydides' *Melian Dialogue* asserts that the strong do what they can, while the weak suffer what they must, the theory of asymmetric relationships suggests that the strong do what is feasible (or cost-effective), while the weak do what they can.[57]

Russia's asymmetric methods may be military, economic, diplomatic, or linked to values and media. In each area, Russia is prepared to challenge the other side—often in a concealed or unpublicized way— while remaining open to cooperation. A greater economic, political, and media openness since the emergence of post-Cold War globalization has provided Russia with additional opportunities to pursue asymmetric actions. Table 3.1 summarizes the differences between symmetric and asymmetric rivalries.

Table 3.1 Symmetric and Asymmetric Rivalry

	Symmetric rivalry	Asymmetric rivalry
International system	Stable bipolarity	Declining unipolarity
Military means	Deterrence and protection of allies	Attacks on vulnerable targets
Economic means	Priority ties with allies	Diversified and flexible ties
Values and media	Consolidating one's own values and those of one's allies	Discrediting the Other
Diplomacy	Established formats	Alternative formats

Russia's military advantages relative to the West do not lie in the area of funding or size. Its military budget is approximately ten times less than that of America and at least twelve times smaller than that of NATO. The Kremlin is not getting ready to fight a major war with the US or NATO, but rather looking to build capacity to prevent the alliance's encroachment on Russia's perceived sphere of influence. Regional geography and ties with neighbors assist Moscow in achieving its objective of preventing the United States from dominating the Eurasian land mass from the Far East to the Balkans and Eastern Europe. Russia maintains a strong nuclear arsenal yet is not interested in matching the American nuclear modernization budget. The Kremlin is also developing a flexible capacity in the areas of cyber and conventional warfare. Russia's military is today driven by considerations of sufficiency, rather than parity with Western forces as during the Cold War. For these limited purposes, it is sufficiently reformed and adequately funded. The recent military operations in Ukraine and Syria have demonstrated Russia's innovative tactics and its ability to achieve its objectives, without the major troop deployments, by exploiting the West's weaknesses and attacking geopolitically vulnerable sites.

Regional geopolitics also assist Russia in securing economic influence in Eurasia. Many of the former Soviet and East European states are dependent on Russia for energy supplies and for access to its markets. Although energy prices have declined relative to the 2000s, Russian gas is likely to preserve its importance and will continue to account for over 30 percent of European demand. Even after placing sanctions on the Russian economy and energy sector, the EU continues to depend heavily on Russian gas. Outside European markets, Moscow aims to develop its role as a global middleman by coordinating its production with other key energy producers and offering its energy expertise across the world. Playing this role also increases its influence in Asia, the Muslim world and the former Soviet region.

Asymmetric rivalry in the area of values and media assumes the need to expose the opponent's weaknesses, while preserving one's own cultural advantages. Russia's media resources are considerably smaller than those of the United States and Western nations, but are sufficient for disorienting the other side and preserving considerable regional influence. In the West, Russia works to undermine the dominant narrative of liberal democratic values, while in Eurasia it capitalizes on common historical legacies and cultural similarities with its neighbors. The latter is possible due to shared borders, the historical experience of fighting the same enemies, and similar linguistic and cultural policies. Segments of the populations in neighboring countries continue to be attracted to Russian economic, cultural, educational and technological products. State-supported bodies such as *Rossotrudnichestvo* (Russian Cooperation) and the Russian Orthodox Church are active in promoting linguistic and spiritual connections to Russia across the post-Soviet region.[58] In addition, relative to some of its neighbors, Russia is perceived by some in the region as having been generally successful in accomplishing state-building tasks, such as providing its citizens with political stability, basic social services, and protection against external threats.

In its relations with the West, however, Moscow relies on negative propaganda by stressing the drawbacks of Western political systems, and seeks to deter the spread of liberal democratic ideas across Russia and Eurasia by filtering domestic information and taking the fight into the West's media space. Russia's contemporary system of state control allows the Kremlin to withstand Western political and ideological pressure by framing it as an attempt to destroy the country's sovereignty and independence. Despite multiple Western criticisms of Russia's system as prone to dictatorship, many Russians support it. The Kremlin's domestic propaganda is effective in part because it stresses the historically resilient value of a strong state in Russia,[59] which it mobilizes when faced with outside pressures.[60] Externally, since the early 2010s, Moscow has practiced its own version of media and information management by relying on lobbying and soft power,[61] developing media tools to challenge Western policies and promote Russia's international image. These tools include the Russia Today (RT) television and internet-based network, the news agency Sputnik, the radio station Voice of Russia, and the *Rosssotrudnichestvo* foundation. In addition, Russia has developed an extensive presence in cyberspace and on Western social media. The country is known for its strong skills in computer science, and supplies programmers across the world.

In the area of diplomacy, Russia's advantages lie both in exploiting established formats and promoting global political ties outside the West. It possesses important diplomatic resources in Eurasia and has used these effectively to resolve several violent conflicts in the region, such as those in Moldova and Central Asia. Central Asian states often welcome Moscow's assistance in security matters, particularly those concerning counter-terrorism and political instability. Here, the Kremlin has built on the example of its cooperation with the Shanghai Cooperation Organization and the Collective Security Treaty Organization. Unable to effectively respond on its own to the security challenge from NATO, Russia is likely to continue to exploit non-Western institutional vehicles such as the SCO, and to develop bilateral ties with China, Iran, India, and Turkey as well as selected European countries such as France, Germany and Italy.

Miscalculations and pragmatism

Russia's relations with Trump have evolved from initial high hopes to a considerably more restrained view. The latter assumes that cooperation with the United States, while important, must be limited and based on the recognition of Russia's power and interests. Following Trump's election, the Kremlin did what it deemed necessary to improve relations. In response to Obama's decision to expel thirty-five Russian diplomats allegedly involved in spying and cyber-interference in the US election, Putin chose to not reciprocate. Instead, he wished Obama Happy New Year and invited the children of American Embassy staff in Moscow to celebrate the holiday in the Kremlin. Two months after Trump's inauguration, Putin sent his envoy to the State Department to propose the full normalization of relations. The plan envisioned the restoration of diplomatic, military, and intelligence contacts and laid out a roadmap for moving in this direction.[62] The plans included consultations on cyber issues with Russia's top cyber official Andrei Krutskikh in April, and special discussions on Afghanistan, Iran, Ukraine, and North Korea to take place in May. The expectation was that by the time of Putin and Trump's first meeting, top officials from both countries would have met to discuss areas of mutual importance. The Kremlin hoped that the promises Trump made during his election campaign could be fulfilled.

As it turned out, however, relations hit another crisis in April when the United States accused Assad of using chemical weapons against rebel forces, and bombed a Syrian military base that was being partly used by Russia. The tough response from Russia included a statement from the Ministry of Defense that suspended an agreement to minimize the risk of flight incidents between US and Russian aircraft operating over Syria. This implied the possibility of Russia shooting down American missiles if a similar attack were to occur. The Kremlin duly issued a statement that the risk of confrontation between the US-led coalition and Russia had "significantly increased."[63]

This incident destroyed Russia's domestic pro-Trump consensus and generated new fears of US pressure in the form of military encirclement and attempts to politically destabilize Putin's system. Shortly after the Syria attack, US Secretary of State Rex Tillerson travelled to Moscow in part to alleviate these fears. Russian analysts such as Fyodor Lukuyanov warned that if Trump were to "keep striking Syria to put pressure on Assad and Russia, then Russia will have no option but to escalate ... That opens up the possibility of war."[64] The trip was symbolically important because Tillerson refused to meet with the pro-Western opposition and focused on issues of mutual importance in his meetings with Russian officials. However, the trip failed to resolve major disagreements or to revive the pre-April hope for increased trust. The Kremlin expected proposals to normalize relations on a mutually beneficial basis. Instead, the United States assumed Russia's weakness and expected it to comply with Washington's priorities regarding Syria, Ukraine, Afghanistan, and nuclear issues, in addition to taking responsibility for interfering in Western elections and ceasing any future such action.[65]

The Kremlin drew its own conclusions from the crisis and concentrated on addressing individual issues. When Putin and Trump finally met on the sidelines of the G20 summit in Hamburg in early July, they reached an understanding on concrete issues of cyber security, Syria, Ukraine, and North Korea. In particular, they proposed to form a joint group to address cyber security and initiated a ceasefire and the establishment of de-escalation zones in Syria.

However, the newly established dialogue was soon broken by the decision of the US Congress to introduce a new package of sanctions against Russia for its actions in cyberspace, Ukraine, and Syria. Under increased domestic pressure, Trump signed the new bill despite his criticisms of it as being unhelpful for improving relations with Russia. In the second half of July, the Kremlin responded by ordering 750 US diplomatic personnel to leave Russia, justifying it as restoring "parity" in terms of the numbers of diplomats working in both countries. The issue was escalated further when on September 1 the United States ordered Russia to close its Consulate General in San Francisco within two days. The US also sent FBI agents to inspect the offices and private residencies of the Russian Consulate.

In addition to this diplomatic crisis, the United States increased the pressure on Russia regarding Ukraine and North Korea. Secretary of Defense James Mattis and the newly appointed State Department envoy on Ukraine, Kurt Volker, travelled to Kiev and indicated that the US was considering providing it with weapons. Trump also issued multiple threats to use force against North Korea if Russia and China failed to prevent it from developing its nuclear program and engaging in further missile tests.

Russia responded with a mixture of sticks and carrots on Ukraine. Putin made clear that US supplies of weapons to Kiev would not alter the balance of power in the region. In addition, in September 2017 he proposed the deployment of United Nations peacekeepers to prevent violations of the ceasefire in eastern Ukraine and to establish the conditions for implementing the Minsk agreement. On North Korea, Russia cooperated with the United States by supporting the latter's proposed sanctions in the UN Security Council. Trump wanted more, stating before his trip to Asia in November 2017 that a good relationship with Russia would be "a great thing" because it "could really help us in North Korea."[66] However, in exchange, the Kremlin demanded that sanctions against North Korea be considerably softened. China also indicated that it did not believe sanctions were the solution to the issue.

Further developments in the two countries' relations served to further caution their leaders against unwarranted expectations. As Russia sought pragmatically to focus on areas of potential cooperation, it kept demonstrating its leverage in Syria and Ukraine, and on other issues. In the meantime, the United States wanted to cooperate with Russia on American terms. Washington continued to increase the pressure on Russia through sanctions, and demanded that the Kremlin cease what Washington saw as violations of the Intermediate-Range Nuclear Forces (INF) Treaty. In response, the White House signaled a new nuclear buildup.[67] US officials also issued Russia with tough warnings not to meddle in the November 2018 Congressional elections.[68] In anticipation of possible Russian interference, Congress announced a new round of economic sanctions following the Putin-Trump summit in Helsinki.[69] Under increasing domestic pressure, Trump accepted these sanctions and in 2018 initiated some of his own over the poisoning of the former Russian intelligence officer Sergei Skripal and his daughter in Salisbury, Britain, on March 4. According to the British government, the substance used was the Novichok nerve agent developed by the Soviet Union and banned by the Organization for the Prohibition of Chemical Weapons. Skripal and his daughter survived the attack and were released from hospital after several weeks. Russia claimed non-involvement and denied all charges, while the United Kingdom, the United States, Germany, France, and other Western governments held Russia responsible.

In response to these developments, many in Russia advocated severing contacts with Washington. Even senior members of the ruling United Russia Party expressed their disappointment with Trump and the way he was handling US-Russia relations. For example, senator

Frants Klintsevich, a member of the Party's governing council, claimed that the relationship with America was "far worse than it would have been under Clinton ... She's an experienced politician and ... her actions would have been based on logic and some kind of discussion. Here we're seeing huge swings in one direction and another."[70] The Kremlin, however, still hoped to continue dialogue with the United States. In particular, the two sides agreed to discuss the INF Treaty, Syria, and oil prices on the sidelines of the G20 meeting in Buenos Aires in November-December 2018. In the event, Trump cancelled the meeting citing a lack of clarity regarding Russia's actions during an incident in the Azov Sea. On November 25, the Russian coast guard had fired upon and captured three Ukrainian vessels trying to pass through the Kerch Strait without prior notification. Russia also detained the Ukrainian sailors. The cancelled G20 meeting, accompanied by American promises of new sanctions and supplies of lethal weapons for Ukraine, only served to further exacerbate US-Russia relations.

The US-Russia rivalry was also evident in relation to the political crisis in Venezuela in early 2019, during which the two countries again found themselves on opposing sides. When the speaker of Venezuela's parliament, Juan Guaidó, declared himself interim president and called on President Nicolás Maduro to resign, the United States supported Guaidó by introducing a series of economic sanctions and pressuring Maduro to leave office. Meanwhile, Russia, which has various interests in Venezuela, acted to help Maduro consolidate his grip on power. The Kremlin insisted Maduro's rule was "legitimate," blamed "outside forces" for destabilizing the country, and vowed to "do everything" to protect the Venezuelan president.[71]

US-Russia relations have thus entered new territory, no longer following the cyclical dynamic of cooperation and conflict that characterized the immediate post-Cold War period. The Ukraine crisis and the sanctions imposed on Russia by the West made it impossible to implement another "reset." Trump's and Putin's efforts notwithstanding, US-Russia relations remained frozen at the conflict stage, with the American political establishment blocking the White House's efforts to initiate a dialogue with the Kremlin. The polarized domestic politics in the United States resulted in the bilateral summits of 2017 and 2018 being accompanied by new sanctions against Russia for its actions in cyberspace, Ukraine, and Syria, and for the alleged poisoning of Skripal.

In addition to their divisive internal politics, Russia and America are also divided over their preferences for world order and their perceptions of each other's power. On the other hand, the two sides are still dependent on each other for resolving vital international security issues and cooperating on counter-terrorism, nuclear non-proliferation, and regional stability. They have had no choice but to look for opportunities to cooperate, yet they have to do so on the very weak foundation of undermined trust and disagreements over each other's capabilities and intentions. From an American standpoint, cooperation with Russia cannot be "anything more than compartmentalized, tactical and transactional—precisely because the core ideological and geopolitical cleavages are so pronounced."[72] The relationship has therefore been pragmatic by default, one in which rivalry and elements of cooperation have had to coexist in an increasingly fragmented and insecure world.

4

European Security

Russia and America have been rivals on various issues of regional and global security, clashing with respect to the stabilization of Europe, the Middle East, and Asia. They have further disagreed on global security in the realms of information and values, nuclear defense, cyberspace, and energy. While the previous two chapters provided a lens for assessing US-Russia relations in various settings, I now turn to addressing their rivalry in a critically important region—Europe.

For a long time, the European continent has been central to understanding the foreign policies of both Russia and America. While Russia traces its roots in Europe to a common Christian heritage, Peter the Great's victories, and the Concert of Vienna, America's influence on the continent—based on deep economic ties, largely shared values, and Europe's dependence on US military protection—has contributed to the United States' international dominance since the end of World War Two. Even if Trump does not place a high premium on shared values, he insists that European nations should increase their spending on NATO and reduce their dependence on Russian energy. He therefore continues with the established American approach to Europe.

Russia's post-Cold War efforts to increase its participation in European affairs were not supported by the West. The Kremlin has thus developed a perception of Europe as disrespectful of Russia's interests and priorities, including those of preserving sovereignty, traditional values, and spheres of security not controlled by the Atlantic alliance. From attempts to cooperate, the two sides moved to disagreements on security, energy, conflict resolution, and human rights. As the United States and European countries set about expanding both NATO and the EU, Russia put pressure on those it deemed insensitive to its interests and worked to strengthen ties with those supportive of its larger role in Europe. Gradually, Moscow shifted toward a policy of containing the West's influence by undermining its unity and preventing former Soviet states from joining European institutions.

It was in this context that the Russia-West rivalry culminated in the Ukraine crisis. Acting on their respective (geo)political logics, each side sought to prevent the other from increasing its economic and political influence on Kiev, thereby contributing to the instability which began with the popular uprising in late 2013. The Kremlin preserves a considerable capacity to achieve its goals in Ukraine and the larger region, and will continue to act to undermine the West's policies insofar as they disregard Russia's European priorities.

The United States and European order

During the Cold War, the United States provided the security umbrella for Western European states and consolidated the continent's unity by "keeping the Americans in, the Russians out, and the Germans down," in the words of Hastings Ismay, the first Secretary General of NATO from 1952 to 1957.[1] With the collapse of the bipolar international system in the late 1980s, the US emerged as the single dominant global power. Because of America's domination and Russia's considerably reduced capabilities following the Soviet disintegration, the overall

European power system can be described as a one-and-a-half polar system.

Today, the coalition of Western states in the region possesses powerful military capabilities in the form of NATO forces and the developing missile defense system (MDS), and preserves its unity through common institutions, economic relations, and shared information space. These capabilities, relations, and institutions served to cement the West's unity following World War Two, and leading American strategists continued to prioritize US involvement in European affairs. In Henry Kissinger's words, "the United States, if separated from Europe in politics, economics, and defense, would become geopolitically an island off the shores of Eurasia, and Europe could turn into an appendage to the reaches of Asia and the Middle East."[2]

The United States has sought to preserve its influence through leadership in European security institutions, maintaining strong bilateral ties with France, Germany, and the UK, and placing limitations on Russia. Following the end of the Cold War, Washington supported the expansion of the most prominent Western institutions—NATO and the European Union. At the same time, Russia was rarely considered a candidate for joining either of these organizations.

The US initiated the process of NATO expansion in January 1994. In response to several security crises in the Balkans and pressure from the former East European states, the White House invited the Czech Republic, Poland, and Hungary to apply for membership in the alliance. Following the conflict in the former Yugoslavia, the US supported extending NATO membership to Romania, Bulgaria and the three Baltic states, all former members of the Soviet bloc. In March 2002 Deputy Secretary of State Richard Armitage endorsed the idea during the alliance's summit in Bucharest, and the process was completed in 2004.

NATO's expansion slowed only after the Bucharest summit in April 2008. Washington was eager to begin a third wave of enlargement by extending a Membership Action Plan (MAP) to former Soviet states. During the summit, US Secretary of State Condoleezza Rice and President George Bush, supported by Poland and the Czech Republic, argued for a MAP for Georgia, Ukraine, and Azerbaijan. Even afterwards, with Russia and Georgia moving towards war in the summer of 2008, alliance officials continued to make the case for the organization's expansion and met with potential aspirants. For example, on June 20, NATO's Secretary General met with Georgia's president Mikheil Saakashvili to discuss the planned conclusion of the MAP for the country, and scheduled a traveling session of the North Atlantic Council to be held in Georgia in September. Less than a month before the Russia-Georgia war in August, Condoleezza Rice traveled to Europe. She found no time to visit Moscow, but on July 9 she went to Tbilisi to demonstrate support for Georgia's territorial integrity and the MAP.

Subsequent developments confirmed the alliance's desire to expand at Russia's expense. NATO leaders rejected Dmitri Medvedev's proposal to establish a new all-European security architecture by moving beyond NATO expansion and the conflict over Kosovo.[3] According to NATO Secretary General Anders Fogh Rasmussen, there was no need for a new security treaty "because we do have a framework already."[4] The expansion process then continued following the crisis in Ukraine, with NATO leaders inviting Montenegro to join the alliance and approving plans to deter Russia's "aggression" and "hybrid war."

The United States has also supported the expansion of the EU so long as it did not include Russia. In 2008 the EU launched the Eastern Partnership program to build special ties with six Eastern European nations—Ukraine, Belarus, Moldova, Armenia, Georgia, and Azerbaijan—yet failed to extend the invitation to Russia. The fact that the program was initially proposed by Poland, Latvia, and Sweden, all known to be especially critical of Russia, served to raise the Kremlin's suspicion that, rather than assisting these former Soviet nations in developing ties with the EU, the Eastern Partnership was a Trojan horse for getting them into NATO. At least some of the states the Partnership aimed to engage—Ukraine, Moldova, and Georgia—aspired to join the alliance. Following Russia's announced desire to establish a Eurasian Economic Union in 2011, the EU warned Ukraine against joining and indicated that Brussels would consider an associate membership agreement for Kiev. In Moscow, this was viewed as confirmation that the Eastern Partnership program was being introduced as a geopolitical competitor to Russia's foreign policy and priorities in Europe. As one scholar concluded, the EU's policies were aimed at limiting Russia's influence, rather than promoting its own stated goals of "good governance, democracy, and economic integration."[5]

In the meantime, Russia's bilateral discussions with NATO and the EU were marked by tensions, and rarely produced substantive agreements. The disagreements concerned energy, economic integration, and resolution of conflicts. Distrusting Russia, the Europeans wanted to have room to change energy partners should such an opportunity present itself. On conflict resolution, the EU promoted the Organization for Security and Co-operation in Europe (OSCE), which Moscow viewed as deviating from its main mission of solving security conflicts to concentrating instead on pushing a particular version of democracy in the region. The Europeans also did not agree with Russia's proposed new all-European treaty to establish a new security architecture "from Vancouver to Vladivostok."[6] There was little progress made regarding the MDS in Europe and the handling of the Middle Eastern crisis. Overall, Russia found itself with no place in the European security system.[7]

Following the election of Donald Trump, US priorities in Europe have remained centered on preserving American influence, now defined, however, in terms of relative power rather than shared values and institutions. Trump's insistence on NATO members contributing their fair share to military expenditure, as well as his attempts to distance the US from Germany by developing bilateral ties with France, Poland, and Italy, indicate a departure from the familiar system of US-centered liberal globalization. For example, on a trip to Europe in July 2017, Trump made a stop in Poland to stress the joint fight against terrorism and to promote economic and military relations rather than common Western values.[8]

The rise of populism, the threat of migration, and the distinct perspectives of Southern, Central, and Eastern European states have further weakened the West's unity. In 2016, criticisms of liberal globalization intensified, resulting in the victory of Euro-skeptics in the British referendum regarding membership in the EU. The vote reflected the continent's economic and migration crises. Europe was suffering from structural imbalances, unemployment, debt, stagnant economic performance, and a large of inflow of migrants fleeing the instability in the Middle East. In 2015 alone, 1.3 million people of Middle Eastern origins reached the European continent.[9] The migration crisis deepened the already existing problem of Europe's coexistence with Muslim immigrants.[10] Those in favor of British withdrawal from the EU, or Brexit, received public support in part for advocating restrictive immigration policies. Hungary, Poland, and several other European states issued strong criticisms of the EU migration policy. Even in Germany the liberal consensus broke down largely over the migration issue, resulting in the weakening of Chancellor Angela Merkel's position. In 2018 she was re-elected with considerably less support, and was forced to enter into a coalition with the opposition Social Democrats. Finally, in

France during the same year, powerful protests over the government's social, economic, and migration policies took place.

Other parts of the world were also entering a period of economic and political uncertainty. Growing economic inequality and the decline of labor markets generated new protectionist sentiments, creating the conditions for a rise in populism and a fragmentation of the global economy, accompanied by increased political instability.[11] Even the traditionally stable European continent—let alone the Middle East, Eurasia, and other parts of the world—was increasingly pushing toward rivalry and competition. As Richard Sakwa argues, the new political tensions in Europe between Russia and the "Atlantic" West reflected larger changes in the international system.[12] The previously strong and authoritative United States was no longer able to arrest dangerous developments on the European continent—developments which have created opportunities for Russia's influence in the region.

Russia's goals and means in Europe

Historically, Europe has been of central importance to Russia. No other region has played a comparable role in validating its claims of identity, its status and its interests. Culturally, Russia views itself as a distinct yet essential part of the European continent. Different schools within Russia's political and intellectual class stress various dimensions of the country's connection to Europe. Conservatives focus on the unifying heritage of Christian values. Statists point to the significance of a common diplomatic experience that has helped to preserve peace and stability on the continent. Liberals highlight their commitment to European values of democracy, liberty, modern economy, and the rule of law.[13]

The Kremlin's approach to Europe has betrayed both its appreciation of the region's importance and its concerns about EU members' potential encroachment on Russia's sovereignty, sphere of influence, and security. As an economically advanced region, Europe is a source of ideas, investment, technological development, and commercial goods. But Russia's identity has been also built on the experience of fighting European armies since the seventeenth century, and includes a great power dimension. Russia's defense mentality remains strong and has only been reinforced by the tensions with NATO.

The Kremlin's main goals in Europe are twofold. On the one hand, it supports those within the EU—at both state and non-state levels—who demonstrate their consideration for Russia's sovereignty, sphere of influence, and ambition to play a larger role in the continent's security. On the other hand, it wants to prevent neighboring states from joining European institutions. Historically, these states formed a protective buffer zone for Russia and have been subject to its strong influence.

Russia's tactics with respect to Europe include asymmetric coercion and co-optation. Coercive means include covert military operations, economic sanctions, and an information war against states that are viewed by the Kremlin as hostile. As noted earlier, while Russia's military budget is not comparable to that of NATO, it is sufficient for meeting its objectives, especially when complemented with propaganda and economic pressures. Russia's co-optation tactic is based on the use of soft power and favorable economic transactions to appeal to segments of the populations within the former Soviet countries. The Kremlin stresses Russia's historic and cultural ties with those Europeans who share its Slavic and Eastern Christian roots. Russians and Ukrainians in particular shared the same state and fought against common enemies from at least the seventeenth century until the late twentieth. Despite the bitter conflict with Kiev since 2014, many Russians continue to see the Ukrainian people as "brotherly," sharing Putin's view of the two nations as parts of the same people.[14] This view is not shared by the EU and the United States, and is only partly embraced by Ukrainians, who remain deeply divided in their views of Russia and the Western world.[15]

Until the mid-2000s, Russia was hopeful that it could persuade its neighbors to respect its concerns and interests by maintaining economic and political cooperation with Moscow and not joining NATO. In 2003 the Kremlin proposed what it viewed as a mutually advantageous plan for restoring the territorial integrity of Moldova. The deal fell apart over the EU's opposition. In 2004 Russia assisted the Georgian leadership in defusing the Adjara uprising and signaled its willingness to assist Tbilisi in resolving the separatist issues of Abkhazia and South Ossetia. In exchange Russia expected Georgia to honor its interests in the Caucasus, rule out the use of force in dealing with South Ossetia and Abkhazia, and consult Russia on vital security issues such as membership of NATO. Georgia did not reciprocate and proceeded to use force against South Ossetia in August 2004.[16]

The Western policy of expanding its institutions contributed to Russia's alienation from Europe. The Kremlin's protests over NATO's expansion were ignored, while the alliance continued to march east and build new military infrastructure in territories bordering Russia. This extinguished Moscow's hopes of transforming the alliance into a non-military one, or of Russia being admitted as a full member. Western military interventions in Yugoslavia and elsewhere exacerbated Russia's historic security concerns and offended its national pride, prompting the Kremlin to mobilize anti-Western sentiments at home.[17]

Russia-EU relations also failed to progress in a cooperative fashion. While trade relations and bilateral ties grew, Europeans remained mistrustful of Russia and its domestic institutions. In 2002, the Kremlin's spokesman complained that European leaders treated Russia as a "mischievous student in the school of democracy."[18] The admission of ten new members to the EU on May 1, 2004 underscored the policy of constructing Europe without any meaningful role for Russia. As one observer put it, "a chagrined Russia finds itself not the architect of this new creation, or even a member, but an outcast relegated to a sideline role."[19]

In response to the sense of growing frustration, the Kremlin shifted from cooperative to increasingly defensive and then assertive policy actions. In the 1990s and early 2000s, due to its domestic disorder and poverty, Russia was in no position to resist the policy of NATO enlargement, but tried to work with the alliance by engaging it in joint security projects such as counter-terrorism. After initially supporting Serbia, Moscow opted to minimize its involvement in the post-Kosovo Balkans and even withdrew its peacekeeping mission from Bosnia and Kosovo in August 2003.

By the mid-2000s, however, Russia was more confident and willing to take action. Following the West's support for the Orange revolution in Ukraine and growing criticisms of Putin's "regime," the Kremlin increasingly shifted to an assertive policy that sought to contain Western expansion, applying economic and political pressure to former Soviet countries looking to join NATO. In June 2007, Russia's Foreign Minister warned that Ukraine or Georgia's membership in NATO could lead to a colossal shift in global geopolitics.[20] As the West had recognized the independence of Kosovo, the Kremlin moved to exploit the issue of secessionism. While US and NATO officials did not conceal their support for Tbilisi and rarely criticized Georgia's actions in public, Russia was increasing its economic and military assistance for the secessionist Abkhazia and South Ossetia. Russia also sent signals that it was prepared to work with separatists in eastern Ukraine.

For example, the Moscow Mayor and leader of the pro-Kremlin Unified Russia Party, Yury Luzhkov, claimed that Sevastopol was legally a part of Russia, and urged Moscow not to extend its treaty of friendship, cooperation, and partnership with Ukraine. The message for Georgia and Ukraine was that their membership in the alliance would come only at the expense of their territorial integrity. In the aftermath of the Bucharest summit, some Russian analysts had already argued that if NATO membership was so important to Georgia then it would come at the cost of losing territory.[21] In addition to economic sanctions, media attacks, and support for separatists, Moscow used military force against Georgia over its intervention in South Ossetia in August 2008 and—covertly—against Ukraine during 2014–15. The so-called "frozen conflicts" in the territories of Moldova, Georgia, Azerbaijan, and Ukraine were now exploited by the Kremlin to force compliance out of states unfriendly towards Russia.[22]

Following the US strategy of global regime change and the 2014 crisis in Ukraine, Russian leaders came to the view that the US was seeking to undermine Russia's political system and values through NATO.[23] That the US became heavily involved in the Ukraine crisis, despite having previously left it to the EU to deal with, served to strengthen this perception, progressively worsening the dynamics of Russia-West relations. The two sides remained locked in a poisonous security dilemma, viewing each other's increasingly active responses as offensive moves that required a tough counter-action. Ukraine, Moldova, Georgia, the Baltics, and other states in the region were now the objects of the Russia-West rivalry.[24]

Outside NATO, Russia has grown ever more skeptical of European institutions more generally. For example, it has severed ties with the Parliamentary Assembly of the Council of Europe (PACE). These ties were never harmonious, but in 2015—in response to PACE's decision to ban Russia from voting due to its annexation of Crimea—Russia temporarily withdrew its participation (and membership fee) from the organization. As of early 2019, the discussion within the Russian political class is over permanent withdrawal from the organization, rather than restoration of Russia's full status within it.

In addition to the Kremlin's attempts to prevent Russia's neighbors from gaining membership of European institutions, Moscow has been working with those in the EU who favor a dialogue over sanctions and military containment. Russia is fearful of instability and does not want to see the EU's disintegration. What Moscow wants is the ability to influence the Union's direction through special relations with its individual members and Euro-skeptic political parties.[25]

Bilaterally, Russia has cultivated ties with Austria, Italy, Hungary, Slovakia, and Serbia. All these states favor relaxing or lifting Western sanctions against the Russian economy, support the Kremlin's energy projects such as Nord Stream 2, and remain skeptical of the EU's liberal migration policies. Hungary, in particular, emerged as an important partner and deepened its dependence on Russia's energy supplies in 2017.[26] In addition, Russia shares special Slavic and Orthodox Christian bonds with several southern European nations. For instance, it has been a tradition for Russian politicians to visit Orthodox monasteries and attend intellectual forums in Greece.

Moscow also enjoys political leverage in those states that it views as pro-American and hostile to Russia. It seeks to influence Estonia and Latvia through their sizable ethnic Russian minority populations, employing targeted media campaigns as well as cyber operations and economic tools. The Kremlin has also exploited Serbian minorities to influence state decisions in Balkan states such as Montenegro and Bosnia and Herzegovina.[27] Russian media outlets RT and Sputnik broadcast in major European countries and NATO member states.

During 2015–17 Russia sought to influence elections in France, Germany, the Netherlands, and elsewhere by strengthening ties with Russia-friendly political organizations and providing favorable coverage in Russian media.[28] These organizations have included the far-right National Front in France and the right-wing Alternative for Germany. The National Front came third in the French presidential election in May 2017, while Alternative for Germany became the third-largest party in the Bundestag after the September 2017 federal election. Ongoing social, economic, and political problems in Europe may provide both parties with new opportunities to increase their influence.

The Ukraine crisis

Of all the East European nations, Ukraine has the most special significance for Russia. It is the place where the cultural, economic, and political dimensions of Russia's connection to Europe intertwine and reinforce each other. In addition to the two countries sharing Orthodox roots, Slavic ethnicity, and a similar language, Ukraine is a large borderland territory that has historically protected Russia from potential military intervention by Western powers.[29] Indeed, the ethno-territorial borders of Ukraine were partly drawn by Stalin in cooperation with Nazi Germany in order to establish a meaningful buffer zone protecting the Soviet Union from the West. Ukraine also connects Russia to Europe economically, as several Russian energy pipelines to EU customers run through Ukrainian territory. Many in the Kremlin perceive the connection to Ukraine as the last pillar of Russia's stability and power, the one that cannot be undermined if Russia is to preserve its sovereignty, independence, and authentic political culture.

It is therefore logical and symbolic that the Russia-West rivalry in Europe has reached its culmination in Ukraine. Washington and Brussels want Ukraine in their sphere of influence. Many within the US political class believe that the key to ending Moscow's influence in Eastern Europe and Eurasia lies in breaking Russia's connection with its Slavic neighbor. Among the first to formulate this idea in the 1990s was Zbigniew Brzezinski.[30] Although the EU leaders are not eager to accept Ukraine as a member, they do not want the country to be excessively influenced by Russia and are themselves in the grip of their own geopolitical logic.[31]

It was in this larger Russia-West context that the Ukraine crisis developed in late 2013–early 2014. When Ukrainian President Victor Yanukovich's decision not to sign up for EU associate membership was met with protests at home, Putin viewed the protests and the subsequent Euromaidan revolution as instigated by the United States, following the script of other revolutions from Serbia in 2000 to the Arab Spring in 2011.[32] Putin was convinced that the compromise agreement brokered by the EU between the president and the opposition on February 21, 2014 had collapsed because of the United States' intervention and the EU's unwillingness to reinvigorate the agreement. Putin acted as if thwarting the US ambition to influence Kiev was his last stand against global American hegemony.[33] Having embraced a policy of assertiveness vis-à-vis the United States since the mid-2000s, he could no longer ignore those inside Russia who have long insisted on protecting the country's values and security from what they see as a dangerous encroachment by the West.

The Ukrainian revolution and the Western backing for it mobilized support for nationalism inside Russia. The nationalist coalition behind Putin's Crimea intervention, his tough stance toward the new government in Kiev, and his support for Ukrainian separatists in Donetsk and Luhansk included security officials known for their close ties with Putin and opposition to NATO expansion. It was in consultation with this group that Russia's president made his decision on Crimea. As explained by Sergei Ivanov, then the head of presidential administration, economic advisors did not participate in the discussion on Crimea because of the decision's urgency.[34] Individuals such as Ivanov and Secretary of the Security Council Nikolai Patrushev formed a close circle of Putin's old KGB friends who have had access to him since his rise to power in 2000. Their decision resulted in the military reinforcement of the peninsula by Russian soldiers without insignia (the so-called Green men), the installation of a new government, the referendum on Crimean status, and Crimea's subsequent formal incorporation as a part of the Russian Federation.

The Western intervention in Yugoslavia, two rounds of NATO expansion in Europe, and the United States' decision to deploy elements of the MDS in Europe had convinced Putin and his entourage that their political system was also under threat. Although Yanukovich scrapped NATO membership plans and signed a long-term lease on Russia's military bases in Crimea, the Kremlin remained suspicious that his desire to strengthen relations with the EU was a path toward joining the Western military alliance. With the ascent of Arseny Yatsenyuk's pro-Western coalition in Kiev, Moscow had reason to believe that Ukraine would resume its drive to join NATO and renounce the Black Sea agreement that allowed Russia to keep its fleet in Crimea until 2042. By intervening in Crimea, Putin acknowledged that his leverage against Kiev—largely based on natural gas supplies and his personal ties with Ukrainian pragmatists—was insufficient to preserve Ukraine's neutral status and the presence of the Russian fleet in the Black Sea.

In addition to these security interests, the Kremlin was concerned about the historical and linguistic ties between the two nations. For a long time, nationalist politicians such as Vladimir Zhirinovski and Dmitri Rogozin had presented ethnic Russians as the largest divided nation and insisted on the imminence of national reunification.[35] Before the rise of political protests in late 2011, the state had perceived nationalists as dangerous, ignoring their demands or banning them from participating in politics. In 2005, Rogozin's popular nationalist party, Rodina, was not allowed to participate in elections to the Moscow City Duma on the basis of its use of ethno-nationalist slogans. The decision undermined Rogozin, who had been gaining influence and was planning to run in the 2008 presidential election. Since then, Putin has co-opted Rogozin into government and restored his movement as a legitimate political organization, thereby recognizing the growing importance of Russian nationalism.

During the Ukrainian revolution, Putin defended those in Ukraine who viewed Russia as their natural protector. Even during the brief war in Georgia in August 2008 he sought to protect not only Russia's security perimeters, but also Russian citizens and other small nationalities in the Caucasus. South Ossetia had on a number of occasions expressed its desire to reintegrate with Russia, and neither Abkhazia nor South Ossetia recognized their status as part of Georgia following the Soviet breakup. In addition, the overwhelming majority of Abkhazians and South Ossetians had obtained Russian passports throughout the 1990s and 2000s. According to the Chairman of Russia's Duma Committee for the CIS and Relations with Expatriates, Andrei Kokoshin, since "Russian citizens constitute a large share of the population living on the territory of South Ossetia and Abkhazia ... Russia must protect their lives, health, property, honor and dignity by all available means, like the United States and other Western nations are doing."[36] Unable to offer such protection previously due to its internal weakness, Russia was now determined to demonstrate that it had not forgotten those loyal to its values and interests in the Caucasus. Putin further embraced ethno-nationalist ideas in response to domestic protests against fraudulent elections to the State Duma in 2011–12.[37] In Crimea, he faced the highest concentration of people with traditional pro-Russian views.[38] Inaction in response to the Ukrainian revolution would have come at the high cost of declining support for Putin's claims to leadership both in Eurasia and inside Russia.

Steps taken following the Euromaidan revolution increased Moscow's suspicion that Ukraine was trying to break its cultural and historical ties to Russia. Kiev canceled the law establishing Russian as the country's official second language. In response to Ukrainians obtaining Russian passports, some deputies in the Rada proposed to punish those with second Russian citizenship with a ten-year jail sentence. The Rada also restricted Russian media coverage and formed a new government in which figures with ties to ultranationalist organizations were heavily represented. These changes prompted Moscow to view the new Ukrainian values as incompatible with those of Russia. In a press conference, Putin referred to events in Ukraine as the "rampage of Nazi, nationalist, and anti-Semitic forces."[39]

In response, Russia mobilized a broad range of instruments. On the coercive side there were covert military interventions in Crimea and eastern Ukraine, political pressure, the severance of economic ties, and a propaganda campaign in the media against the Ukrainian government. The Kremlin refused to recognize the latter without fresh elections and introduced new restrictions on energy supplies to Ukraine. The Russian state-controlled media referred to the Ukrainian government as a "fascist junta,"[40] and presented developments in the country as a confrontation between the values of the "Russian world" and those of Nazi-descendants backed by the West.[41] On the co-optation and soft power side, Moscow extended economic assistance to those in Donetsk and Luhansk who had lost their pensions and other forms of support from Kiev, and made it easier for residents in separatist territories to obtain Russian citizenship and work permits. In addition, the Kremlin found ways to shape and frame discussions on the internet.[42] By July 2018, Putin was sufficiently confident of support for Russia among eastern Ukrainians to propose a referendum in Donbass as a step toward resolving the conflict.

Western leaders reacted to Russia's actions by imposing several further rounds of sanctions and building up NATO's capacity to respond to Moscow's potential aggression. In addition, the US and UK have been active in arming and training the Ukrainian military, navy, and special forces. The expectation was that Russia could be prevented from further attempts to destabilize Ukraine and the European continent more generally. NATO moved to establish a Very High Readiness Joint Task Force, extended membership to Montenegro, and stationed four battalions in Poland and the Baltic states indefinitely on a rotation basis. The alliance also conducted massive military exercises in Eastern Europe involving over 30,000 troops and thousands of combat vehicles from twenty-four countries.[43] Western sanctions targeted individual Russian officials and included limitations on Russian banks' access to European capital markets and a ban on sales to Russia of energy-related equipment and dual-use technologies that could be used for military purposes. In December 2017, the United States approved sending lethal weapons to Ukraine, including Javelin anti-tank missiles. In late 2018, the State Department's Special Representative for Ukraine, Kurt Volker, raised the possibility of increasing arms support to Kiev, particularly for its navy, following the Russia-Ukraine crisis in the Kerch Strait in November of that year.

These combined efforts had a limited effect in terms of restraining the Kremlin and resolving the Ukraine crisis. Neither Moscow nor Kiev was ready for a compromise. During 2015–16, Russia drew up two agreements for a peaceful settlement after assisting Donetsk and Luhansk in defeating the Ukrainian army. Known as Minsk 1 and Minsk 2, these agreements were not implemented. In September 2017 Putin proposed that United Nations peacekeepers be deployed to eastern Ukraine to facilitate the implementation of Minsk 2 and assist the OSCE mission. The proposal remains on the table because of Russia and Ukraine's disagreements. Even the limited Minsk 2 conditions of non-use of force and negotiations with eastern Ukraine are not acceptable to a Kiev determined to restore its territorial integrity on its own terms. Russia's July 2018 proposal for a referendum in Donbass was also rejected by both Kiev and the United States.[44] Although Moscow is not powerful enough to force Kiev to accept its conditions for peace, its asymmetric power is sufficient to prevent Ukraine from using force in the east and to block its efforts to join the Western institutions.

Overall, American and European leaders have failed to force Russia to comply with their demands to relieve the pressure on Ukraine and conduct a restrained foreign policy. These demands cannot conceal the fact that the West is playing a weak hand. The United States' attempts to arm Kiev may increase casualties and suffering in the country, but will not change the military balance on the ground. Russia has significant geopolitical advantages and will not be shy to exploit them in defending its interests. The economic measures taken against Russia have had little success. Even accompanied by a major decline in oil prices, the sanctions have failed to change the Kremlin's behavior. In the meantime, most Russians have rallied behind Putin on the grounds that he is defending Russia against encroachment by the West. The more Western governments try to squeeze the Kremlin, the more nationalist and anti-Western the Russian public becomes.

Future rivalries in Europe

Russia and the Western nations have failed to build a common economic and security space on the European continent. Increasingly this space is being fragmented along various lines of competition within and outside the EU. While Washington influences the region by strengthening its military presence and developing bilateral economic and political relations, Moscow works to undermine US influence and make room for its own participation in European security. The Kremlin will continue to sabotage the development of the MDS and the expansion of European institutions at Russia's expense.

Moscow has failed to gain the West's recognition of its sovereignty, area of influence, and balance of power in the region. The Kremlin has not achieved what it wanted: the freedom to build a domestic political system free of Western interference; a sphere of friendly or neutral states along its western border; and a meaningful participation in European security structures. The United States and some members of the EU firmly believe in the virtues of isolation and containment as the right course with respect to Russia.

Having concluded around the mid-2000s that its soft power methods were not working for cementing its influence in Europe, the Kremlin moved toward implementing a plan B based on exercising asymmetric power and forcing the West to consider Russia's security preferences. In order to achieve this, the Kremlin was prepared to accept suboptimal outcomes, or a minimum of its initial preferences. Such minimal goals had less to do with Russia making a positive contribution than with the negation of Western interference. This included nationalist, anti-Western mobilization at home (negative sovereignty), frozen conflicts and controlled destabilization inside peripheral anti-Russian states (negative sphere of influence), and asymmetrical military defense (negative security).

Moscow has been able to sustain this approach because it continues to possess a set of powerful asymmetric tools. Its response to the internal crisis in Ukraine in late 2013— annexing Crimea and supporting separatists in Donetsk and Luhansk—exacerbated the relations with the West but helped to secure the Kremlin's accepted suboptimal outcomes. Domestic support for Putin remains strong; Ukraine is not likely to join NATO any time soon; and Russia's capacity to preserve its favored balance of power in Ukraine looks solid.

Russia remains capable of preventing the West's domination in areas of vital geopolitical influence in Europe. Its military, economic, diplomatic, and cultural resources are sufficient for the task. It has responded to NATO's military preparations in Central Europe and the Baltics by announcing the deployment of advanced nuclear-capable missiles into Kaliningrad and Crimea by 2019.[45] Despite NATO's fears of the Russian military marching west, Moscow is defensively oriented and seeks to perfect its asymmetrical or "hybrid" response.[46]

Russia has also persevered economically and politically. By 2017, the Russian economy had adjusted to the sanctions regime by finding alternative markets and incentives for growth. In addition, the sanctions have hurt the West's own economy. European producers in particular are increasingly deprived of opportunities inside Russia and are losing billions of dollars due to Berlin's decision to join Washington's sanctions. The Kremlin also reciprocated by implementing a package of food sanctions against Western nations specifically designed to affect those European economies dependent on trade with Russia. Russian elites have supported Putin and are in the process of shifting their assets away from Western to Asian economies. The larger population too is not in the mood to protest against Putin or pressure him to bow to the West's demands. The regime itself has further tightened its control over domestic political and information space.[47]

The West furthermore has failed to isolate Russia diplomatically, as non-Western powers have not been eager to follow the United States and Europe in their determination to punish Russia. Chinese and other international companies did not participate in the sanctions against Russia, and in fact gained from them. The Kremlin has also been effective in capitalizing on the image of Russia as a power working to assist those seeking to improve their position in the world. For example, during the G20 meeting in St. Petersburg many states declined to support the US position on Edward Snowden in part because Moscow managed to frame the issue in terms of resistance to US global hegemony. Most non-Western countries do not see the issue of Ukraine as demonstrating Russia's "revisionist" ambitions and do not feel threatened by Russia. On the contrary, the dominant perception is that the Kremlin's policies in Ukraine are largely defensive, even if they have not been respectful of international law.

Finally, Russia has preserved an important measure of cultural influence in Ukraine. Public opinion polls indicate that despite Kiev's effort to present Russia as the main cause of Ukraine's instability, half of Ukrainians maintain a positive attitude toward Russia, and this only increased in 2018 relative to the previous year.[48] Russia's religious influence is also significant. Many Orthodox Christian parishes in Ukraine are a part of Moscow's Patriarchy, and thus belong to the same spiritual space. Although Kiev has worked to establish independence from Moscow's Patriarchy by obtaining autocephaly from the Ecumenical Patriarch Bartholomew of Constantinople, most Orthodox parishes have not transferred to the newly established church. The Kremlin has indicated that it reserves the right to interfere by "political and diplomatic" means if the religious divide in Ukraine takes a violent turn.[49]

There have also been important divisions in the Western approach to Russia. While the United States—frequently supported by the United Kingdom, Poland, and the Baltic states—has favored supplying weapons to Ukraine and stronger sanctions against Russia, other European nations have been skeptical of piling pressure on the Kremlin and advocate more dialogue as a way to resolve the conflict. Germany, France, Italy, Austria, and others favor a moderate Russia policy and have been cautious on sanctions. This division has been often on display. For example, following the Kerch incident America called for more sanctions and military support for Ukraine, while the European Union opposed both. During its summit in December 2018, the EU extended the sanctions against Russia for six months yet refrained from introducing additional sanctions. These divisions continue to be an important diplomatic, political, and economic resource for the Kremlin.

Such differences notwithstanding, the overall Western approach to Russia's role in Europe has made it more difficult for the West to prevent the development of a rivalry with the Kremlin. Sanctions against Moscow and support for Kiev have already contributed to an escalation of the conflict in Ukraine and continue to serve as obstacles to peace. Ukraine is thoroughly demoralized and will remain unstable for years to come. The Ukraine conflict has resulted in a large degree of human suffering and social instability, with thousands killed and over 2 million refugees.[50] Eastern Ukraine may continue to depend on Russia's support, as most likely will Transnistria, Abkhazia, and South Ossetia. In other areas, the asymmetric rivalry will affect the belt of Russia's unfriendly neighbors to the west (the Baltics, Moldova, and Georgia) and those inside and outside the EU that remain vulnerable to foreign interference. The EU's relations with Russia will suffer further. The risk of a military confrontation will increase, as both Russia and NATO continue to feel threatened by each other's actions.

Short of major changes inside Russia or Ukraine, or a change in the West's approach to Moscow, European security will continue to be characterized by this asymmetric rivalry. Progress in solving the Russia-Europe conflict will therefore remain limited at best. The United States remains convinced that it has the power to restrain Russia and stabilize Ukraine, even if this is going to take a considerable amount of time. In the meantime, foreign pressures only strengthen anti-Western attitudes inside Russia, weakening the Kremlin's incentives to cooperate with the West. Many in Russia view NATO's recent military exercises as indicative of the West's offensive strategy and its intention to dismantle Russia's political regime and system of values.[51] The Kremlin is unlikely to bow to Western pressure when its core interests and domestic stability are at stake. Even those who favor sanctions acknowledge their limited effect and the fact that they have failed "in their most ambitious goal, to nudge Russia toward fulfillment of the Minsk agreements," because "Russia is prepared to incur large costs to maintain its influence in Ukraine."[52]

The current Western approach is therefore unlikely to safeguard the two sides from future dangerous crises.[53] As the Kerch incident suggests, such crises may develop as a result of Kiev's attempts to benefit from the Russia-West rivalry. Russia considers the Kerch Strait part of its territorial waters; if, by sending navy gunboats through it, the Ukrainian President Piotr Poroshenko sought to increase his domestic support and further isolate Russia from the West, then his attempt worked. He improved his ratings before the presidential election in March 2019, while American and European leaders condemned Russia for its use of force in detaining the Ukrainian sailors. As mentioned earlier, Donald Trump cancelled his scheduled meeting with Putin in Buenos Aires and State Department Representative Kurt Volker cancelled his planned trip to Moscow in December 2018. Since then, Ukrainian officials have vowed to send more vessels to the Azov Sea. In the absence of high-level diplomacy, such developments may provoke a hard response from Russia, strengthening anti-Russian attitudes in Ukraine and Western countries and further undermining security in the region and in Europe more widely.

Short of engaging Russia in a joint effort to ensure European security, Russia-West relations will remain frozen and, given the level of fear and mistrust, may even escalate into a military conflict. Sanctions and other pressures on Russia mask the lack of vision regarding the stabilization of Ukraine and the larger region on the part of US and European leaders. Joint steps toward normalization must include Kiev's military neutrality, guarantees for ethnic Russian minorities, and provisions for Ukraine to develop economic relations with both the EU and the Eurasian Economic Union.

5

The Middle East

The Middle East is yet another area marked by US-Russia rivalry and limited cooperation. Despite President Trump's initially proclaimed desire to reduce America's obligations and military presence in the region, he soon followed the traditional US policy of maintaining a strong political and military influence in the Middle East. In August 2018, national security officials in the Trump administration announced that US military personnel would remain in Syria even after the defeat of Islamic State, in order to train local troops, facilitate political transition, and contain Iran.[1] An unidentified official went as far as to say that "Right now, our job is to help create quagmires [for Russia and the Syrian regime] until we get what we want."[2] Earlier, in September 2017, Trump had made a similar U-turn by increasing the number of American troops in Afghanistan. The United States never supported Russia's increased role in the Middle East and has remained critical of Moscow's decision to intervene in Syria on the side of Assad. In December 2018, Trump announced yet another withdrawal of US military forces from Syria. His occasional announcements of America's reduced commitments notwithstanding, the US remains keenly interested in preserving its influence in the region.

In the meantime, Russia's radically expanded role in Middle Eastern affairs since the early 2010s has served the Kremlin's objective of undermining US global priorities and expediting a transition to a more multipolar and multilateral world order. While its intervention in Syria was in part a response to domestic imperatives such as fighting Islamic radicalism in the Northern Caucasus, Russia's international priorities included strengthening a multipolar balance of power in the Middle East, restoring traditional state sovereignty, and stabilizing Syria on non-American terms.

The results of Russia's intervention have been far from conclusive. The complexity of the region's political interests led to several incidents of Russian casualties, including the downing of civilian and military planes in October and November 2015 and September 2018, and attacks on Russian paramilitaries from the private company Wagner in May 2018.[3] The strategically important Idlib province is not under Assad's control and is not free of terrorism. Russia and Turkey's agreement to cooperate by establishing a demilitarized zone in the province and separating moderates from radicals is yet to bring peace and stability. On the positive side, Russia has largely completed its military campaign in Syria, established strong diplomatic and military ties with all major players in the region, and gained the reputation of a major power with a considerably enhanced political standing in the world.

US goals in the region

The United States' goals in the Middle East correspond with its ambition to remain the preeminent global power by protecting pro-American regimes, preventing the rise of threats from potentially hostile powers, and providing security in the region. The latter includes efforts to prevent nuclear proliferation, the spread of terrorism, and regional instability.

These goals have historically translated into five specific policies: containing Soviet/Russian and Iranian influences; ending nuclear weapons programs in Iran and any other state outside Israel; fighting Islamic radicalism and terrorism in Syria, Iraq, and other parts of the region; supplying military aid to US allies including Israel, Egypt, Saudi Arabia, Jordan, and Turkey; and promoting democratization and regime change in those countries opposing American policies (Iran and Syria).

The US record in the region has been one of gradual withdrawal since the second half of the 2000s. The 2003 invasion of Iraq changed the regime in Baghdad, but also gave Iran an opportunity to fill the geopolitical vacuum and increase its influence in Iraq and the wider region. Russia-Iran ties grew stronger and the overall influence of Russia has risen significantly since Moscow's 2015 intervention in Syria.[4] Instability spread from Iraq to other territories and resulted in a humanitarian and refugee crisis, with ISIS taking control of important parts of Iraq, Syria, and Libya.[5] The US also failed to impose political changes in Syria and Iran. As a reflection of these developments, and in anticipation of the region's approaching realignment, US allies in the Middle East—Turkey, Israel, Egypt, and Saudi Arabia—have each aspired to stronger economic and military ties with Russia. As a result, American power in the region has been challenged and undermined.[6]

The Trump administration responded to these developments by seeking to preserve US influence in the region. It grew critical of the Russia-Iran-Turkey initiative to launch a Syrian peace process in Astana, Kazakhstan. The US military became more aggressive in preventing Assad from seizing full control of Syria. On several occasions, the White House accused Assad of using chemical weapons and ordered the bombing of critical military infrastructure in response.

Finally, Trump rebuilt US ties with Israel that had been damaged under Barack Obama, and increased the pressure on Iran to limit its influence in Syria and elsewhere. The United States fully supported Israel's military strikes against Iranian forces in Syria as motivated and justified by Israel's right to "self-defense."[7] In May 2018, Trump also withdrew from the nuclear deal with Iran in an attempt to pressure Teheran into complying with more stringent regulations of its nuclear energy program and to curtail its ambitions to play a larger role in the region. While not seeking a regime change in Iran, Trump does seek to constrain the country's power.

Trump's decision in December 2018 to withdraw troops from Syria after defeating ISIS, while potentially significant, may not indicate a break with US goals in the Middle East. In December 2017, Putin had also declared victory in Syria and promised the withdrawal of a significant number of Russian troops, yet the Russian military continued to operate in the country. Besides defeating terrorism, American goals in Syria include containing Iran and preventing Assad from centralizing political power. These goals can be and partly have been accomplished without major troop deployments. Instead, the US has relied on air strikes, limited military contingent bases in Syria, special forces operations, and the support of American allies inside and outside the country. In addition to assisting ethnic and political groups in Syria, the US has an interest in rebuilding relations with Turkey as a counterweight to Assad and Iranian influence in the country. Alongside declaring its military withdrawal from Syria, the US announced a possible $3.5 billion sale of the Patriot surface-to-air missile system to Turkey.

Russia's Middle East priorities and threat perception

Russia's priorities in the Middle East follow from its favored global perspective in which civilizations and great powers consult each other on fundamental international decisions and negotiate acceptable rules of behavior. In this increasingly multicultural, multipolar, and multilateral world Russia sees itself as a state-civilization and great power with an important voice in shaping the global order.

The dominant self-image in Russia is that of a civilization that incorporates both Western and Eastern influences while preserving its own distinctiveness. A Christian nation, Russia has nevertheless developed strong ties with Muslim communities in Eurasia. Despite historically difficult relations, Russians have over time learned to coexist with Islam. Since the era of Catherine the Great, the Russian empire developed special ties with Islam by supporting those Muslim authorities who were willing to submit to its general direction, and even served as arbitrator in disputes between Muslims from the Volga River to Central Asia.[8] Indeed, since the second half of the nineteenth century, Russian thinkers have challenged Eurocentric assumptions by turning to the East, increasingly viewing it not as barbaric and backward but as a source of learning. In the aftermath of Russia's defeat in the Crimean War, philosophers such as Nikolai Danilevski and Konstantin Leontyev grew especially fearful of Europe and asserted that Russia was a "special cultural-historical type" that could not be viewed as a part of Europe. In the early twentieth century, some émigré intellectuals, building on these ideas, developed the notion of Russia as a principally non-European, "Eurasian" civilization—an idea that continues to be influential today.[9]

In line with this civilizational perspective, Russia's foreign policy debate is increasingly framed in geopolitical cultural categories.

In response to the growing global instability, Russian pundits have advocated a new civilizational project to strengthen the country's cultural foundations and preserve its complex relations with the outside powers. Some of them want Russia to strengthen its international influence by taking advantage of the country's "intersection" in the middle of Eurasia, linking its southern, western, and eastern peripheries through the development of transportation routes across Russian and ex-Soviet territory. Moscow also views the Middle East as critically important for transporting Russian oil to Chinese and European markets. Its influence in Syria allows Russian companies to control the transit route for Iranian and Qatari energy to Europe. In 2016 Russia also reached a deal with Saudi Arabia to boost oil prices by limiting production.[10]

Russian officials have identified two prominent threats to their vision of Russia as a civilization at the intersection of the Western and Islamic worlds. The first of these threats is a radicalized and militant Islam, or Islamism. Russian analysts and politicians often speak of special relations with Muslims, but differentiate between Islamic "fundamentalism" and Islamic "extremism." For example, Yevgeni Primakov viewed most Muslim Arabs as fundamentalists who observe traditional Islamic rituals but do not engage in violence and therefore are not threatening.[11] He made a sharp distinction between the Islamic states and the Taliban's form of Islam, which he described as "Islamic Extremism." Primakov wanted Russia to engage with the former and isolate the latter. In a similar move, Putin has on numerous occasions expressed his respect for traditional Islam as integral to Russia's religious, cultural, and social fabric, but separates it from "all forms of religious intolerance and extremism."[12]

Russia's fear of militant Islam has strong historical and domestic roots.[13] During the late Soviet era, Moscow learned a painful lesson about Islamic radicalism and cross-border Muslim solidarity when it invaded Afghanistan.[14] Following the Soviet breakup, the growing influence of Islamist ideologies, rising Muslim immigration from ex-Soviet republics, and inadequate state policies on the Northern Caucasus' economic and political integration created an explosive environment. Originally contained in Chechnya, Islamist terrorism spread to other parts of the region—Dagestan, Ingushetia, Kabardino-Balkaria, and North Ossetia. Following the Russia-Chechnya war in the 1990s, Chechen jihadists staged multiple violent actions in Russia by seizing a hospital, a movie theater, and a school, bombing the Moscow metro and airport, and sending suicide bombers to assassinate moderate Muslim leaders. These attacks claimed the lives of thousands of innocent civilians.

The second threat to Russia's perspective comes from a highly ideological trend within Western civilization that presents its values as being superior to those of the rest of the world, thereby justifying its unilateral, frequently military, actions against those it views as threatening its hegemonic worldview. An example of such biased perception is the mirror image of the Orient developed by Europeans to justify Western imperialism in the Muslim world, as documented by Edward Said in his classic work *Orientalism*.[15] Like others in Russia's political circles, Putin views such a perception as dangerous. The Russian position is that terrorism is a stateless phenomenon that can only be defeated through coordinated state efforts, and not by taking on relatively established states, such as Iraq. Related to this is the fear that military intervention will provoke a violent global Islamist response. In Russia's perception, what began as a counter-terrorist operation in Afghanistan with relatively broad international support turned into a "war of civilizations," an American crusade against Muslims, their beliefs and lifestyles. Instead of engaging moderate Muslims, US policies isolated them and handed the initiative to the radicals. Westernist and Islamist trends were therefore colliding, spreading violence and instability across the world. For Russia—a country with 20 to 25 million Muslims—involvement in such a "war of civilizations" would mean setting fire to its own home.

Russia's perspective is therefore principally different from that of the West and poses a challenge to the United States' role in the Middle East. Ever since NATO bombed Yugoslavia the Kremlin has treated the West's tendency to use force to solve global crises as a threat to the world's stability. Russia supported the United States in its war on terrorism after 9/11, but advocated a measured response within the United Nations' jurisdiction. The Kremlin supported the US intervention in Afghanistan but not its invasion of Iraq or its regime change policy and intervention in Syria. Russia wanted to reduce the terrorist threat, but saw the Iraq war as a deviation from the global war on terrorism.

To counter the threats of Islamism and Westernism, Russia advocates three policies, each designed to consolidate the multicultural, multilateral, and multipolar world order: preservation of sovereignty; dialogue; and strengthening the balance of power.

Russia's principles of sovereignty and dialogue

The Arab Spring greatly alarmed Russia for its potential to destabilize the region and bring Islamists to power. The Kremlin viewed it as a continuation of the US-facilitated process of regime change that had begun with the color revolutions in Eastern Europe and Eurasia. In order to prevent the further spread of instability, Russia has sought to reinforce sovereignty as the main principle of international law and restrain Western leaders from military intervention or imposing additional sanctions on Iran, while welcoming negotiations. The Kremlin remains fearful of a new war along civilizational lines and tends to view any kind of Western pressure on Middle Eastern nations—political or economic—as a prelude to a future military intervention. In response to the Western tendency to rely on force, demonstrated from Yugoslavia to Libya, Russia acts on the basis of assuming the worse-case scenario, and the West-skeptics in the Kremlin tend to prevail over those favoring cooperation with Western nations.

The Kremlin has applied the principles of sovereignty and dialogue to Iraq, Libya, Syria, and Iran with varying degrees of success. Russia was highly critical of the United States' military interventions in Iraq and Libya, but failed to prevent both. The Libya intervention became possible due to the then president Dmitri Medvedev's decision not to veto the United Nations resolution on a no-fly zone. Immediately after the West-sponsored resolution had been passed, Putin compared its language to "medieval calls for crusades." Medvedev took a personal risk by rebuking Putin. His mistake proved to be politically costly, with some observers noting that Putin's decision to remove him from the presidency in 2011 might have been partly determined by the confrontation over Libya.[16] As Putin expected, the West used the resolution to remove Gaddafi from power. Medvedev had to backtrack, and from that point on was critical of the Western nations for what he saw as their abuse of the UN mandate.

Having learned its lessons over Libya, the Kremlin emerged highly critical of the American position regarding Syria and Iran. In February 2012, Putin warned that the consequences of a military strike on Iran "will be truly catastrophic."[17] Acting jointly with China, Russia vetoed the US and Europe-sponsored Security Council resolutions on Syria.

Fearful that such resolutions would lead to a military intervention and regime change in Syria, as had happened in Libya, the Kremlin instead pushed for negotiations between Assad and the opposition. In May 2012, the Kremlin was even considering accepting the possible removal of Assad, but not at the cost of dismantling the Syrian regime.[18] On various occasions Putin expressed concern about instability in the country and the wider region post-Assad.[19]

With the Syrian crisis underway, Russia concluded that the West, emboldened by the regime change in Libya, was moving toward military intervention. In response, Moscow insisted on continuing to pressure the Syrian government to negotiate with the opposition over a transitional governing body, as was agreed by the Geneva Communiqué of June 30, 2012.[20] The document proposed that, once established, the transitional government would be in a position to prepare elections and a new constitution. The Communiqué was initiated by Kofi Annan and signed by five members of the UN Security Council as well as a number of prominent representatives from countries in the region and beyond. As Western nations and several Syrian neighbors moved to support the Syrian opposition, Russia held them responsible for reneging on the earlier deal and thus creating further instability in the region.[21]

The Kremlin noted the irony of Western political support for peaceful protests in Tunisia, Egypt, and Yemen turning into military assistance in civil wars in Libya and Syria, in which the West acted in concert with its mortal enemy, Al Qaida. In Putin's sarcastic remarks: "They might as well open the gates of Guantanamo and unleash all its prisoners against Syria. At the end of the day, this is the same thing."[22] With the West's support, countries such as Saudi Arabia and Qatar provided Syria's opposition with money and small arms, while denying them heavier weapons such as shoulder-fired missiles.[23] As some

Western and Middle Eastern supporters argued for supplying them with heavy weapons, the media reported that the arms flow to the rebels was benefiting radical Islamists and Al Qaida fighters in Syria.[24]

Despite these disagreements, the Kremlin remained keenly interested in cooperating with Western nations on vital security issues. As noted in Chapter 2, Russia provided important intelligence to the FBI and the CIA warning them about the radicalization of Chechen individuals residing in the United States ahead of the Boston Marathon bombing in April 2013. Russia also cooperated with US intelligence services over developments in Syria and Afghanistan, and was further instrumental in negotiating the nuclear deal with Iran in 2015.

In addition to defending the principle of sovereignty, Russia sought to facilitate dialogue with those whom it viewed as moderate and US-critical political forces in the Middle East. Following the US intervention in Iraq and the rise of violence in the country, the Kremlin proposed an international conference accompanied by an American phased withdrawal from the country. In order to address the growing suspicions about Iran's intent to develop nuclear weapons, Moscow encouraged Teheran to send its spent nuclear fuel to Russia. Although this proposal was rejected, the Kremlin continued its dialogue with Iran and increasingly strengthened its influence there. In 2015 Russia was instrumental in negotiating jointly with the United States the nuclear agreement with Teheran. In Afghanistan, Russia fostered ties with its official leadership but also established separate lines of communication to the Taliban leadership.[25] Despite Russia's traditionally strong ties with the Palestinians, Syria, and other Arab states, the Kremlin also worked to develop its relations with Israel and Turkey by developing energy projects and cooperating on improving security in the Black Sea area. Furthermore, it opened a political dialogue with leaders of Hamas, who won the

Palestinian elections but refused to renounce violence against Israel or recognize its right to exist as an independent state. Russia also condemned the "inadmissible" provocations against Muslims in the West, such as the publication in some European nations of cartoons satirizing the Prophet Mohammed, or the anti-Islam film *Innocent Muslims* in the United States, both of which resulted in violence against Western journalists and officials.

Following the conclusion of the most active stage of the civil war in Syria, and the US decision to withdraw from the nuclear agreement with Iran in May 2018, Russia has continued its efforts to preserve the fragile stability in the region. It has contributed to multiple rounds of negotiations within the framework of the Astana peace process. Launched in January 2017 by Russia, Iran, Syria, and Turkey, the process has focused more on ceasing hostilities and creating several "de-escalation zones" in Syria, and less on political transition in the country.

In addition to seeking a political settlement inside Syria, the Kremlin has sought to prevent a military escalation between Israel and Iran over their influence in the country. Tel-Aviv and Teheran both view Syria as critically important for their security and have long viewed each other as potential enemies. This has caused serious tensions between Russia and Israel. In September 2018 the Israeli air force bombed Iranian targets in Western Syria. Responding to the attack, Syria accidentally shot down a Russian transport plane killing fifteen people, for which Russia blamed Israel. With reports of further Israeli strikes on Iranian targets in Syria, Russia has been put in a difficult position when it comes to brokering a compromise in the region that does not threaten its relations with Iran and Israel. Indeed, some analysts have suggested that Russia is the only country currently preventing a war between the two.[26] As discussed above, Moscow views the challenge as one of preventing a wider inter-civilizational confrontation.

Russia's power

In attempting to increase its influence in the Middle East, Russia cannot compete with Washington in terms of military support or economic trade in the region. However, the Kremlin has effectively mobilized two other dimensions of power, capitalizing on its reputation as an honest broker committed to the region's stability, and providing targeted military assistance for those states not under US influence.

Russia's reputation as a state committed to stability and fighting terrorism has grown stronger over time. The Kremlin's insistence on negotiations and its critique of the regime-change strategy has found strong support inside Russia. Even liberal observers were frightened by the West's endorsement of what they saw as militant Islamist developments in the region. They feared not only the loss of Russia's influence, but escalation leading to a war between Israel and Iran, possibly involving the US, and with the consequence of further instability on Russia's periphery.[27] In the colorful language of the *Kommersant* daily, "The West, in painting [the Syrian opposition] as freedom fighters, doesn't understand that these guys are blood-sucking vampires and if they come to power there will be hell to pay, and for the Americans, too ... Russians understand it better. They understand that this is a conflict between the civilized world and the suicide bombers who cry 'Allahu akbar!'"[28]

If anything, these developments in the Middle East prompted Russian political and intellectual elites to push the Kremlin further away from the West. Conspiracy theories about the United States' intentional support for Al Qaida have been in circulation since 9/11 and continue to proliferate.[29] In particular, Western support for Islamists and regime-change in the Middle East has emboldened hard-liners within Russian Eurasianism who view the West's interventionism as resulting from its civilizational aspirations. Eurasianists anticipate greater instability in the Middle East, Afghanistan, and Central Asia as a result of Western interventions, and advocate a close alliance with Iran, Syria, and China in order for Russia to develop a "civilizational mission" and defend itself against Western influences.[30]

Outside Russia, support for its position has also grown considerably. China, India, Brazil, and Middle Eastern nations have not been critical of Russia or its human rights record in the region. Building on non-Western resentment of US hegemony and interventionism, Putin has strengthened his global reputation as an advocate for sovereignty, national unity, and cultural values. While meeting with Obama during the G20 summit in St. Petersburg, Putin secured the support of most non-Western leaders present for his position on Assad and the Middle East.

Russia has also worked jointly with other non-Western partners. The BRIC summits supported negotiations in Syria such as those that began in Geneva in February 2014. In addition, with the continued destabilization of Syria and Iraq by Islamic radicals, the focus of Russia and other powers has been on countering the region-wide threats posed by ISIS. By early 2015, ISIS had emerged as the leading force with the capacity to topple Assad and secure important territorial gains in Iraq. In particular, ISIS militants had conquered western Iraq and eastern Syria, claiming to control a territory with 6.5 million residents.[31] In June 2014, they took control of Mosul, Iraq's second-largest city, and in May 2015 seized the ancient UNESCO-protected town of Palmyra in Syria. To contain and defeat ISIS, Russia consulted both Western and non-Western nations, especially Iran. Moscow continued to bolster its economic and political relations with Teheran, in part for the purpose of jointly assisting in the stabilization of Syria and Iraq. Increasingly, it was also reviving strong ties with Egypt and,[32] disagreements on Syria and Iran notwithstanding, seeking to strengthen relations with Saudi Arabia.[33]

In addition to focusing on stability across the Middle East, Russia has identified potential sources of influence. Its relations with Iran and Turkey have been growing since the 2000s, in particular in the area of energy, one example being a deal involving the barter of oil in exchange for building electricity stations in Iran worth \$10 billion.[34] Russia also removed the ban on delivering the S-300 air defense system to Iran and supported its bid to join the SCO.[35] Although Russia and Turkey have supported different sides in the Syrian conflict, and experienced a crisis resulting from Istanbul's decision to shoot down a Russian fighter jet over the Syrian-Turkish border in November 2015, their overall perspectives have been compatible. The two states have been critical of the Western role in the region and they share the identity of a modernizing state with a civilizational status.[36] In addition, they have cooperated on energy issues, seeking to build an alternative transportation route to Europe outside Ukraine and Turkey, and aiming to become a major energy hub.

Due to its military success in Syria and its engagement in negotiations with all the relevant actors, Russia has further strengthened its ties in the region, including with leading critics of Assad such as Saudi Arabia, Turkey, Israel, and Egypt. In October 2017, during the Saudi King Salman's visit to Moscow, Russia reached an important agreement with Saudi Arabia on limiting oil production and came to a new political understanding of the region's realities based on the premise of Assad remaining in power.[37] Although Turkey remains a difficult partner for the Kremlin, Russia continues to develop relations, including negotiating the construction of an additional natural gas pipeline. Moscow has also continued to foster military and energy ties with Egypt. Finally, links with Iran have been strengthened, partly in recognition of Russia's still limited economic ties with its neighbors and its relatively marginal involvement with China's Silk Road initiative. During his trip to Teheran in the fall of 2017, Putin negotiated the development of a South-North transportation corridor that would complement the Silk Road by connecting India and the western part of Russia via Iran and Azerbaijan.[38]

The Syria intervention

Following Putin's trip to the United States in September 2015, Russia began a military operation in Syria. The intervention was not supported by the US and was designed to assist Assad in strengthening his position against his opponents, including ISIS. The military operation had complex goals and sought to win support from different audiences. It must be understood in the context of Moscow's attempts to increase its "geopolitical relevance" by restoring the balance of power and the prevalence of traditional international law in the Middle East.

First, Russia sought to protect the traditional Westphalian norm of international law defined in terms of sovereignty and non-interference in internal affairs. It wanted to cooperate with the West as far as possible, but never supported what the Kremlin viewed as the illegal forced removal of Bashar al-Assad from power. When the United States accused Assad's regime of using chemical weapons, Russian officials responded by rejecting the accusations, characterizing them as driven by the United States' geopolitical objectives and its desire for regime change in Damascus. The Kremlin aimed to boost its reputation as a legitimate defender of international law by acting on the invitation of Syria's official leadership and fighting terrorism in the interests of all established states—unlike a

United States that was covertly supporting questionable non-state groups.

Second, by defending international law, Russia also aimed to confirm its status as a power responsible for negotiating the conditions of world order. Many in the Kremlin understood that resolving the Syria crisis was crucial to the future political architecture of the wider Middle East and beyond. The intervention was viewed as a necessary battle for a future multilateral and multipolar world, especially given that many in the United States had been eager to demonstrate their superiority and military strength in response to the crisis. As already mentioned, a number of prominent non-Western powers, such as China, Brazil, and India, were also supportive of the Kremlin's position.

Third, the Kremlin was protecting its security interests in the Middle East and at home by defending its relations with Syria and continuing to fight against terrorism. Historically, Russia has had strong relations with the Assad family, and maintains a significant military presence with two bases in Tartus and Latakia.

Finally, despite its sharp disagreement with the West's understanding of the conflict, the Kremlin kept looking for ways to engage it in a joint project of counter-terrorism and stabilization. If Russia and the West could coordinate their actions in Syria, they could jointly inflict a major blow on ISIS and emerge as important participants in defining the political future of the region. The Kremlin was hoping to build on the previous experience of security cooperation with the West, such as the September 2013 agreement with the United States on a phased elimination of Syria's chemical weapons. The two countries had also cooperated on counter-terrorism by maintaining intelligence contacts over developments in the Syrian civil war. During his trip to Moscow in May 2015, Secretary of State John Kerry sought Russia's cooperation in isolating Islamic extremists in Syria and other parts of the region, and even acknowledged "catastrophic errors" in the US handling of the Middle East.[39] Finally, there was also room for cooperation on nuclear non-proliferation, as demonstrated by the joint agreement between the US, the UK, France, Russia, China, and Iran to limit the Iranian nuclear program in exchange for the lifting of international sanctions.[40]

The Kremlin's Syria intervention was risky despite the potential payoffs. Putin was widely despised and mistrusted in the West—partly due to his perceived efforts to undermine the West globally and by his attempts to centralize power on an anti-Western platform at home. In addition, the region's politics are extremely complex, involving the competition of powers such as Iran, Turkey, Saudi Arabia, Israel, and Iraq for influence and resources. Russia's anti-ISIS coalition ran the risk of remaining Shia-based, which would only strengthen Iran and so undermine Russia's relations with Israel and Sunni states.

There were also important risks to consider given the radicalization in the Middle East and Russia's problems in the Northern Caucasus, the potentially unstable Central Asia, and its own economic weakness. The Russian public was initially skeptical of the military intervention in Syria, with only 14 percent supportive of it.[41] Although Putin promised "no boots on the ground," the trauma of the Soviet war in Afghanistan remains unhealed and could play against further involvement in the Middle East. Active military engagement in Syria could have exacerbated problems at home, if the Kremlin overplayed its hand.

The tentative record

The results of Russia's Syria intervention have been both encouraging and disturbing. On the military front the Kremlin calculated that its hard power was sufficient for the task, especially if accompanied by the soft power of reputation. It ruled out the deployment of ground troops, relying instead on air strikes against multiple targets such as groups of militants, command points, oil fields and refineries. While precise figures for Russia's military expenditure in Syria are not available, some estimates assess it at $2.5–2.8 million per day, relative to the United States' spending on its fight against ISIS in Syria and Iraq of about $11.9 million.[42]

Russia's military participation in the Syria war can be divided into three distinct stages: strategic adjustment from October 2015 to March 2016; growing assertiveness up to September 2016; and significant victories thereafter. During the adjustment stage, Russia suffered a major ISIS terrorist attack against its civilian airline in Egypt, with 224 people killed. Soon after that incident, in November 2015 Turkey shot down a Russian military plane on the border with Syria, indicating Istanbul's radically different view of the situation. The Kremlin also faced the West's growing opposition and refusal to coordinate its military actions in Syria, as well as pressures from Assad and Iran to increase its level of deployment. However, in February 2016, Russia and the US agreed on a cessation of hostilities and made progress in separating militants from moderates among the opposition to Assad. The Russia-supported forces also liberated the major city of Palmyra from ISIS.

It was partly in response to these developments that the Kremlin sought to draw the line by announcing a "withdrawal" of its main forces from Syria in March 2016.[43] Russia calculated that it had significantly strengthened Assad, weakened ISIS, and consolidated its role in any future political settlement in the region. It now also felt strong enough to contain influences from Turkey and Saudi Arabia. Moscow also found a way to conduct a dialogue with the West and to send a message to both domestic and supportive Middle Eastern audiences about its relatively limited objectives in Syria.

Russia soon resumed military operations with full force, however, striking against ISIS and the militant opposition to Assad, especially the al-Nusra Front, with elements of air, naval, and ground forces. Inevitably many civilian casualties resulted from Russia's intervention. Moscow even employed its advanced S-400 air defense system and deployed Iskander ballistic missiles. This new stage of assertiveness lasted until September 2016 and included additional political and military victories, including seizing the city of Aleppo, which was critical to the defeat of ISIS. Politically, Russia reconciled with Turkey, came to an understanding with Saudi Arabia, Israel, and other states in the region, and reached an agreement with Washington on the moderate opposition to Assad, which was to take part in the political negotiations launched in Astana.

After September 2016, however, Russia found that its military tactics were increasingly being opposed by the United States. The two sides clashed in September and October, blaming each other for the collapse of the ceasefire in Aleppo. In April 2017, the US attacked a Syrian military base partly used by the Russians, over Assad's alleged use of chemical weapons in western Syria. The US continued to attack Damascus's forces in part to serve Washington's geopolitical objectives. By October 2017, US-supported Syrian rebels had taken control of Raqqa, while Assad's troops had captured the last ISIS stronghold of Deir ez-Zor.

As a result of this geopolitical competition, political settlement in Syria has been difficult. In Dmitri Trenin's words, "military action is only effective as long as it furthers a general political strategy,"[44] yet such strategy was lacking. ISIS was defeated but the country was divided into several zones of geopolitical control by rival powers.[45] The US reached an agreement with Russia on three de-escalation zones in southern Syria, but the sides continued to compete for influence in the country. The goals of the main participants in the conflict did not line up. Assad wanted to defeat the rebel forces and sabotaged negotiations with the opposition. The United States sought to control the area to the north of the Euphrates River, while restraining Assad in the south. In April 2018, the US again accused Damascus of using chemical weapons, this time in Douma, and ordered military strikes on Assad's positions, with Russia threatening to "take retaliatory measures" if its forces were affected.[46] In the meantime, Turkey wanted to secure control over the Kurdish area, while Israel and the Sunni states acted to reduce the Iranian role in Syria.

Overall, Russia managed to achieve some of its key objectives: it had defended Syria's sovereignty in not allowing Assad to be removed by the US-supported opposition, greatly contributed to defeating ISIS in the country, and enhanced its reputation as a major power and essential mediator in the region. The progress in fighting terrorism was partly due to its cooperation with Washington, which allowed both sides to coordinate their military activities and reach political compromises. US-Russia disagreements, however, remain deep, and the future of Syria continues to be a source of geopolitical rivalry in the region. The Kremlin's position made a peace deal possible but did not deliver a settlement. Russia's strategy was to strengthen Assad, with only 14 percent of its strikes being conducted against ISIS.[47] Its effective use of force made the United States recognize the limitations of its own power in Syria and fight to preserve its geopolitical influence, rather than domination, in the region. The US announcement of its military withdrawal from the country in December 2018 was a partial acknowledgment of this reality.

6

Asia and China

In Asia—the largest and arguably most important region of the twenty-first century—Russia has built strong economic, political, and military ties with China. Against Western expectations, these ties have continued to grow, Moscow and Beijing's distinct international priorities notwithstanding. Following the two sides' largest military exercise in September 2018, held jointly with Mongolia, some analysts have even raised the prospect of a Russia-China alliance in the making.[1]

Washington has remained skeptical of such an alliance's prospects. US Secretary of Defense John Mattis, for example, was dismissive: given their divergent security interests he saw "little in the long term that aligns Russia and China."[2] Viewing Russia and China as the most important threats to US national security, Washington has pursued a policy of containment with respect to both countries' international ambitions. By insisting on its America First approach to global affairs, the Trump administration has unwittingly created the conditions for increased Sino-Russian cooperation on economic and security issues. Following the crisis in Ukraine, and the introduction of Western sanctions against the Russian economy, the Kremlin's pivot to Asia has been accelerated. More recently, the US decision to raise tariffs on Chinese exports and its plans to impose sanctions on China for purchasing military equipment from Russia have further strengthened Moscow and Beijing's determination to cooperate.

This chapter analyzes Sino-Russian cooperation in Asia as a foundation for preserving the region's stability and prosperity. Relative to Eastern Europe/Ukraine and the Middle East/Syria, the Asian region, with the exception of Afghanistan, has been less affected by radicalization and violence. Russia and China have gradually built up the trust required for widening and deepening their relations, including on the most sensitive issues of national security. Their perspectives on the global order and their regional priorities—from the security of the Korean peninsula to coordination between the Russia-led Eurasian Economic Union (EAEU) and China's "One Belt, One Road" project— are now compatible. Moscow and Beijing have also developed a power arrangement that has helped to preserve stability in Central Asia by keeping American influence at bay. The more the US commits to the policy of dual containment, the more extensive Sino-Russian cooperation will be. As one analyst observes, the potential estrangement of China from the West may now serve as an additional incentive for it to cooperate with Russia and side more openly with Moscow in the latter's conflict with the US.[3]

America's declining influence in Asia

The American objective of preserving its global preeminence is increasingly being challenged by a rising China and Sino-Russian cooperation in economic, political, and military affairs. Despite the United States' intent to prevent the emergence of "revisionist" powers, as stated in its national security documents, Washington will have to adapt to new international realities and adjust its policies in the Asian region.

The first and most important US policy is to contain Chinese economic, political, and military influence in northern and eastern Asia.

Fear of China within the US political class is widespread and growing. That China presents a major national security threat is a point of departure for US discussions that are largely focused on strategies for addressing the threat.[4] Many experts increasingly favor containment over engagement, and propose measures such as investment in US military technologies, support for allies including by conducting joint military exercises, and increasing economic pressure on Beijing.[5] More recently, Donald Trump has introduced increased tariffs on Chinese goods in order to reduce the trade deficit in bilateral relations. In Beijing's perception, this policy of introducing trade barriers is a new form of the old containment strategy.[6]

The technology gap remains wide, but China is increasingly challenging the United States' political and military influence in Asia by involving members of the region in various geo-economic projects. Among these is the One Belt, One Road initiative, which Beijing is seeking to develop in cooperation with many countries and organizations, including the Russia-influenced EAEU. The EAEU serves as an area of Chinese investment and a transportation bridge connecting China to Europe. Beside Russia, the EAEU includes Kazakhstan, Belarus, Armenia, and Kyrgyzstan. Other examples of Beijing's economic activities in Asia include the Asian Infrastructure Investment Bank and the 16+1 group, which is developing Chinese-financed projects in Eastern Europe and the Balkans.[7] China has sought to organize trade around its interests and has reacted to US commercial barriers symmetrically by introducing its own restrictions on American goods and technologies.[8]

The second US policy related to the containment of China involves the protection of American allies, including Taiwan, South Korea, and Japan. Despite Trump's initially stated desire to adopt a commercial "transactional" approach to protecting Japan and South Korea, the United States later confirmed its military commitment to its allies.

However, because of China's growing clout and Trump's wavering commitment, all the US allies have now begun to strengthen their own military forces and develop their own direct relations and understanding with Beijing. Despite their multiple disagreements, China and South Korea have shared concerns over North Korea's nuclear program, international trade, and Japan's moves to revive its military. China and Japan have also increased their communication. For example, Japanese Prime Minister Shinzo Abe, in the first official visit in seven years, travelled to China in October 2018 to discuss North Korea, trade, and the disputed Senkaku Islands. In addition, Japan and Russia have been discussing a new agreement that would resolve their territorial dispute over the Kuril Islands and expedite their economic and political cooperation.

Thirdly, Washington refuses to accept the idea of a nuclear North Korea and is determined to ensure that Pyongyang terminates its nuclear program. Still, many observers are skeptical that the policy of denuclearization can be successful. Sanctions and political and military pressures, short of war, are unlikely to convince a Pyongyang that has no trust in American assurances and is mindful of the West's war on Libya following the termination of its nuclear program. Any arrangement to be made with North Korea will therefore have to partially accommodate it and be conducted with the involvement of regional powers, especially China.

Fourthly, the United States wants to reduce the influence of Russia and China in Central Asia and Afghanistan. In particular, President Obama initiated economic and security projects for developing bilateral ties with the region's leaders, with Secretary of State John Kerry visiting all five Central Asian states in November 2015 to reveal the new vision.[9] The Trump administration has also demonstrated its interest in building ties with Kazakhstan and Uzbekistan by hosting their leaders in Washington in 2018 and proposing cooperation on economic and security issues.[10] However, due to Russia-China cooperation and power in the region, these efforts have not succeeded in the past and are unlikely to succeed in the future. Pursuing a policy of "dual containment" of two major powers is not prudent,[11] including in Central Asia. Due to its geography, the Central Asian region is destined to be heavily influenced by Russia, China, and Iran.

Finally, the US goal of defeating terrorism and ensuring stability in Afghanistan and Central Asia is also dependent on Russia's and China's cooperation. The American presence in Afghanistan remains limited and is insufficient to ensure a robust political settlement, as the region's stability and security is increasingly handled by the SCO, with Russia and China as its founding members. Afghanistan's West-supported government does not command strong internal support. Although following his election Trump increased the number of US troops in Afghanistan, in December 2018 he announced a partial military withdrawal. In recognition of the country's instability, Russia and Uzbekistan have sponsored a new process of Afghan reconciliation involving anti-government Taliban forces in political dialogue.

Russia's priorities and power in Asia

Geographically, Asia is home to Russia, as almost two thirds of its territory lies outside Europe. Hence Asia's security and stability translates into security and stability inside Russia. Issues of North Korea's nuclear status, the stability of the Korean peninsula, and the struggle with terrorism and narcotics in Central Asia concern Russia directly. With the destabilization of the Middle East and Afghanistan, the

Kremlin is especially fearful of Islamist radicals and drug trafficking. In Russian geopolitical theory, the Central Asian region is viewed as an area located in between Russia and other "civilizations" that tends to be destabilized, exporting violence to the outside world.[12]

As an engine of global economic development Asia is also a source of Russia's modernization. Siberia and the Far East remain heavily underpopulated and underdeveloped relative to the European part of Russia. Building transportation and energy infrastructure, creating jobs, and attracting trade and investment are critically important priorities for Russia in relation to its pivot toward Asia.[13] These projects allow for the greater involvement of China, the two Koreas, Japan, and other neighbors. Russia has viewed the American proposal to build a free-trade zone in Asia as potentially diverting trade and investment if it does not include China.[14] Russia also seeks to capitalize on opportunities in Central Asia by exploiting existing energy pipelines and building new ones, engaging Central Asian leaders in common projects, and investing in their economies. As a strategic space between central and northern Europe, on the one hand, and the Middle East and eastern Asia, on the other, Central Asia—alongside Afghanistan, the Caucasus, and the Balkans—has the potential to connect nations and continents economically.

Russia's presence in Asia is also important for validating its status as a great power capable, in coordination with China, the United States, and other states, of serving as a guarantor of international security. Western analysts often stress the danger of Moscow becoming dependent on Beijing's foreign policy in the emerging world order.[15] In the meantime, rather than becoming a junior partner of either China or the United States, Moscow wants to remain a global actor on a par with both countries.[16] This quest for status partly reflects Russia's psychological need for recognition.[17] In addition, the Kremlin seeks to be active in ensuring that the outcome of the current world order transition will be favorable to Russia.

Russian officials have made clear that building strong ties in Asia is a priority. In September 2012, while hosting an APEC summit in Vladivostok, Putin positioned Russia as "an intrinsic part of the Asia-Pacific region."[18] He stressed the importance of strengthening his country's Pacific identity, and proposed to build a new Eurasian Union as "a bridge between the European Union and the Asia-Pacific region" by pursuing "closer integration of economic models, regulation and technical standards."[19] Following the Ukraine crisis in 2014, Russia established an annual Far Eastern economic forum to discuss prospects for developing the region and accelerating its pivot toward Asia.[20] Russia's contemporary geopolitical vision is one of a "Greater Eurasia" which includes China and Europe but excludes the United States. Such a vision was proposed by Russia's president at the International Economic Forum in St. Petersburg in June 2016, and involves the creation of various economic agreements between the Eurasian Economic Union, China, member states of the SCO and ASEAN, as well as the EU.[21]

The dimensions of Russia's power in Asia include its diplomatic ties, sophisticated military, and energy resources. With respect to diplomacy, Moscow has built a reputation as an experienced, trustworthy partner committed to preserving sovereignty and stability in the world. Russia has improved its standing by fostering bilateral ties and participating in international coalitions such as the SCO and BRIC (Brazil, Russia, India, and China). Relations with China, Russia's largest neighbor, have a strategic dimension and the two have demonstrated an increased convergence in their global priorities and proposals for solutions to existing issues in world politics. At the same time, Russia made sure that India too became an SCO member, thus limiting China's potential dominance within the organization. It has also worked on improving ties with South Korea and Japan, seeking to diversify its economic and energy relations away from China. In Central Asia, Russia is perceived as generally successful in state-building and continues to attract millions of labor migrants from Kyrgyzstan, Tajikistan, and Uzbekistan.

The military is another source of Russian power in Asia. Although China's military budget is larger and continues to grow, Russia possesses advantages in tactical nuclear weapons, air defense, and other types of systems. As a rule, Moscow does not sell its most advanced military technologies to foreign countries, but is actively engaged in arms trading with China, India, and other powers in Asia. Responding to China's growing military power, Russia strengthened its Pacific Fleet and its forces in the Far East region. In Central Asia, it has military bases in Tajikistan, Kyrgyzstan, and Kazakhstan. Russia is also a signatory to the Collective Security Treaty Organization (CSTO) and the SCO, and holds regular military exercises within the CSTO and SCO framework.

What makes Russia a necessary, even indispensable partner to Asian countries is its energy resources combined with its geographic location. Given that Asia is resource poor, Russia has much to offer, and has cooperated with China and other Asian nations on energy and transportation projects since the early 2000s. In addition, it has sought to unify the Trans-Siberian and Trans-Korean railways, viewing the latter as a contribution to the security of the Korean peninsula. Another logistical initiative was to utilize the Northern Sea Route to transport goods from Asia to Europe via the Arctic. The route is much shorter than via the Suez Canal, although it is open only four months per year. Russia also increased its diplomatic contact with Japan in order to eventually solve the territorial dispute over the Kuril Islands and open a new page of economic relations with the eastern power.

The Russia-China power division

Moscow's relations with China are based their similar systems of perception and partly shaped by their mutual concern about the United States' global ambitions. The roots of this similarity in perception lie in a common history, values, and national identity. The enduring legacy of communism provided Russia and China with a similar lens through which to assess the international system and their own development priorities within it. Both nations advocate the importance of patriotism in their system of values and identity construction, present their histories as continuous, stress the advantages of a centralized state, and see their state system as superior to that of Western nations.[22] Since the mid-1990s, Russia and China have been issuing bilateral declarations on their preferred multipolar international system. In 1997, the two countries signed their first "Joint Declaration on a Multipolar World and the Formation of a New International Order," which reflected their vision of multipolarity as a work in progress. Both powers have also been critical of Western interventions in internal conflicts, which they regard as violations of state sovereignty.[23] Western interventions in Yugoslavia, Iraq, and Libya, plans for the creation of a US-Japanese missile defense system, and the West's global democracy promotion have further consolidated Russia's and China's shared preference for a less West-centered international system.[24]

By building on their similar perceptions, Russia and China have developed a complex division of power. The two countries recognize each other's advantages in performing the shared task of containing US ambitions in Asia. Beijing views itself as an increasingly global power, while recognizing Russia's energy capabilities, military strength, and diplomatic capital. Moscow has its own interests in mind, while accepting China's economic expansion and seeking to find a niche in Chinese commercial and logistical schemes. As early as May 2003, China signed a twenty-five-year oil supply agreement with Russia's state company Rosneft, worth 90 billion US dollars. Since then, Russia has completed an oil pipeline connecting to northeastern China and plans additional pipelines and energy supplies. In 2014 and 2015, the two countries signed additional agreements on delivering natural gas from Siberia. If Beijing does not press Moscow for excessive commitments, and acts as a partner on important international issues, the Kremlin may win the time necessary for domestic modernization.

The complementarity in Russia-China power relations is further strengthened by their growing bilateral ties. Institutionally, these develop through the SCO, progressing partnerships between the Russia-dominated EAEU and the China-initiated Silk Road project, as well as through state-to-state contacts. The latter are not always harmonious or free of tensions. For instance, Moscow has long advocated that the two countries use their own currencies, rather than US dollars, for conducting all bilateral economic transactions. As of the end of 2018, Beijing opposed the transition to a national payment system out of fear that it may complicate its trade negotiations with the United States.[25] However, the overall dynamics of Russia-China commercial and financial relations are positive and continue to improve. All these ties, along with their regular military exercises, solidify their shared perception of threats having to do with internal instability, terrorism, and what they see as dangerous intrusions by the United States in the region.

The two nations' views of regional security issues are compatible as well, at least in the medium term. In Central Asia, the Kremlin favors the resolution of security problems through a systematic coordination of state efforts, and not through the use of force by ad hoc coalitions. It developed the SCO framework to address the regional security vacuum and threats from terrorism. In East Asia, Moscow has advocated a multilateral solution to the North Korea nuclear crisis, and in 2003 contributed considerably to the creation of the six-party format for dealing with it. During the US-North Korea stand-off in the first half of 2018, Moscow and Beijing cooperated in diffusing tensions by seeking to soften the American sanctions against Pyongyang and maintaining diplomatic dialogue with North Korea. In addition, Russian officials have extended their support for the unification of the two Koreas if it takes place in an orderly fashion and on the basis of inter-Korean dialogue. Russia supports this view with the objective of further diversifying political influences and limiting China's power in the region.

Finally, Russia and China have successfully resolved territorial disputes and issues of cross-border immigration. They have largely compatible perspectives on territorial integrity and have consistently denounced separatist movements within each other's territories, whether in Chechnya or Taiwan. The two states formally disagreed on the issue of Russia's recognition of Georgia's breakaway territories, Abkhazia and South Ossetia, with Beijing refusing to publicly endorse Moscow's action out of concern for its own territorial integrity, particularly in the light of Uighur activities in the largely Muslim province of Xinjiang. Informally, however, the Chinese supported Russia during the crisis in the Caucasus, and the issue has not complicated relations between the two nations. The Chinese media were on the whole sympathetic to Russia's position during the conflict, and Chinese analysts have tended to support Russia's suspicion of NATO enlargement.[26]

The division of power between the two can be demonstrated using the example of Central Asia. Here, as Marcin Kaczmarski writes, "Moscow and Beijing found ways to divide their influences, with China dominating the energy realm and Russia the security realm."[27] Russia's power in Central Asia is primarily, though not exclusively, based on its military capabilities. The Kremlin has worked on consolidating its military presence in the former Soviet region since the mid-2000s and possesses important military and geopolitical advantages.

On the other hand, the power of China in the region is largely economic, based on its ability to finance important regional projects and offset various threats to Central Asian economies. While Russia wants to preserve its economic influence in the region, it is increasingly unable to compete with Beijing and has learned to accept China's lead in exchange for the latter's recognition of its military and political dominance in the former Soviet region. In the meantime, Chinese military attention is directed less toward Central Asia than to the regions of East Asia and the Asia Pacific. Beijing has deployed no troops in Central Asia, and has expressed no desire to lease any military facilities there.[28] Therefore, from a military standpoint, Russia remains the regionally dominant power. This is acceptable to Beijing, which focuses on fighting local separatist and terrorist threats.

Challenges and solutions in Central Asia

The Central Asian region illustrates the above-described process of the United States' gradual withdrawal from Asia. Despite various efforts by Presidents Obama and Trump to strengthen the American presence in the region by initiating various bilateral proposals, Central Asian leaders have continued to center their international policies on China and Russia. Although they value economic and security assistance from the US and European countries, they don't view this as critical in fulfilling their foreign policy objectives. Indeed, in some cases, as observers have noted, "it was precisely Western disengagement that opened the door for change" in the region, with Russia and China both favoring it.[29]

Central Asia is, however, potentially dangerous and unstable. Destabilizing conditions include its proximity to the conflicts in Afghanistan and the Middle East; an authoritarian, non-transparent, and clan-based politics; a lack of resources; and limited experience of modern statehood. Externally, the Central Asian states have been negatively affected by deteriorating conditions in Afghanistan, economic slowdown in Russia, and increasingly unstable conditions in the Middle East following the Arab Spring. Should neighboring Afghanistan be destabilized further, the vacuum may quickly be filled by Sunni or Shi'ite radicals. The Central Asian region has also been an area of intense competition between the major powers for resources and geopolitical influence,[30] with "pivotal" states such as Uzbekistan and Kazakhstan often subject to rival pressures that have dramatic consequences for their own stability.[31]

Domestically, most political systems in the region are authoritarian and clan-based.[32] In the case of Tajikistan, a clan confrontation resulted in a civil war, while another in Kyrgyzstan contributed to a popular uprising in March 2005.[33] States with a strong national identity are in a better position to overcome the dominance of clan or ethnic affiliations, but Central Asian states appeared on the political map only in 1991 and therefore lack national identity and statehood experience.[34] In addition, they suffer from a shortage of resources such as fresh water and energy. Kazakhstan, Turkmenistan and Uzbekistan are richly endowed with natural resources, but are dependent on external water supplies, whereas Kyrgyzstan and Tajikistan depend on external supplies of oil and natural gas.

Despite the dangerous mix of internal and geopolitical conditions,[35] the region has been relatively stable in recent years. Since 2006, the Central Asian states have not experienced economic or political breakdowns, nor the degree of violence and instability that affected

Uzbekistan and Kyrgyzstan in 2005, let alone that of Tajikistan's civil war in the 1990s. Nor has the region had to confront refugee crises, which contrasts not only with the extreme example of the Middle East, but also with Central and Eastern Europe.

The region has displayed a generally positive outlook and demonstrated modest, albeit uneven growth. Economic developments in Kazakhstan, Uzbekistan, and Turkmenistan have been especially impressive. All of them have fully revived their economies, exceeding the 1990 level considerably, while Kazakhstan and Uzbekistan have made considerable progress in fighting poverty.[36] Most Central Asian economies grew during 2009–12, with a considerable increase in trade with Russia, although the latter's financial crises and recessions have affected Central Asia negatively.[37] Despite their authoritarian and non-transparent politics, Turkmenistan and Uzbekistan conducted stable leadership successions in 2006 and 2016. And despite the activities of radical groups such as the Islamic Movement of Uzbekistan, Hisbu-Tahrir, Al Qaida, and ISIS, the region has remained largely stable.

These positive developments contrast with the pre-2006 period that witnessed civil war in Tajikistan, the breakdown of the Kyrgyz and Tajik economies, the spread of radicalism and terrorist violence in Uzbekistan, and the rise of narcotics-related corruption in the states bordering Afghanistan and Iran. The 1992–97 Tajikistan civil war resulted in enormous economic devastation, around 1.2 million refugees and displaced people, and up to 100,000 killed. In March 2005, Kyrgyzstan underwent a regime change after mass protests accompanied by violence and looting. The relative stability since has largely been thanks to the Russia-China understanding and division of power in the region.

Their similar perceptions have helped Russia and China to build a mutually acceptable regional arrangement based on respect for sovereignty, non-interference in internal affairs, and recognition of spheres of influence. This has been expressed in their multiple bilateral declarations on their preferred rules for international order. The two countries have acted to block UN Security Council resolutions with respect to Middle Eastern states that they found to violate principles of sovereignty. Moscow and Beijing have sought to demonstrate that they are more concerned with meeting internal stability challenges than with assertion of their power.

The two countries' agreement on spheres of influence is informal and assumes China's recognition that Central Asia remains in the area of Russia's geopolitical aspiration. Beijing does not perceive Russia to be a security threat in Central Asia and does not seek to balance against it. While China has economic and counter-terrorist interests in the region, it has no ambitions to develop a military presence there; its aid is limited to non-military materials and involves little military training.[38] Nor does Beijing aim to culturally transform Central Asia. This attitude of restraint partly stems from various phobias about China's "expansion" into Central Asia that are particularly strong in Kazakhstan, Kyrgyzstan, and Tajikistan.[39] The attitude also has historic roots in China's old Middle Kingdom mentality which was based on tributary relations with its neighbors—Beijing demanded payments but otherwise did not interfere with their cultural and international priorities.[40]

On important occasions the two powers have acted in concert in support of sovereign decisions by local states. For example, both Russia and China expressed concerns over the Tulip revolution in Kyrgyzstan in March 2005, which replaced the Russia-supported President Askar Akayev with the pro-American Kurmanbek Bakiev. The latter was to receive considerable financial aid for agreeing to expand the US military facility in Manas.[41] Moscow and Beijing did not like the outcome and worked quietly behind the scenes, seeking to influence the new Kyrgyz government.

Another example of Russia and China's shared approach was their attitude to the events in Uzbekistan in May 2005. Fearful of a revolution similar to that in Kyrgyzstan, the Uzbekistan government used force against a crowd of protesters in the city Andijan, resulting in several hundred deaths.[42] In response to the West's criticism, President Islam Karimov ordered the removal of the US military base in the southeastern part of the country, and moved to strengthen political and military ties with Russia.[43] While Western states condemned Uzbekistan's actions, Russia and China extended their support for Tashkent by endorsing Karimov's justification for the use of force. The Kremlin stressed the importance of preserving order and legality, placing responsibility for the unrest on "outside extremist forces" from Afghanistan, including the neo-Taliban.[44] Both Moscow and Beijing invited Karimov to visit their countries. Chinese President Hu Jintao told Karimov he "honor[ed]" Uzbekistan's "efforts to protect its national independence, sovereignty and territorial integrity."[45]

Russia and China also refrained from intervening in Kyrgyzstan in June 2010, when the country went through another cycle of ethnic riots and a revolutionary change of power. Washington urged Moscow to send troops,[46] but Russia chose not to. As Foreign Minister Sergei Lavrov stated, "the Kyrgyz authorities must stabilize the situation on their own, and external assistance should be limited to only those forms that suit the Kyrgyz authorities themselves."[47] China too kept a low profile, limiting itself to providing humanitarian assistance and supporting Russia in its decisions. A Chinese Foreign Ministry spokesman even expressed support for the CSTO role in the conflict: "China has taken note that the CSTO has convened a meeting to discuss the situation in Kyrgyzstan and acknowledges its efforts to maintain peace and stability in Central Asia."[48] Again, Russia and China worked through official channels to advance their interests and seek to reduce the US military presence in Kyrgyzstan.[49]

In each of these cases Russia and China coordinated their actions. This was evident in their joint assessments of the threats and challenges facing Central Asia, as well as in the practical steps taken by Moscow and Beijing individually or through the SCO, including regular joint military exercises and high-level diplomatic consultations on sensitive political issues. Seeking to limit US influence, Russia also mobilized its organizational ties in the region. In particular, the Russia-controlled CSTO, which also includes Armenia, Belarus, Uzbekistan, Tajikistan, Kazakhstan, and Kyrgyzstan, amended its mission by pledging to defend its members from internal "unconstitutional disturbances." Although in June 2012 Uzbekistan withdrew its membership of the CSTO, it has maintained strong relations with Russia and refused to host any Western military forces.[50]

The Russia-China coordination should not be viewed as the consolidation of stagnation in Central Asia. The contemporary reform agenda in Uzbekistan is a case in point. Since the election of Shavkat Mirzioyev as president in December 2016, the country has moved in the direction of controlled economic change, media freedom, and international openness.[51] Against the common expectations of Western analysts, Mirzioyev felt able to pursue these reforms because Russian and Chinese support gave him a sense of geopolitical security.

Overall, the Russia-China division of power and its success in Central Asia presents a model for potential solutions to other problems in Asia, such as North Korea's nuclear ambitions, its economic development, and the future unification of the Korean peninsula. Increasingly, such solutions are being worked on without the United States' involvement and at the expense of US global interests. In all the prominent political and security issues in Asia where Moscow has acted jointly with Beijing, it has been able to advance its objectives of preserving Russia's great power status and delivering stability on its own rather than American terms. The Kremlin has fostered negotiations with North Korea, developed special relations in Central Asia, and made counter-terrorism and the resolution of the Afghanistan conflict part of the SCO agenda. It has also made progress in attracting Asian investors, despite the US insistence that Asian nations uphold sanctions against Russia. As the American presence in the region shrinks, the scope for US-Russia rivalry in the region also declines.

7

Values and Information

The US-Russia rivalry takes place not only in regional but in global contexts as well. The remainder of the book analyzes the two sides' rivalry over several distinct global issues—values and the management of information, nuclear and cyber power, energy, and sanctions.

This chapter engages with the question of values and information. In the United States a struggle over values and the control of national discourse has been taking place between the liberal media accusing President Trump of "collusion" with Russia, and Trump's supporters who refer to CNN, the *New York Times*, and other mainstream media outlets as purveyors of "fake news" and agents of the "deep state." On the international front, America and Russia frequently refuse to accept their respective presentations of events, accusing each other of propaganda and lies. For example, the US Ambassador to the United Nations Nikki Haley repeatedly accused Russia of covering for Syria and North Korea by resorting to a strategy of "denying, distracting, and lying" that had become "the new norm of the Russian culture."[1] The Kremlin has reciprocated by accusing the United States of lying about the Syrian government's chemical weapons attacks, Russian meddling in American elections, the poisoning of former Russian spies, and other developments.

The US and Russia differ in how they work with media and manage their global image presentation, yet they both have a strong interest in influencing the coverage of international news. From the mid-2000s both sides grew increasingly critical of each other's values, describing them in mutually disparaging terms—"neo-Soviet autocracy" on the one hand, and a greedy and corrupt oligarchy on the other. Both used propaganda and various methods of shaping global media discourses. Unable to match the United States' financial resources, the Kremlin engaged in an asymmetrical information war seeking to expose the West's own weaknesses and disorient Western readers, rather than convince them of the superiority of Russian values. This rivalry in the area of values and information is likely to continue and intensify given the high stakes and the available power resources.

The US global information strategy

Governments care about how they are perceived abroad and develop strategies for managing information and working with media. One such strategy is that of soft power influence, which aims to win the support of others through an open media discourse and persuasion by the power of example.[2] However, when governments are challenged from outside, they may shift from soft power to the strategy of propaganda, manipulation, and/or information war. The latter involves state efforts to impose certain frames and priorities in news coverage, presenting the "other" as uncooperative, lacking moral values, or even outright evil. Such strategies are commonly employed during international crises and wars. In those cases, media assists government in discrediting its opponents.

The influence of the US government on mainstream media's perception of the world has been essential. Despite its autonomy and formal independence, the media frequently relies on the state for information. Through briefings, interviews, and articles by government officials, news writers and commentators may receive information not known to the public. While conveying that information, the government also signals what it views as the appropriate tone and frame of the coverage. Government therefore may be in a position to set the agenda and directly engage with the general public.

During the Cold War, the US government successfully influenced the agenda of various media and non-governmental organizations to engage in the fight against communism. For instance, organizations created since World War Two with the agenda of protecting freedom and human rights globally, such as Freedom House and Human Rights Watch, were partly transformed into tools for fighting the Soviets. Freedom House's slogan, "United States: country of freedom," removed all doubts about the organization's missionary objective to liberate America in choosing its means for undermining the "evil empire." The organization consistently abstained from criticizing the United States, choosing to instead direct its attention outside.[3] As the space for inter-state dialogue shrank, the mainstream media too linked the democracy and human rights agendas to that of defeating the Soviet Union.[4] As the Soviet side was fighting its own cultural Cold War via media and propaganda, international power competition increasingly defined perceptions of self and other. When pressured from outside, nations tend to react defensively by embracing ethnic prejudices, empowering nationalist voices, and engaging in exclusionary discourses.

After the Cold War, the US state remained a major influence on the media by suppressing fears of Russia in times of cooperation and encouraging them during periods of interstate tension. Up until the early to mid-2000s, the United States followed the strategy of soft power influence with respect to Russia. The US media and policy makers were widely expecting Russia and other non-Western countries to become market democracies. The strategy of influence resulted from the world's generally high regard for American values and the confidence of the US political class in the superiority of its system. The leading establishment journal *Foreign Affairs* summarized the dominant triumphal mood: "the Soviet system collapsed because of what it was, or more exactly, because of what it was not. The West 'won' because of what the democracies were—because they were free, prosperous and successful, because they did justice, or convincingly tried to do so."[5]

In the second half of the 2000s, and especially following the reelection of Barack Obama as US president, the government role in influencing the media changed. By that time, the United States' global reputation had suffered, while Russia was growing more assertive, aiming to further limit the West's global influence. In this environment, rather than discouraging the newly emerging narrative of Russia as a growing threat, the US government sought to exploit it to its own advantage. As the US media was shifting from a "hopeful transition" tone to that of castigating Russia as a corrupt, autocratic, and illegitimate state, the government was pressuring the Kremlin to not restrict the activities of media and foreign NGOs, while increasing its financial assistance to domestic opponents of Putin. In response to Russia's propaganda and media attacks on Western values, members of the US political class and expert community began discussions of policies to counter the Kremlin's information campaign.

The US government refrained from confrontational rhetoric, but made clear its highly critical view of Russia's political system and increased its support for the country's pro-Western opposition. A 2007 report on Russia by the State Department condemned the "centralization of power in the executive branch, a compliant State Duma, corruption and selectivity in enforcement of the law, media restrictions, and harassment of some NGOs," pledging various types of assistance to media and "democratic organizations" inside the country.[6] In 2006, the US government had financed training for 2,700 broadcast journalists in Russia, and the following year it provided technical assistance for over 1,200 independent media outlets.[7]

The Kremlin's international assertiveness in the wake of the color revolutions in the former Soviet region, its intervention in Georgia in August 2008, its practice of limiting space for political opposition, and its annexation of Crimea all provided a fresh context for viewing Russia as the leading threat to the West. Obama's approach shifted in the assertive propaganda direction in response to the growing perception that Putin's return as president indeed made Russia a threat—the image that many within media and political circles had promoted since 2005. At the same time, the view emerged that more resources were needed to successfully promote Western values in the context of global media competition. In March 2011, while testifying to the Committee on Appropriations in Congress, Secretary of State Hillary Clinton called for the post-Cold War strategy of influence to be abandoned in favor of a Cold War-like strategy of propaganda and shaping the media: "During the Cold War we did a great job in getting America's message out. After the Berlin Wall fell we said, 'Okay, fine, enough of that, we are done,' and unfortunately we are paying a big price for it … Our private media cannot fill that gap … We are in an information war and we are losing that war."[8] Responding to the perceived threat of Russia's information power, the government-controlled Broadcasting Board of Governors (BBG) sought to increase funding for Radio Free Europe/Radio Liberty to help it become more competitive relative to Moscow's Russia Today (RT), which was described as "generously funded, slick, and unconstrained by moral scruples."[9]

Putin's return as president in 2012 prompted new fears about Russian propaganda, pressuring US officials to react. In March 2015,

Secretary of State John Kerry said he was concerned that the US was falling behind when it came to putting out information. He asked for additional funding to be provided for the BBG, stressing that RT's influence was growing worldwide and that the US didn't have "an equivalent that can be heard in Russian."[10] By then, Congress had organized hearings on propaganda and the information war and supported the United States International Communication Reform Act of 2015, intended to make the country's international broadcasting more effective in the face of state propaganda from Russia, China, Iran, and the Islamic State.[11] The Act was introduced by California Congressman and Chairman of the House Committee on Foreign Relations, Ed Royce, and New York Congressman Elliot Engel. The day before the hearing, Royce published an op-ed in the *Wall Street Journal* titled "Countering Putin's Information Weapons of War," in which he wrote that Russia's information power "may be more dangerous than any military."[12]

Following Trump's election as president, it seemed that the US government would no longer be speaking in the same voice, as the new president signaled his intent to improve relations with Russia. However, the growing tensions between the two countries on various issues, as well as Trump's rhetoric of American nationalism and exceptionalism, provided support for presenting Russia as the main threat to US values and interests. Congressional pressures on the administration to provide additional funds to "counter Russian propaganda and disinformation" also increased. In November 2017, the body overseeing media access to the US Congress revoked the press credentials of the Kremlin-funded RT news channel on the basis of its employment by a foreign government.[13] In March 2018, members of the House Armed Services Committee demanded that the US president invest more money in the Global Engagement Center, the wing of the State Department that counters foreign propaganda.[14]

Russia as the "dark double"

Over the last thirty years, US-Russia relations in the realm of values have gone full circle, from confrontation between "communism" and "capitalism" during the Cold War, to convergence, growing divergence, and then a return to a confrontation that a number of observers view as a new Cold War.[15]

Following the Cold War, the US ceased to view Russia and its values as threatening. The perception developed that the new Russia was becoming a part of the West, embracing its ideas and governing principles. The end of the Cold War was interpreted as a victory for the West's "universal" values. Russia's leaders at the time themselves proclaimed their commitment to such values and sought to integrate with Western economic and security institutions.[16] In their own words, Russia was becoming "normal" again and was eager to reunite with the West. For instance, Foreign Minister Andrei Kozyrev stated that the country's system of values was to be changed, as Russia now accepted the priority of the individual and the free market over society and state, and wished to develop a "natural partnership" with Western countries.[17]

The contestation of values, however, did not end with the Cold War. Although the old ideological dichotomy of "communism" and "capitalism" was in the past, the two nations were increasingly at odds in how they viewed each other. By the mid-1990s, it became clear that Russia was not converging with Western values. Although it had abandoned the old Soviet system, Russia also began to reproduce familiar strong state principles, with a highly concentrated authority of the executive and few checks and balances. The new 1993 Constitution incorporated these principles by giving the president a degree of power comparable to that of Russian tsars. During the 2000s, Vladimir Putin continued to consolidate state power as the country's president, acting on the belief that "a strong state is not an anomaly that should be got rid of ... [but] ... a source and guarantor of order and the initiator and main driving force of any change."[18]

In the United States, the perception of Russia as threatening American values appeared in the mid-2000s, articulated by various groups in Washington as well as the mainstream media.[19] Responding to multiple developments in Russia's domestic and foreign policy, the US media introduced the narrative of a neo-Soviet autocracy, according to which everything in the country is controlled by Vladimir Putin, who perceives America as the main enemy. The narrative of a neo-Soviet Russia had existed in the US since the end of the Cold War, but did not dominate the media space until the mid-2000s. Now some seasoned observers were describing the new perception of Russia in the media "as a concerted effort to alienate Russia from the West,"[20] and as displaying an attitude that was "more anti-Russian than was our policy toward Soviet communist Russia."[21]

Leading US newspapers and TV networks presented a view of Russia in which an authoritarian police state was systematically eliminating political opposition, harassing foreigners and minorities, and aggressively vilifying the United States. Developments inside Russia that did not fit such a binary narrative received little media coverage. For instance, the mainstream media rarely reported on the revival of the Christian faith in the country, its struggle with corruption, or its attempts to strengthen relations with neighbors and Western nations. By contrast, the American economic and political system was presented as incomparably superior and largely devoid of serious problems. With respect to practical relations with Russia, the media's advice for US policy makers was consistently on the side of exerting pressure on the Kremlin and containing its international "expansion," rather than proposing cooperation and joint solutions.[22]

This shift in the US media to a view of Russia and Putin as "evil" and "neo-Soviet" occurred partly in response to Russia's move toward a more centralized system of authority and to its growing deviation from what the American media viewed as the appropriate value standards by which to assess others. Various researchers found the US media to be dependent on negative stereotypes and narratives of otherness.[23] Searching for negative others in support of a US-centered binary "freedom-oppression" narrative, the media found such an other in Russia. Increasingly, Russia became associated with a dangerous autocratic system rooted in the Soviet political model. It was assessed not on the scale of how far it had gotten away from the Soviet Union, but by how much it had become a Soviet-like "one-party state" driven by a "KGB mentality" and dependent on the use of propaganda, "Cold War rhetoric," and the repression of internal opposition in order to consolidate state power.[24]

This activation of fears about Russia became possible due to the dominance of liberal views in American political and media circles. Under the liberal narrative of the global march of "universal" democratic values promoted by the *New York Times*, the *Washington Post*, CNN, and other networks, Russia's state consolidation and stress on order and sovereignty were viewed with suspicion. The US media's dependence on a unifying narrative with which to cover foreign countries increasingly complicated US-Russia relations, and the activities of special interest groups with anti-Russian agendas contributed to an increasingly hostile perception of Russia in mainstream media and political circles.

The perception of Russia as the leading threat reached a new height following the Euromaidan revolution in Ukraine in February 2014 and the election of Donald Trump as president of the United States in November 2016. Russia's annexation of Crimea and support for separatists in eastern Ukraine exacerbated fears of the Kremlin's "autocratic expansionism" and drive to conquer Europe. Some writers in the *Washington Post* and the *New York Review of Books* went as far as to compare Russia's actions to those of Nazi Germany,[25] which had incorporated Austria in 1938 before breaking up Czechoslovakia and igniting a World War. The implication was that the West must not appease an aggressive Russia and that only a tough response would stop it from further expansion.

Russian propaganda became an important object of Western media fears. The *Wall Street Journal* raised the alarm over RT propaganda, which it found to be achieving its objectives in "vulnerable states on Europe's eastern periphery and in the South Caucasus," and called on the West to respond by modernizing its public diplomacy.[26] Ann Applebaum and Edward Lucas frightened their audience with a report on the "troll factories" that are a much more powerful part of "Russia's disinformation empire" than RT.[27] Peter Pomerantsev, co-author of a report on Russian propaganda, testified before the House Foreign Affairs Committee that "Russia has launched the most amazing information warfare blitzkrieg we have ever seen."[28] The scare campaign was effective, as evident in government-controlled media requests for additional funds.

Russian values and asymmetric propaganda

Russia's perception of the United States has reflected both its culturally distinct values and interstate tensions. Historically, under the traditional tsarist and Soviet systems, the Russian state formally controlled the media and sought to demonstrate a state-society unity in the face of external pressures. Following the end of communism, the state no longer imposes formal restrictions, but has developed various informal ways of shaping and influencing the media. In part due to its control of important TV channels and other types of media, the Russian state has retained a strong ability to ensure favorable media coverage and influence the public.[29] In seeking to strengthen the state, Putin built a system in which political competition and media freedom are restricted by the authorities' perspective on what is necessary for preserving internal stability at a time of economic transition and reform.

Relative to the American media, the Russian government's system of managing global information has not been nearly as powerful and has been largely defensive in its initial objectives. As acknowledged by Putin, "We do not have so-called global media, mass media with global reach. This is the monopoly of the Anglo-Saxon world, primarily the United States."[30] In Daniel Kennedy's analysis, "If there is an 'information war' being waged, it is an asymmetrical one, where Russia is at a disadvantage in the West."[31] RT's popularity on social media—judged by followers of its official Twitter account—is only slightly more than one-tenth that of BBC World News, let alone CNN. RT's performance on Facebook is better, yet still five to eight times lower than that of the mentioned Western stations.[32] If one judges by funding, Russia is again not in a very competitive position. RT's annual budget is $220 million, whereas the official budget for the BBG is over $721 million, in addition to an estimated $100 million to support independent news publications' overseas and other programs within the US government.[33] Finally, the picture is different judging by the popularity of Russia abroad. In the United States its popularity declined very considerably. In March 2014, 68 percent viewed Russia as either an unfriendly or an enemy country, while favorable views of Putin were less than 10 percent.[34]

Despite being less effective than US media in influencing the global audience, Russian propaganda has assisted the Kremlin in controlling the information narrative at home and spreading its critique of the West abroad. Domestically, the official message has worked because it emphasizes the protection of Russia's distinct values against Western pressure and because the state has preserved the ability to greatly influence the media. The central message of Russian media changed around the mid-2000s. Responding to West-supported regime changes in the former Soviet region and the Middle East, it began to reflect the government's search for indigenous Russian values and to present US foreign policy as a promotion of American values. Even moderate newspapers such *Nezavisimaya gazeta* and *Kommersant* now viewed US democracy promotion as a dangerous attempt by the West to "impose" its own "political model" on parts of the world where it would not be sustainable, leading to greater instability and human rights violations.[35] As for sanctions and the various forms of pressuring Russia politically, the Russian media widely speculated that such actions revealed the United States' intention to destroy the Russian economy, preserve US dominance, and provoke mass political protests in the country in order to hasten Putin's downfall.[36]

The United States' internal political system has been presented as inherently flawed and as encouraging an aggressive foreign policy.[37] Rather than stressing American achievements, Russian journalists have frequently presented the United States as a nation in decline and under growing pressure domestically. This negative image was briefly softened following the election of Trump, before Russia's hopes for improving ties with America dissipated.[38] Since the late spring of 2017, Russian media has resumed its highly critical coverage of US domestic and foreign policy. Russia's TV and newspaper commentators often present American politicians as incapable of dialogue and as driven to preserve the United States' global domination at any human cost. Thoroughly disappointed by Trump, the Russian media frequently attack him as someone prepared to launch a war on Russia. While some present him as weak domestically and dependent on the "deep state" for his own survival, others view him as reckless and itching for a global confrontation with Russia to demonstrate America's power.[39]

In foreign coverage, Russian media have engaged in targeted attacks on the West's values, seeking to expose their weaknesses and discredit them in the eyes of Westerners. No longer satisfied with defensive and internal measures, the Kremlin has increasingly taken the fight into the West's media space. In his July 2012 meeting with Russia's ambassadors, Putin called on them to actively influence international relations by relying on the tools of lobbying and soft power.[40] The Kremlin established an infrastructure for influencing the formation of Russia's image in the world. The RT network became the TV and internet-based outlet through which Russia's worldview was to be promoted globally. The Voice of Russia and Sputnik were established as radio stations. Several state-supported foundations and the Russian Orthodox Church actively promoted linguistic and spiritual connections to Russia across the post-Soviet region. In 2012 the state also set up *Rossotrudnichestvo* (Russian Cooperation) as an organization through which to connect to those in Eurasia with ties to Russia by distributing foreign aid and creating the "optimal conditions for promoting Russian business, science, education, and culture."[41] There was also evidence of Russian activity on American social networks such as Facebook and Twitter.[42]

Given their limited capabilities, RT and other Russian media outlets have been reasonably successful if judged by the criteria of foreign recognition of their influence. Not having the luxury of dominating the global information space, Russia responds in an asymmetric way by seeking to confuse and discredit its Western opponents. The United

States' deepening social and political polarization has assisted the Kremlin in accomplishing this objective.[43] Instead of trying to impose its values, Russia's goal is to strengthen its bargaining position and deter the United States from possible future interference in Russian affairs. Rather than trying to outperform the West, Russia is fighting a defensive information war. It is in the business of influencing and leveraging rather than attacking and destroying. Despite lacking comparable financial resources, Russia possesses the propaganda skills to expose the limitations of the West's global media and cyber dominance. Moscow does not have the capacity to win an information war, nor does it expect to. Instead, the Kremlin aims to confuse and disorient the West and compel it to negotiate with Russia.

Why the information rivalry will continue

The clash of values in US-Russia relations was not inevitable, in the sense that alternative strategies and ideas existed in both countries. Influential intellectuals, organizations, and members of the political class voiced their support for cooperation based on mutual interests in fighting terrorism, ensuring regional instability, and restricting weapons proliferation. Yet each time, those advocating exclusive values rather than inclusive solutions prevailed.[44] The United States shifted toward negative presentations of Russia in response to the perceived challenge to its interests and values globally. The Kremlin's value strategy was more regional and local, resulting from perceived Western pressures and internal confidence. Driven by such perceptions, ruling elites postponed the search for cooperation and adopted policies for the unilateral protection of their own interests.

These value conflicts have their roots in both cultural and political divisions. Against some initial expectations, the age of globalization has not replaced the world of nation-states but has introduced new conditions in which national identities, values, and institutions tend to express themselves by reviving old, historically established ideas and practices. As one American commentator has noted, it is abundantly clear that many in the West "underestimated the role of nationalism and other forms of local identity, including sectarianism, ethnicity, tribal bonds, and the like ... it turns out that many people in many places care more about national identities, historic enmities, territorial symbols, and traditional cultural values than they care about 'freedom' as liberals define it."[45]

Following Trump's election the US media's perception of Russia as the main threat to American values reached a new level of intensity. The Kremlin was now presented as winning the information war and infiltrating the country. The political divide that pushed the mainstream US media toward embracing the narrative of Trump-Russia "collusion" was largely internal. The division has its roots in the United States' crisis of identity and political polarization. The media now criticizing Trump was largely supportive of Hillary Clinton and her vision of a liberal world order with America as its guarantor. However, the 2016 presidential election revealed various constituencies both within and outside of the Republican Party that were critical of the mainstream liberal perspective. The election exacerbated the already existing divide over the country's role in the world, with Russia serving as a tool for accentuating two principally different visions—globalist and nationalist. This stage of the media's Russophobia involved large segments of the population becoming dependent on the Russia-threat image for America's own psychological confidence. If the United States and Russia fail to foster a constructive dialogue, one can expect the US media to continue promoting this ideological and highly negative coverage of Russia.

8

Nuclear and Cyber Security

The US-Russia rivalry is especially dangerous in the area of nuclear and cyber security. Russia and America are world leaders in nuclear and cyber weapons' development and they have largely comparable—if divergent—capabilities in both. The United States seeks to dominate in both areas, including by acting unilaterally and disregarding Russia's priorities. For instance, on October 2, 2018, the US Ambassador to NATO Kay Bailey Hutchinson warned Russia over secret nuclear missiles and threatened to "take them out" if Moscow developed them in violation of existing treaties.[1] American cyber strategy also assumes the importance of domination for the purposes of influencing global public and information gathering. The Trump administration's approach includes the possible deployment of cyber weapons against its adversaries.

The chapter analyzes the steps that Russia has taken in response to the United States' efforts to establish primacy in the nuclear and cyber areas. The Kremlin advocates nuclear and cyber dialogue with America, while being prepared to act unilaterally if such a dialogue is not successful. Among other issues that concern Russia are Washington's plans to deploy the missile defense system (MDS) in Europe, the announced US intention to withdraw from the Intermediate-Range Nuclear Forces (INF) Treaty, the possibility of a non-renewal of the strategic START II agreement, and the US refusal to engage in negotiations over cyber security. In response, the Kremlin has developed an asymmetric approach that combines several methods of reacting to potential Western aggression. In addition to developing new military capabilities, Russia has accelerated its military coordination and training with China and initiated new steps in defense of "cyber-sovereignty," including by proposing resolutions to the United Nations. In the absence of political will on both sides to engage in comprehensive discussions, the rivalry in nuclear and cyber areas may intensify further.

The US quest for primacy

George W. Bush and then Donald Trump abandoned old policies of arms control and strategic deterrence in favor of establishing primacy in nuclear and cyber capability. Although many in the political and expert community have advocated arms control, cooperation with Russia, and even nuclear disarmament,[2] the Trump administration, like its Bush predecessor, has chosen to capitalize on the United States' economic and technological power to develop nuclear and cyber superiority. US strategic objectives include the development and consolidation of that superiority, the non-proliferation of nuclear weapons and materials, and the reduction or denial of advanced nuclear and cyber capabilities to Russia and other major powers.

The quest for nuclear primacy began with Bush's withdrawal from the ABM Treaty in December 2001. A new National Security Strategy called for reliance on an overwhelming military superiority to discourage arms races around the world: "Our forces will be strong enough to dissuade potential adversaries from pursuing a military build-up in hopes of surpassing, or equaling, the power of the United States."[3]

This approach had been earlier formulated by the Project for the New American Century think tank, which favored abdication of the ABM Treaty, achievement of a global first-strike ability, and control over space and cyberspace.[4] In March 2003, Assistant Secretary of State for Nonproliferation John S. Wolf told the Senate Committee on Foreign Relations that while the Nuclear Nonproliferation Treaty (NPT) "remains the cornerstone" of US nonproliferation policy, international agreements alone "are simply not enough" to stop the spread of weapons of mass destruction.[5] In January 2006 the then US Ambassador to NATO Victoria Nuland declared that the US wanted a "globally deployable military force" that would operate everywhere—from Africa to the Middle East and beyond.[6]

The new approach was also revealed in the United States' unwillingness to engage in nuclear arms control or sign treaties with mechanisms for enforcement and verification. Only in 2006 did Washington respond to Moscow's invitation to negotiate a new agreement to replace the START I Treaty, which was due to expire in December 2009. During the same year, the United States also announced an agreement with the Czech Republic and Poland to deploy elements of the MDS—silo-based interceptor missiles and radar stations—on their territory. Washington argued that the MDS was intended to protect Western nations against attacks from "rogue states" such as Iran, and was not a threat to Russia with its vast weapons arsenal.

In its efforts to ensure nuclear primacy, the United States dismissed the concerns of Russia and of America's own generals as unwarranted. US generals and admirals argued that it was "highly unlikely that any state would dare to attack the US or allow a terrorist to do so," and called on the president to focus on preventing terrorists from acquiring weapons of mass destruction.[7] However, George W. Bush and other US officials insisted on the MDS idea as a necessary, global, and not anti-Russian response to foreign security threats. By that time, the US had already deployed elements of the missile system in the Pacific, the Hawaiian Islands, Alaska, California, Japan, and South Korea. Europe was next in line.

President Obama's approach, while different, showed continuity with his predecessor. Obama's efforts to "reset" relations with Moscow included negotiating a new START Treaty that further limited the number of strategic nuclear missiles to 1,500, renewed a verification mechanism, and banned the deployment of strategic weapons outside of national territories. US officials also indicated their interest in further nuclear reductions. The US president wrote to the Kremlin explaining his interest in reducing strategic nuclear warheads by an additional one-third beyond the START levels. The United States also wanted a reduction in Russia's arsenal of short-range missiles. In the administration's assessment, while America had "hundreds," Russia had "thousands" of tactical nuclear weapons at the level of 2,000–4,000 out of 4,000–6,500 missiles overall.[8] Finally, Washington sought to cooperate with Russia on banning the nuclear program in Iran. However, the United States showed no interest in cooperating on the MDS issue, which Russia considered central for preserving the nuclear balance.

Trump's nuclear views bear a strong resemblance to those of George W. Bush. Already during the election campaign Trump had indicated that he wanted to develop nuclear primacy based on his America First approach, and that he was prepared to consider a nuclear strike in order to achieve US goals. According to some reports, Trump as presidential nominee asked foreign policy advisors why the United States could not use nuclear weapons more readily.[9] He further signaled his preparedness to not renew the START agreement signed by Obama, proclaimed his intent to renegotiate the nuclear deal with Iran, and committed to an ambitious program of nuclear modernization.[10]

Trump also announced his readiness to create a Space Force to ensure "American dominance" beyond the Earth.[11]

In the meantime, Washington accused Moscow of conducting tests in violation of the INF Treaty. In particular, it argued that the new Russian 9M729 (SSC8) missile exceeded the range permitted by the treaty and thereby threatened the security of the European continent. The United States expressed its fear that Russia's doctrine of "escalate to de-escalate" implied the Kremlin's readiness to use nuclear weapons, and proposed to increase sanctions against Russia to ensure its compliance.[12] In October 2018, citing Moscow's violations, Trump announced his intent to withdraw from the treaty and sent his National Security Advisor John Bolton to Russia to explain America's position. In December 2018, in a joint statement with NATO, Washington clarified that it would withdraw from the treaty if Russia did not comply with it within sixty days.

The United States also sought to preserve its dominance in the cyber area. As revealed by the Snowden affair, cyber primacy is necessary for conducting foreign espionage, but it also has to do with influencing foreign publics. The Obama administration prioritized social media and internet freedom in order to promote American values and improve the image of the United States following the Bush years. The 2010 National Security Strategy highlighted the internet, smartphones, and other technologies as offering "powerful new opportunities to advance democracy and human rights" by "fueling people-powered political movements."[13] In her statements and memoirs, Secretary of State Hillary Clinton advocated involving marginalized foreign activists in the political process through various techniques of "digital diplomacy."[14] Her advisor for innovation, Alec Ross, described the internet as "the Che Guevara of the twenty-first century" in terms of challenging incumbent governments, and prepared a strategic plan for the development of digital diplomacy as a way to engage and influence foreign activists.[15]

Despite attempts to build a sustained dialogue with such activists, the key thrust of the cyber approach was still to activate propaganda and prevent the non-Western powers from extending their cyber and media influence. US intelligence officials stated that Russia and China posed significant security threats due to their cyber and espionage activities and that Putin's return to the presidency would make it more difficult to develop relations with Russia. In February 2012, Congressional testimonies from Director of National Intelligence James Clapper and CIA Director David H. Petraeus confirmed that this assessment had become the consensus view. The 2015, the US cyber defense strategy directly identified Russia and China as adversaries with "advanced cyber capabilities and strategies."[16] This assessment was reinforced by the US allocation of additional funds to confront what it viewed as potentially dangerous ideas in the global media space.[17]

Trump's priorities in the cyber area reflect his unilateral America First approach. As reported by David Sanger, the Pentagon has authorized the United States Cyber Command to take a more aggressive approach to defense against cyber attacks by raiding and disrupting activities in foreign networks and seeking to disable cyber threats preventatively.[18] Cyber Command was also elevated to a status equal to that of the Indo-Pacific Command, the European Command, the Space Command and the Joint Special Operations Command, although this change was not formally debated inside the White House, reflecting Trump's policy of giving military commanders a greater authority.[19] In September 2018, the Trump administration released a new cyber security strategy promising a more aggressive approach to Russian and Chinese hacking.[20]

During Trump's meeting with Putin in July 2017 the US president indicated a desire to discuss the cyber issue and proposed setting up an impenetrable security system to prevent election hacking and other negative developments. However, soon after the meeting, Trump tweeted: "The fact that President Putin and I discussed a Cyber Security unit doesn't mean I think it can happen."[21] This was partly a response to growing opposition at home and the perception within the American establishment that any cyber cooperation with Moscow would give it access to secret US technology and information. In the meantime, the US authorities were continuing their investigation of Russia's interference in the 2016 presidential election. On February 16, 2018, the office of the US Special Counsel Robert Mueller charged thirteen Russians and three Russian companies with interference in the election by promoting Trump on social media sites. Among the indicted was Yevgeni Prigozhin, who controlled a company called the Internet Research Agency and was viewed as responsible for financing and organizing the interference. As a result of these indictments, the US-Russia meeting on cyber security scheduled to be held in Geneva on February 27–28 did not take place due to a last-minute cancellation by the US.[22] Developments following the US-Russia summit in Helsinki in July 2018 followed a similar pattern of reversing attempts at cooperation. During the summit the two presidents agreed to establish a group for addressing issues of cyber security. Soon after the decision was made public, Trump unilaterally abolished an Obama-era rule against deploying cyber weapons against adversaries.[23]

Russia's nuclear deterrence

Russia's response to the US drive for nuclear primacy has proceeded along two tracks. The first track is based on Moscow's commitment to negotiations and the preservation of bilateral and multilateral treaties on nuclear arms limitations. The second track has developed as a suboptimal yet necessary unilateral response in case the Kremlin fails to convince the United States of the benefits of nuclear diplomacy and mutual agreements.

Russia advocates nuclear dialogue and cooperation despite the US decision to withdraw from the ABM Treaty. The Kremlin's initial response was muted and non-threatening, as it hoped that the two nations could focus on counter-terrorism and develop the trust required for deepening bilateral cooperation. Russia was also interested in arms control in order to reduce the economic burden of maintaining one of the two largest nuclear arsenals in the world. Putin demonstrated his commitment to nuclear arms reduction when he convinced the Duma to ratify the START II Treaty in 2002 and when he supported the new START I Treaty in 2009.

Even as the Kremlin was increasingly worried about Washington's plans to deploy MDS elements closer to Russian borders it continued to seek engagement with the United States. For instance, following his tough criticism of the US in his Munich speech in February 2007, Putin surprised Washington by proposing that it share the early warning radar system in Gabala, Azerbaijan, thereby making "it unnecessary for us to place our offensive complexes along the border with Europe."[24] After the White House dismissed the proposal as insufficient to address its security concerns, Putin went as far as to draw a parallel between the plans for MDS in Eastern Europe and the deployment of Soviet missiles in Cuba that led to the US-Soviet crisis in 1962.[25] The subsequent US-Russia summit in Sochi in March 2008 again failed to resolve the two sides' differences.

The issue remained unresolved during Obama's two terms in office. Having signed the START II Treaty, Russia was prepared to consider additional nuclear cuts only on condition of making progress on the MDS. The Kremlin continued to view nuclear force as the basis of national defense and international stability. In the words of Russia's Deputy Foreign Minister Sergei Ryabkov, "Before discussing the necessity of a further reduction of nuclear weapons we need to arrive at an acceptable solution of the ABM [anti-ballistic missile] problem."[26] Russia was worried about being isolated from Western security developments and viewed as potentially threatening the expansion of US military infrastructure closer to Russia's borders, which had been taking place both within and outside NATO. Although Obama's approach differed from Bush's in basing some MDS elements at sea rather than on land, the Kremlin remained concerned that the Aegis Ashore system was potentially dangerous because it could function in both an offensive and a defensive capacity.

Russia has continued to advocate nuclear arms control with the United States under Trump. The Kremlin remains interested in extending strategic treaties, maintaining the INF Treaty, and preventing the militarization of outer space. Despite the secrecy surrounding the 2018 US-Russia summit in Helsinki, a leaked Russian document revealed that Putin proposed to extend the new START, "reaffirm commitment" to the INF agreement covering missiles with ranges of between 500 and 5,500 kilometers, and engage in discussion on "the non-placement of weapons in space."[27] The Kremlin maintains that it has never violated the INF Treaty and that its newly developed 9M729 missile is under the 500 km range.

Track two first emerged in the late 2000s and reflected an important shift in Russia's strategic thinking. In the 1990s, Russian strategists were focused on deterring the West's superior conventional threat with nuclear weapons, and had developed a theory of de-escalation. However, from around 2010, strategic deterrence was redefined to include conventional, nuclear, and even non-military components. A Ministry of Defense document described the concept as a "coordinated system of military and non-military (political, diplomatic, legal, economic, ideological, scientific-technical and others) measures taken consecutively or simultaneously ... with the goal of deterring military action entailing damage of a strategic character."[28] According to analysts, the shift in Russia's thinking reflected American military-technological advances and the emergence of non-military threats and "new-generation" warfare dominated by non-military tools.[29]

Following the Ukraine crisis, Russia's strategic thinking was consolidated further around the notion of an asymmetric approach to perceived Western aggression. As summarized by Dmitry (Dima) Adamsky, this approach employs

> a complex of means unequal to those of the adversary and may include causing apprehension with regard to the adversary's intentions and responses; demonstration of resolve and capabilities to repulse the invasion with unacceptable consequences; military actions aimed at deterring the potential aggressor by assured destruction of its vulnerable and strategically important objects and persuasion that aggression is doomed to failure.[30]

Russia's 2015 National Security Strategy identified as the main threats NATO's expansion and military activities and attempts by the United States to preserve its global economic, political, and military domination.[31] While the Atlantic alliance was worried about protecting the Baltics from potential attack, Russia feared for the security of its enclave in Kaliningrad. Rather than challenging NATO in the Baltics, Russia concentrated its troops in its southern and western regions.[32]

The Kremlin's response to US nuclear policy has included demonstrations of new Russian capabilities. Assessing the danger posed by NATO's growing military presence in Poland and Lithuania, attempts to pull in neutral states such Finland and Sweden, and further MDS deployment in Europe, Russia has pursued the development of systems capable of breaching the MDS. The Kremlin threatened to deploy advanced nuclear-capable missiles into Kaliningrad, targeting new US installations in Europe, and confirmed it would not be reducing its arsenal of short-range missiles unless its concerns about MDS developments were addressed. Without much publicity, it has continued to work on developing and testing non-strategic weapons.[33]

Russia further signaled the possibility of resuming its production of medium-range missiles, thereby rendering obsolete the Intermediate-Range Nuclear Forces (INF) Treaty. Although the Kremlin did not state its official opposition to it, some within the military establishment argued that the treaty was not meeting Russia's defense interests. For example, in June 2017, Lieutenant-General Evgeny Buzhinsky and Deputy Director of the Institute of Political and Military Analysis, Alexander Khramchikhin, rejected the claim that Russia had violated the INF but argued in favor of restoring a type of medium-range missile. According to them, this is necessary given that many of Russia's neighbors possess such weapons or are interested in obtaining them.[34] In December 2018, Putin also criticized the treaty as a one-sided concession to America by the Soviet Union. While rejecting US concerns as unwarranted, he said Russia would quickly develop mid-range missiles and would have to target sites in Europe should the United States withdraw from the INF Treaty and deploy nuclear missiles on territory of its NATO allies. US officials have expressed multiple concerns at Russia's failure to comply with the treaty since 2015.[35]

In response to what it viewed as NATO's highly provocative military exercises and air patrols, Russia conducted massive exercises of its own and engaged in bold asymmetric behavior testing the West's patience. In several cases, Russian planes flew unusually close to Western warships, running a high risk of casualties or a direct military response. In December 2018, Russia also sent two nuclear-capable bombers to Venezuela for training, and made public its plans to build up a military presence at a Venezuelan base on the island of Orchilla in the Caribbean Sea.[36] These were actions intended to demonstrate that the Kremlin was more "determined" than NATO and in command of its perceived spheres of influence.[37]

Well aware of its inability to match the American strategic arsenal, the Kremlin also developed new weapons that could be used in an asymmetrical response. Already in 2006 Russia had tested new missiles that were "hypersonic and capable of changing their flight path" and therefore of penetrating any MDS.[38] The Kremlin also announced plans to re-equip its new single-warhead intercontinental ballistic missile Topol-M (SS-27) with multiple warheads.[39] On March 1, 2018, addressing Russia's Federation Council, Putin revealed the country's new weapons systems capable of penetrating the MDS, including the hypersonic nuclear cruise missile Kinzhal and hypersonic intercontinental ballistic missile (ICBM) Avangard. In the same speech, Russia's president presented the heaviest of the already known ICBMs, Sarmat, designed to replace the older Voevoda or the SS-18 Satan.[40] Along with several other unveiled systems, the three weapons challenged the United States' earlier decision to withdraw from the ABM Treaty and the White House's new nuclear plans stated in its Draft Nuclear Posture Review. Putin's presentation further repositioned Russia as a leading force in a potential nuclear arms race.

In addition to its own military expansion, Russia increasingly cooperates with China in developing a strategic deterrence to the United States' nuclear policy. Both Moscow and Beijing have opposed the development of MDS and the US deployment of weapons in outer space. While being wary of each other's nuclear capabilities, both countries have coordinated their own space programs and military build-ups. Unable to compete with US military expenditures, both have pursued the development of hypersonic weapons against which the United States cannot defend.[41] Russia has also indicated that in order to maintain the strategic balance, China, along with other nuclear powers, will need to be included in future missile control negotiations.[42]

Russia's cyber priorities and power

Russia's cyber policies are similar to those on nuclear deterrence. In the cyber area the Kremlin favors establishing mutually agreed principles expressed in bilateral and international treaties, yet is also prepared to act unilaterally to defend what it sees as Russia's essential interests.

Moscow has been proposing to negotiate rules of cooperation in the cyber area since the early 2000s. Motivated by an insistence on "cyber-sovereignty," Russia regularly proposes resolutions at the United Nations to prohibit "information aggression." In a 2011 letter to the UN General Assembly, Russia proposed an "International Code of Conduct for Information Security," stipulating that states subscribing to it would pledge to "not use information and communications technologies and other information and communications networks to interfere with the internal affairs of other states or with the aim of undermining their political, economic and social stability."[43]

In its relations with the United States, the Kremlin has favored negotiation of a bilateral pact of non-interference in cyber affairs similar to the one the US signed with China during President Obama's state visit in September 2015.[44] Moscow also had in mind the model of its cyber security pact with Beijing, negotiated in May 2015 on the basis of principles of sovereignty and non-aggression in cyberspace.[45]

Russia's bilateral proposals, however, have not been successful, which may have prompted the Kremlin to rely on last-resort actions in protecting its interests. Experts assess that Russia's basic motives remain largely defensive and that its conception of cyber and information power serves its overall purpose of protecting national sovereignty from perceived encroachments by the United States.[46] Even when the Kremlin relies on assertive tactics, its assertiveness is of a reactive nature and a response to US policies, including in cyberspace. Rather than getting involved in a full-scale cyber or information war with the West, Russia seeks to increase its status and strengthen its bargaining position in relations with the United States.[47] Despite the widespread Western fears of Russia described earlier, the Kremlin's goals have been much more modest than getting a Russian proxy into the White House, destroying American values, or replacing them with its own. Its actions have had more to do with the defense of the Russian state and the calculation that this can be accomplished by demonstrating its ability to erode the stability and cohesion of the United States, and by claiming the status of a major cyber power equal to the US. In domestic politics, these external efforts by the Kremlin have been accompanied by restrictions on internal cyberspace aimed at defending the state from perceived political destabilization.

Following the election of Trump, Putin tried to reach out to the US administration to negotiate a new agreement by sending his envoy to Washington in March 2017. Russia's new roadmap for improving relations included negotiation of cyber issues with Putin's special advisor Andrei Krutskikh.[48] When this did not materialize, Putin again raised the cyber issue during his meeting with Trump in Hamburg in July 2017, proposing to form a joint group to address the issue. In February 2018, Krutskikh led a delegation of seventeen Russian officials, including representatives from the military and special services, to negotiate cyber security in Geneva, but the scheduled meeting did not take place.[49] The issue was again raised during the US-Russia summit in July 2018 but did not result in any agreement. In October 2018, the head of Russia's Federal Security Service, Alexander Bortnikov, called for international steps to prevent the spread of computer viruses.

As the cyber area remains poorly regulated, Russia retains a strong capability and is in a position to engage in asymmetric assertiveness. While its overall defense budget is no match for that of the United States, cyber capabilities are relatively inexpensive. The development of such capabilities largely depends on human investments, a strong engineering background, and computer science skills, for which Russian universities are globally renowned.[50] The Kremlin hopes to demonstrate its leverage by relying on low-cost methods and revealing US vulnerabilities. The Kremlin does not have the power to fight or win an information war, but it believes it has sufficient capacity to confuse and disorient the West and compel it to negotiate. The aim of sowing confusion also explains the secrecy of its cyber attacks and their denial by the Kremlin. In the cyber and information area, taking asymmetric action means attacking secretly and confusing one's opponent, rather than promoting one's own values. He who attacks has the tactical advantage. Analysts disagree over the effectiveness of Russia's actions, yet most argue that "the preponderance of Russia's activity is disruptive rather than degrading ... [and] ... represents the actions of a restrained and declining power."[51]

This explains the motives behind and the limited magnitude of Russia's interference in the United States' 2016 presidential election. Although definitive evidence of such interference is not available, it is likely that the Kremlin was indeed involved. However, its motives and the extent of its involvement were likely limited to power-demonstration purposes. Following the Ukraine crisis, Russia has become disillusioned by the United States and is more prepared to escalate issues for the purpose of getting the White House's attention as a step toward a future bilateral negotiation. Even if Putin had the capacity to wreck the US electoral system, he would be careful not to overexploit it because the costs would be excessively high and all bargaining power would be exhausted. Demonstrating an additional power resource was likely all that the Kremlin intended by the cyber attacks and, if so, any future such attacks are also likely to be limited.

This wariness about not overexploiting its cyber power also explains the Kremlin's lack of any serious effort to interfere in the US Congressional elections in November 2018. Although many in Washington expected major Russian interference, this would not only have provoked a strong counter-response but would also have reduced, rather than increased, the likelihood of a dialogue between Putin and Trump on cyber security.

Future nuclear and cyber rivalry

The two sides' interests in the nuclear and cyber areas differ significantly. The US aims for primacy by investing in nuclear weapons development, expanding the MDS infrastructure, pressuring Russia to reduce its arsenal of short-range missiles, and refusing to engage in cyber negotiations with the Kremlin. Russia seeks to balance relations with the United States by placing limitations on MDS developments, retaining and developing its short-range missiles, and negotiating a bilateral cyber pact. According to some sources, the Kremlin is prepared, under certain conditions, to resume development of medium-range missiles.

Lack of trust and perceptions of status in US-Russia relations exacerbate the difference of interests that otherwise could constitute a basis for meetings and negotiations. The United States believes in its overwhelming superiority and wants to negotiate from a position of strength. Washington has indicated on multiple occasions that its position on MDS is not negotiable. The refusal of negotiations over cyber issues implies that the US has opted to wait until more favorable conditions appear. The US thinking could be that sanctions and concerted Western pressures on the Kremlin will make it accept the American position in the future. In the meantime, Russia too views the other side as a strategic threat. The Kremlin is prepared to negotiate on some issues but not others, and its list of preferences diverges significantly from that of the White House.

These disagreements are asymmetric and take place in the context of increasingly multipolar developments in the world. In order to strengthen its bargaining position vis-à-vis the US, Russia increasingly coordinates its nuclear and cyber policies with those of China. At the same time, Russia must also consider nuclear and cyber developments in China, India, and other parts of the world. At least some nuclear and cyber-related issues need to be addressed in a multilateral, rather than merely bilateral, format.[52]

The US-Russia INF disagreement also illustrates the emergence of an increasingly multipolar world. Both America and Russia are well aware of their growing disadvantages in the area of short- and medium-range nuclear missiles relative to China and other rising powers. They therefore have a mutual interest in cooperating on the issue. A number of experts and politicians have proposed to modify the INF Treaty rather than abandon it, in order to prevent a new arms race. For instance, the Director of the Nuclear Crisis Group, Jon Wolfsthal, has proposed that Russia make a 9M729 missile available for inspection,[53] while former Soviet president Mikhail Gorbachev and former US Secretary of State George P. Shultz have called on the two countries' leaders to jointly address the issue of verification and compliance.[54] However, the trust required for making progress in nuclear or cyber areas is in short supply.

Although US-Russia differences do not constitute a new Cold War, they are likely to persist and even progress, further deepening the rivalry. While the two sides' nuclear and cyber capabilities are compatible,[55] the leaders' priorities and perceptions are not. Russia's defensive posture and readiness to remain assertive, and America's perception of the need to develop strategic superiority, may result in stalemates and arms races. In the worst-case scenario, START will not be renewed, the INF Treaty will be abandoned, nuclear programs in Iran and North Korea will be accelerated, and cyber attacks will become more ambitious and devastating. These dangerous developments will open up the space for a new nuclear and cyber competition that will last until a more adequate perception of US-Russia capabilities emerges and pushes the two sides toward negotiations.

9

Energy and Sanctions

In the era of global economic relations and interdependence, Russian and American energy policies have implications both for their respective national security environments and for global security. Following the discovery of its shale oil and gas reserves, the United States has increased its exports of oil, coal, and natural gas and has plans to influence European, Asian, and Middle Eastern energy markets. President Trump has frequently blamed OPEC for its monopoly and high oil prices, and has sought to convince energy producers such as Russia and Saudi Arabia to increase their production levels. Trump has also attempted to limit the ambitions of other energy powers by imposing conditions for entering into economic relations with them. American sanctions against the Russian and Iranian energy sectors are partly connected with these objectives. Trump has further made clear his opposition to Germany's dependence on Russian natural gas.

Russia's energy priorities have included maintaining strong relations with Europe and strengthening ties with Asia, Eurasia, and the Middle East. The Kremlin has sought to maintain its image as a reliable energy supplier and a transportation bridge between Asian and European markets. In response to US sanctions, Russia has been cautious about reciprocating in kind. In seeking to preserve its ties to European markets, it has stressed common interests and interdependence, siding with Germany and other European countries on issues from the construction of the Nord Stream 2 pipeline to preserving Iran's nuclear deal and opposing Trump's protectionism. The current chapter analyzes these issues in greater detail.

US global energy priorities

Preservation of the United States' international primacy partly depends on its ability to influence markets and secure access to global energy sources. This is required for both domestic and foreign policy purposes. Domestically, the US remains dependent on oil and gas imports even though it has become more self-sufficient during the 2010s. In foreign policy, the ability to influence global energy markets is crucial in the context of limiting the ambitions of rising powers such as Russia, China, and Iran. To achieve its objective of restraining these powers, America seeks to control their energy development, discredit their energy policies, impose sanctions on their energy companies, and build alternative transportation routes.

With respect to Russia, this policy often translates into steps to exercise control over Russia's resource capacity and limit its access to international markets, including by building energy ties with countries in Europe and other regions and by imposing sanctions on Russian state-controlled companies and state-connected oligarchs. The idea that controlling and containing Russia is essential for US energy dominance was first formulated in the 1990s. Influential analysts such as Zbigniew Brzezinski presented Eurasia as "the chief geopolitical prize" for America, one that could only be won by controlling Russia. This was to be achieved by supporting Chechnya's independence, expanding NATO, and blocking Moscow's energy relations with Europe.[1] In 1999—before the US intervention in Iraq and the sharp rise in oil prices—soon to be vice-president Dick Cheney indicated that controlling Russia's energy reserves was no less important than controlling those of the Middle East, and that the way to achieve this would be by securing access to global energy for the four oil giants, Chevron Texaco, ExxonMobil, BP, and Royal Dutch Shell.[2] Cheney's National Energy Policy, released on May 17, 2001, defined access to oil as a key component of national security and recommended increasing its availability.[3]

This approach resonated with many in the private sector and was pursued under several US presidents. Bill Clinton sought to exploit the Caspian Sea reserves by encouraging American companies to invest in Azerbaijan and constructing non-Russian pipelines such as the one from Baku via Tbilisi to Turkey's Mediterranean coast, known as the BTC or Baku-Tbilisi-Ceyhan pipeline. The BTC proved to be extremely expensive to build yet was considered of strategic significance as the only route circumventing energy-rich Iran and Russia. The 1,750 km long pipeline was completed in 2005 and is able to carry one million barrels per day.[4]

Several prominent officials in the George W. Bush administration had strong ties to the energy industry and wanted to limit the competition to American energy expansion in Europe and Eurasia. In the early 2000s, the United States even entered into negotiations with prominent Russian companies about purchasing shares and assets. For example, Russia's largest oil company, Yukos, had been discussing a merger with American companies before its head, Mikhail Khodorkovski, was arrested in October 2003.[5] In addition, Washington condemned Russian integration initiatives such as the Eurasian Union, worked with Kazakhstan to persuade it to build Russia-alternative pipelines, attacked the Russian gas company Gazprom for threatening the economic security of Europeans, and discouraged EU members from entering into integration schemes with Russia.

President Obama continued with these policies by appointing a special envoy to pursue US energy goals in the Eurasian region. Although his environmental approach was significantly different from that of his predecessor, Obama shared the objective of US energy domination at Russia's expense. The Ukraine crisis presented an opportunity for the United States to take additional steps to limit the Kremlin's energy power. In response to Russia's annexation of Crimea, the US imposed heavy sanctions on prominent Russian officials and energy companies.

Donald Trump's energy policy has included the development of US self-sufficiency by allowing more drilling inside the country, the introduction of additional sanctions against Russia's and Iran's energy sectors, and attempts to expand US energy exports to European and Asian markets. Some analysts have directly linked Trump's economic approach to the shale-led revival of America's energy sector that had begun before his arrival in office.[6] Shale gas increased as a percentage of US natural gas production from 1 percent in 2000, to 20 percent in 2010, to 50 percent in 2015, and is expected to reach about 20 percent of the world's LNG volume by 2020.[7] Trump's reduction of corporate tax rates, attracting industrial investment to the United States, as well as his imposition of higher tariffs on European and Chinese goods, also reflect an important change in thinking. The new American philosophy is that of a neo-mercantilist advancement of fair, rather than free, commerce, balancing international trade and developing political and military relations in conjunction with economic reciprocity.[8]

The United States has occasionally tried to cooperate with the Kremlin on energy issues. Examples include the period following the 9/11 terrorist attacks when the two countries recognized their mutual importance as energy partners,[9] and the more recent effort by Trump's Secretary of State Rex Tillerson to rebuild ties with Russia. Tillerson had previously been ExxonMobil's CEO, had worked with Russian companies, and was even awarded Russia's Order of Friendship medal in 2013 by the Kremlin. Both periods proved to be brief, and were soon followed by the more common US policy of seeking global domination at the expense of relations with Russia.

Russia's power and energy interests

Russia's energy power has multiple dimensions and areas of application. It is based on the country's large share of the world's known reserves of oil and natural gas—13 percent and 34 percent respectively[10]—and its geographic capacity to export energy to both European and Eastern markets, as well as to serve as a transit for energy exported from Central Asia and the Caucasus into Europe. Due to its central geographic location and diverse political ties, Russia has been able to maintain diverse and flexible arrangements with partners in Europe, Asia, the Middle East, and Eurasia by negotiating with both producers and consumers of energy in these regions. The largest share of Russian energy exports goes to Europe. Since the Ukraine crisis and the introduction of Western sanctions, this share has been declining in favor of China, yet is still likely to remain the largest due to the high European demand for Russian gas.

In a global political economy in which the United States remains the dominant actor, Russia must be careful to exercise its energy power in a way that preserves its opportunities and minimizes conflicts. Vulnerable to potential pressure from the Western countries, Russia does not have the choice of de-linking itself from the global system and therefore seeks to attract foreign investors by preserving a relatively open financial and economic system. Furthermore, Moscow hardly has a choice not to develop its capacity as a global middleman by coordinating its production with other key energy producers and offering its expertise in building energy infrastructure across the world. This capacity has already helped Russia to absorb the pressure of Western sanctions by strengthening its energy ties with China and Middle Eastern countries. With such capacity also comes international political influence.

These considerations have determined the Kremlin's sense of its energy interests and priorities. Russia's economic and energy goals match those of its overall foreign policy, which aims to preserve the country's status as a great Eurasian power. As such, it must ensure access to European, Asian, and Middle Eastern markets and maintain its capacity to serve as a global energy power with diverse international ties stretching as far as Africa and Latin America. While implicitly recognizing the West's dominance, Moscow cherishes its sovereignty and its right to influence the conditions under which it participates in the global political economy, with the aim of building a genuinely multipolar world based on "a more equitable distribution of resources for influence and economic growth."[11] Already in the early 2000s, Putin stressed the need for Russia to succeed in the geo-economic rather than military sphere, since "the norm of the international community and the modern world is a tough competition—for markets, investments, and political and economic influence."[12]

In order to achieve these foreign policy goals, the Russian state must withstand domestic and international business pressures and exploit the energy sector. As explained by Putin, the state should go beyond relying on market forces and shape economic outcomes by actively seeking to control social resources, coordinating the activities of key social players, and assisting the country in finding its niche in the global economy.[13] This approach explains the central role of energy in Russian foreign policy as well as Putin's early crackdown on oligarchs who did not want to submit to the state's direction and economic preferences.[14] It also explains why the Kremlin has sought to consolidate its influence over the economy, increase its shares in energy companies such as Gazprom and Rosneft, and pursue the construction of pipelines in all geographic directions.[15]

In response to Western economic pressures, Moscow has worked in various regional and global formats such as BRICS and the SCO to increase its global economic and financial opportunities. It has developed several energy projects with China, promoted cooperation with South Korea and North Korea, and worked to secure foreign investments from Japan. In the Middle East, it has strengthened its relations with Iran and signed an agreement with Turkey to build a gas pipeline through its territory to reach European markets. Moscow has also sought to coordinate its energy production with the most important oil-producing state, Saudi Arabia.[16]

In Eurasia, Russia's energy priorities have to do with maintaining the political relations and economic openness necessary for its transportation of energy to European, Asian, and southern markets. Putin's proposed Eurasian Economic Union also reflects Russia's desire to capitalize on its geography by bringing together markets in Asia and the EU.[17]

As discussed in earlier chapters, following the Ukraine crisis and new attempts by the United States to limit Russia's opportunities, Moscow redoubled its efforts to strengthen its economic ties with Asia and the Middle East. Alongside the sanctions imposed by the West, the considerable decline in energy prices since 2015 has undermined Russia's power. Especially painful were the sanctions against Kremlin-connected oligarchs and operations in the energy sector in response to what the US described as "malign" activities across the globe.[18]

The negative effects of the US sanctions have been increasingly felt. In the assessment of Russian energy experts, although in the short run the effect of sanctions is minimal, they "operate with an accumulating effect: the more time passes, the greater the potential technological backlog, financing gap, and negative consequences will be."[19] The latter will affect the volume of Russia's energy production, its pipeline infrastructure and access to foreign markets, and the stability of the Russian economy.[20] In particular, sanctions will limit its access to the technology needed to develop next-generation energy reserves in the Arctic, offshore, and in deep water. A number of high-profile joint projects with Western companies such as ExxonMobil and Statoil have already been disrupted.[21] Most Russians recognize the negative effects of the sanctions, with 47 percent identifying their effect as "major."[22]

Nevertheless, Russia will preserve its capacity to influence global energy markets by resisting the pressure of Western sanctions. Aware of the dangers, Moscow has sought not to overplay its hand. The Kremlin has maneuvered by maintaining macroeconomic stability and social services,[23] avoiding a symmetrical sanctions fight, and diversifying economic relations with individual countries in the West and beyond. The domestic effects of sanctions have included a policy of import substitution and the strengthened perception that the economy must reflect national security priorities. Richard Connolly refers to this effect as the securitization of the economy, meaning that it is increasingly operating in accordance with state-determined political and military, rather than strictly economic, needs.[24]

In its relations with European nations, Russia responded to sanctions with counter-sanctions but aimed at a differential bilateral impact in order to preserve its bargaining space. In selecting which agricultural and food imports to ban, the Kremlin inflicted considerably greater damage on those states it viewed anti-Russian while placing fewer restrictions on major European states including Germany, France, Italy, and the UK.[25]

In its relations with Middle Eastern countries, Russia sought to strengthen its ties with OPEC in order to reduce the potentially negative impact of the decline in global oil prices. The Kremlin has succeeded in developing closer relations with Saudi Arabia and other oil-producing states in the region by agreeing on cuts in production. In December 2018, despite opposition from Trump, Russia and OPEC reached a deal to reduce oil production by 1.2 million barrels per day for the first six months of 2019.[26]

In its relations with the United States, the Kremlin has also been careful to not damage its own economic interests. In response to the series of US sanctions, Putin signed a law on counter-sanctions that gave him an opportunity to act but did not identify specific areas. The initial draft was restrictive of exports to the US, which elicited strong opposition from Russian business. In particular, exports of titanium, rocket engines, and nuclear materials would be affected if sanctions were imposed on US companies such as Boeing, which relies on Russia for about 40 percent of its titanium.[27] Russian companies would also be negatively affected by losing important markets and development opportunities, on top of the risk of inviting even more severe US sanctions. As a result, the Kremlin decided against supporting the bill, and it was left for the president to ultimately determine whether and how to respond to the sanctions.[28]

In August 2018, the US announced a new round of sanctions in response to the Kremlin's alleged attempted assassination of its former intelligence officer Sergei Skripal and his daughter in Salisbury. The ruble lost 10 percent of its value, while Russian energy companies began to prepare for additional restrictions on their access to Western markets, technology, and supplies. The Kremlin's spokesman Dmitry Peskov called the sanctions "absolutely illegal" under international law, while Prime Minister Dmitry Medvedev described any action taken against Russian banks as an act of economic war and threatened retaliation against the United States by unspecified "economic, political, or, if needed, by other means."[29] Despite the rhetoric, the Kremlin again refrained from action, aware of its limited ability to hurt the US economy without damaging its own. The likely international impact of the new sanctions will be the further reorientation of Russia's energy exports to Asia, while it continues its efforts to maintain strong ties with Europe. Rather than becoming isolated or de-globalized, the Russian economy is therefore experiencing a degree of re-globalization.[30]

Sanctions and US-Russia gas rivalry in Europe

The case of US-Russian rivalry over gas supplies to European markets illustrates how an economically weaker power may preserve its limited competitiveness in the global system despite pressures from the dominant power and the hierarchical structure of the system. The conditions for Russia's limited competitiveness include its regional advantages, longstanding ties with diverse European nations, and ability to exploit their divergent economic and political relations with the United States.

Washington has traditionally worked to limit the Kremlin's influence in Europe, including by warning Europeans against their "dependence" on Russia's energy. For example, the United States sought to block Russia's North and South Stream projects to transport gas to Europe, by pressuring Bulgaria and other Balkan nations not to cooperate with Moscow, supporting Poland and Ukraine's opposition to these projects, and criticizing Turkey for its plans to serve as an intermediary in transporting Russian gas.

Thanks to the discovery of its shale oil and gas reserves, the United States has emerged as Russia's competitor in European markets. The US began Europe-bound shipments of LNG in 2016 and in 2017 it pioneered gas exports to Lithuania and Poland. During the same year, Washington increased pressure on Germany by threatening sanctions against any country planning to cooperate with Russia on constructing the second line of the Nord Stream under the Baltic Sea. In June 2017 the US Congress passed a wide-ranging sanctions bill that set restrictions on Russian energy by prohibiting Western companies from working with Russia on Arctic offshore, deep-water, and shale projects.[31] The bill included an option to activate sanctions against any country supportive of the Nord Stream 2 if the White House decides to employ it. The bill also allows—in consultation with Western European partners—the blocking of any Russia-related project worth more than $5 million a year that helps to build new gas pipelines or maintain old ones, if they "threaten US national interests."[32] On December 10, 2018, reflecting the growing concern over Russia's influence in Europe, the US House of Representatives passed a non-binding resolution in opposition to Gazprom's Nord Stream project and urged European governments to do the same. Two days later, the European Parliament passed a similar resolution on the project.

Reaction to the bill from Europeans interested in preserving ties with Russia was highly critical. Influential analysts such as Germany's former ambassador to the United States, Wolfgang Ischinger, argued that instead of strengthening transatlantic ties, the bill would compromise European energy security and damage US relations with Europe.[33] He suggested that Washington was seeking to "advance US commercial interests at Europe's expense," defended the EU position on the Nord Stream, and argued that the new US policy could potentially damage gas supplies from Azerbaijan, not only Russia, via the emerging Southern Corridor.[34]

Russia reacted to the US sanctions by capitalizing on shared Russia-European energy interests and seeking to build a new capacity for LNG exports to European markets. Russia's energy relations with Europe remain strong, despite disagreements over principles of market diversification and the nature of bilateral contracts. These disagreements are not political and concern differences in business preferences between energy consumers and producers. As an energy producer, Russia prefers long-term contracts and full control over its transportation networks, while the EU wants more flexibility in contract negotiations and access to Russia's pipelines.

In seeking to counteract the effects of Western sanctions, the Kremlin has energized its relations with China and other non-Western nations, but it has not turned away from Europe, with which it wants to keep its traditionally strong energy ties. Gazprom has negotiated the South Stream pipeline under the Black Sea, advanced integration with European companies, and signed intergovernmental agreements with multiple countries that are recipients of Russian gas.[35] Despite the Western sanctions, the Kremlin has preserved such ties with German, French, Austrian, and other companies. In order to partly compensate for the sanctions-related losses, Russia also reactivated the Yamal LNG project in the Arctic. In addition to Chinese shares, the project is 20 percent owned by France's Total and connects to European markets through Belgian gas-distribution companies. The project's first phase was completed in December 2017, and its LNG offered to European, Asian, and Middle Eastern nations.[36]

In addition to actions on the energy front, the Kremlin has sought to exploit the political opportunities presented by the growing division between the United States and European states over Iran's nuclear deal and trade.[37] In April 2018, Trump announced the United States' withdrawal from the Iranian deal, insisting on new negotiations and threatening to punish those companies that continue to do business with Teheran. On June 1, the White House also introduced high tariffs on European, Canadian, and Mexican imports of steel, aluminum, and other products. European governments widely condemned both actions, pleading for the US to preserve the deal with Iran and promising counter-actions on trade.

Russia used this momentum to stress its common economic interests with Europeans, including lifting mutual sanctions and promoting the Nord Stream and the idea of a South Stream through the Balkans. In May 2018, Putin hosted the leaders of Germany and Bulgaria to discuss European security and future energy cooperation. Chancellor Angela Merkel confirmed the German interest in Nord Stream 2, provided that it is not built at the expense of Russia's pipelines through Ukraine. Bulgarian Prime Minister Boiko Borisov even apologized to Putin for not acting in 2009 on the opportunity to build the South Stream pipeline under the Black Sea, and thanked the Russian leader for not "holding a grudge."[38] The Kremlin then announced the possible construction of the second pipeline, running from Turkey to Europe via Bulgaria, Serbia, and Hungary.[39]

The United States responded to these developments by promising additional sanctions against the Russian energy sector and all international energy projects that involve the participation of Russian companies. The US placed the head of Gazprom under sanctions and announced the possibility of further sanctions to punish those companies cooperating on the Nord Stream 2 project. According to some sources, as of August 2018 the US was ready to activate these sanctions, but had yet to decide whether to impose them only on the companies laying the pipes or to extend them to the banks and financial companies funding the project.[40]

The reaction from Europe has been ambivalent. In July 2018, Gazprom's European partners confirmed their intent to build the pipeline despite the US warnings about sanctions and its claim that Moscow was using the project to sow division.[41] It remains to be seen whether the EU has the capacity to resist American pressure. The response of European companies to the US threat to restore sanctions against Iran suggests that such capacity may be limited. Despite the EU's assurances that it would stick to the nuclear deal with Iran and continue doing business with the country, by late summer 2018 around a hundred Western financial and energy companies had left Iran, including Boeing, General Electric, Peugeot, Siemens, and Total.[42]

As of the end of 2018, multiple US-introduced sanctions against Russia have not been supported in Europe, while attempts to sabotage construction of the Nord Stream 2 have been met with strong opposition from Germany, Austria, and other EU members. Finland and Sweden have agreed to allow the pipeline to run through their territorial waters, with Denmark the only one yet to grant permission. Putin's meeting with Merkel on August 18 further confirmed the two sides' commitment to the project. Following the new tensions between Russia and Ukraine due to the November 25 Kerch Strait incident, the United States renewed its call for the Europeans to abandon cooperation with Gazprom. In concert with Ukraine, Poland, and the Baltic states, the US State Department also urged the EU to introduce additional sanctions against Russia. On December 13, EU leaders extended existing sanctions for six months but did not introduce new ones. The US-Russia rivalry over European energy markets thus continues with uncertain prospects.

Future of energy security

The US-initiated sanctions against Russia weakened its economy but failed to achieve the intended objective of restraining the Kremlin in its foreign policy. Although Russia has suffered financial and technological losses, the Kremlin has refused to concede on Ukraine and has not been isolated from Europe economically. Politically, Russia has demonstrated its resilience, with both elites and the general public showing support for the Kremlin in its refusal to bow to American pressure.[43] In some areas, the US sanctions backfired and had to be softened, demonstrating yet again that they are no substitute for a broader strategy and, used by themselves, cannot work. One example involved Russia's largest aluminum company RUSAL, owned by Oleg Deripaska. Following the sanctions on RUSAL introduced in April 2018, the company lost 50 percent of its value; due to the company's global operation this meant that prices for aluminum rose greatly, thus affecting jobs in Europe and Australia. After two weeks the US Treasury had to soften the policy, stressing that it was "not targeting the hardworking people who depend on RUSAL and its subsidiaries."[44] Another example concerns the United States' reinstatement of sanctions against Iran, which provided the Russian economy with an unintended boost due to the weakened ruble and increased export capacity.[45] Both examples highlight the problems with attempting to isolate an economy as big as Russia's.

Russia has been greatly assisted by its diverse ties with various European countries and companies, with Turkey and Iran in the Middle East, and with China. Despite the perception that Moscow overplayed its hand in Ukraine, the energy interests of important outside powers were more in line with those of Russia than the United States. Although US exports of LNG to Europe may increase dramatically by 2020, the notion of pushing Russia out of European markets is misplaced. The economic realities are such that American LNG will have to compete in markets with abundant demands, and "where Norway and Algeria are often larger players than Russia."[46]

The energy rivalry will persist and may intensify further if the

United States shows a determination to increase its LNG supplies to European markets and to reduce Russia's role on the continent. American attempts to pressure Germany against establishing strong energy ties with the Soviet Union did not succeed during the Cold War, and are unlikely to succeed today. Not only does Russia and Europe's mutual economic dependence remain strong, but the contemporary US-Russia competition takes place in an increasingly global energy setting, with more opportunities available for both countries. Trying to make energy serve geopolitical objectives in this context is more difficult than ever, even as the great power rivalry continues.

10

Where to from the Asymmetric Rivalry?

Russia, America, and the new world disorder

The world is now in transition away from the US-centered system established after the Cold War. While the United States still occupies the key position in the international order, rising non-Western powers are increasingly challenging American power in various global and regional settings. If we are to learn from history, then the contemporary world order transition will likely take as long as the previous transitions from the settlements reached at Vienna, Paris, and Versailles did, each lasting several decades. Indeed, the current one may last even longer, given that the United States remains asymmetrically more powerful than other states and that the major powers, due to their nuclear status, are not likely to resolve their contradictions through war, as they did previously.

In the West the relative power shift began following the US intervention in Iraq. This contributed to the Middle East's destabilization and the rise of ISIS, empowered Iran, and resulted in a domestic and international backlash against American interventionism. The greater Middle East is now an area of competition among several prominent local and global players, with the US increasingly looking for ways to reduce its presence in the region. If it wants to remain a global leader in addressing international security issues, from nuclear proliferation to terrorism and regional instability, then the United States must refrain from unilateral interventionist practices and seek cooperation with other powers.

An alternative to becoming a better global partner is to abandon the position of leadership in favor of the role of a superpower with limited international obligations. In an increasingly chaotic and insecure world, the latter role is potentially destabilizing, yet it is increasingly being embraced by the United States.[1] Donald Trump has demonstrated his lack of commitment to the accepted global economic rules, security alliances, and international institutions. He remains an economic nationalist interested in restoring American power by engaging in trade protectionism and actively securing new markets, including in the area of energy. The main threats for Trump are China, the European Union, and Iran, each of them in their own way impeding the realization of US economic goals. In 2018, Trump withdrew from the nuclear agreement with Iran, launched trade wars with China and the European Union, refused to sign a joint statement by G7 leaders in Quebec, and announced significant military withdrawals from Afghanistan and Syria. It is no coincidence that Trump's main ideologist was Steven Bannon, who advocated not only toughening up migration policy, but also abandoning the post-World War Two Bretton Woods agreements.

Residual liberal elites in Europe continue to oppose Trump's worldview, yet they are unlikely to put up a strong unified resistance. Europe's continued dependence on NATO for protection, and the prospect of a trade war with the United States, weakens the European opposition. Faced with US economic pressure, European companies are withdrawing from Iran, while European governments remain eager to preserve American commitment to the continent's security.

Under these conditions, Russia is neither supporting Trump nor siding with the Europeans. Nor is it launching a new Cold War on the

United States. Rather, the Kremlin seeks to adjust its policies to the global transition of power and international rules. During this transition, Russia aims to preserve its international interests and great power status using the foreign policy tools available. It remains dependent on the West and is not likely to engage in actions fundamentally disruptive of the existing international order. Despite its internal institutional differences from Western nations, Russia also sees itself as an indispensable part of the West, and will continue to reach out to Western leaders in order to demonstrate its relevance as a great power. This part of Russia's historic identity is well established and will keep the country open to the West on international matters even when the latter refuses to recognize its potential contribution. Russia's frequent attempts to engage the United States in cooperation—following 9/11, over Iran and Syria, and on nuclear and cyber security—demonstrate the principal importance to the Kremlin of being recognized as a major power in its relations with the outside world.

On the other hand, Russian cooperation with the United States is conditional on actions viewed by the Kremlin as reciprocal and respectful of Russia's equal status. The Russian foreign policy community, while including groups with diverse views, shares the belief in the country's great power status, based on its global military capabilities, spheres of influence, and internal sovereignty. All groups within the establishment favor the preservation of Russia as a major power, accept the annexation of Crimea as a strategic necessity, and recognize the need for a strategy of internal development. Although committed to engaging the West in meaningful cooperation, they maintain that such engagement must not be conducted at the expense of Russia's right to protect its interests and act as a great power.[2]

Russia's economic weakness may temporarily restrain but will not change the overall direction of its foreign policy. Even with a stagnating economy, the Kremlin commands strong domestic support and can employ a wide range of informational, military, and economic tools to defend itself against any perceived American encroachment on its interests. In the global and still largely open world, Russian power is often deployed asymmetrically. Its methods are evolving yet its objective of securing an "appropriate" place in the international system remains constant.

The preceding chapters have documented specific steps taken by the Kremlin to defend Russia's interests and position in the international system. Unable to match America's global capabilities, Moscow has built multiple economic, political, and military relations with non-Western powers and strengthened its capacity to undermine US policy globally. The asymmetric methods of Russian foreign policy include the selective use of media and information technology, cyber power, hybrid military intervention, and targeted economic sanctions.

Russia's new policy toward the United States combines asymmetric rivalry and cooperation. In response to NATO expansion and Ukraine's drive to join European institutions at the expense of its ties with Russia, the Kremlin annexed Crimea and continues to support Donetsk and Luhansk by insisting on their meaningful autonomy from Kiev. By securing the status of Assad in Syria, Russia has positioned itself as a major power in the Middle East, capable of maintaining dialogue with all key players in the region including Iran, Saudi Arabia, Turkey, and Israel. In Asia, Russia has reached a strategic understanding with China about the two countries' division of labor and spheres of influence. Russia-China relations are now being built on the assumption that America's presence in Asia complicates the security environment and that the greater Eurasia area should be developed without the United States.

Russia and America have also competed in global settings. The Russian media has presented US political values as those of an oligarchical state with an inherently aggressive foreign policy, while the American media has focused on the Kremlin's corruption, international aggression, and oppression of domestic opposition. The two countries have also further disagreed on nuclear priorities and accused each other of violations of existing international treaties. They have failed to resolve the issues of cyber security and interference in each other's elections and domestic affairs. Finally, the two countries proceed from principally different perceptions of their energy interests. They increasingly compete for European and Asian markets, showing little desire for cooperation or compromise.

Attempts by Russia to cooperate with the United States have brought limited results. They have not found a formula for stabilizing Ukraine or engaging on other issues in a meaningful way. Exceptions include the two countries' limited efforts to coordinate their military actions in Syria, attempts to encourage North Korea to negotiate over its nuclear tests and further nuclear development, and an ongoing conversation on the future of strategic stability. However, on all these issues progress remains restricted by the need to avoid an escalation of tensions.

Any attempt by Trump to enlist Putin as a partner in fulfilling the United States' international objectives is therefore likely to have a limited effect. For instance, by initiating a summit with Russia in July 2018, Trump wanted to achieve his goals in various regional settings: in the Middle East, to reduce Iran's influence in Syria and the wider region; in Europe, to both confirm US relevance and pressure NATO allies to increase their defense budgets; in Asia, to reduce the influence of China and to secure Russia's help with denuclearizing North Korea. In exchange for the Kremlin's cooperation, the US president has indicated that he is prepared to consider Russia's interests, revisit the question of sanctions, and even discuss the recognition of Crimea.

Neither Putin nor the Russian establishment is prepared to make a serious change in foreign policy unless it is accompanied by a lifting of sanctions and the recognition of Russia's international interests and status. Moscow is not ready to exert pressure on Teheran, make significant concessions in Syria, stop supporting Donbass, reduce its energy-related activities in Europe, accept US nuclear arrangements, or reconsider relations with China. The Kremlin is also aware that Trump's internal political problems persist and that he is perceived as an impulsive and unpredictable leader. Moscow remembers the symbolism of closing the Russian Consulate General in San Francisco on the day of the new Russian US ambassador's arrival, as well as Trump's decision to "punish" Russia and Iran by bombing Syria.

In the meantime, Trump's ability to build ties with Russia remains severely limited by US domestic politics. The American political class is deeply suspicious of and hostile toward the Kremlin. In addition to being viewed as a leading threat to US global interests and its political system, Russia has become a hostage in a bitter struggle for decision-making power between American elites. Congress, the liberal media, and some intelligence circles have exploited the issue of Russia and the Kremlin's possible collusion with Trump to curtail his ability to make policy.

The case of Maria Butina illustrates the volatile nature of US-Russia relations. In July 2018, she was arrested in Washington, DC and charged with espionage and actions on behalf of Russia without prior registration as a foreign agent. Butina subsequently pleaded guilty in December 2018. The charges against her were likely pressed by the US prosecutor in connection with attempts to establish unofficial channels between Russia and American conservatives and Russia's possible role in the 2016 presidential election.[3] In this highly polarized political environment, it was extremely difficult for Trump to develop relations with the Kremlin or even to meet with Putin for discussion of vital international issues. Following their cancelled meeting in Buenos Aires in November 2018, the two presidents will likely continue to face difficulties in maintaining high-level contact. Perhaps mindful of Trump's domestic problems, the Kremlin initially refrained from reacting harshly to the Butina case. During his annual press conference on December 21, 2018, Putin referred to it but limited his remarks to a rhetorical critique of the US as having no grounds for prosecution. His press secretary Dmitry Peskov, commenting on the case after the press conference, said that Russia's actions are most effective when pursued in asymmetric fashion. However, in early 2019, the Kremlin announced it had arrested an American spy, Paul Whelan; this was likely a delayed retaliation for Butina's arrest, and an invitation to exchange her for Whelan.

Future US-Russian rivalry

Two principal factors that have determined US-Russia relations concern the global balance of power and domestic perceptions. While the global balance of power began to shift after the 1990–2005 period, the position of the United States within the international system will remain dominant for many years to come. The second critically important factor is each country's perception of the global challenges and the policies adopted for meeting them. Based on these factors, one can envision three alternative scenarios for US-Russia relations unfolding within the next five to ten years. The first two are less likely than the third.

The first scenario assumes that America and Russia will follow a steep learning curve by developing a rare appreciation for one another's interests and come to recognize the commonality in their perception of global threats and opportunities. The Kremlin's initial hope for a grand bargain with Washington may then be realized in the form of agreements on nuclear and cyber security, a roadmap on lifting sanctions, a joint strategy for fighting terrorism, coordinated regional security efforts, and a concerted movement toward establishing new global rules. Some observers continue to believe in the possibility of such a great power compact.[4]

The likelihood of this scenario is, however, low. The conflict between the two countries has developed over a long period, making it difficult for either to trust the other's intentions. Historically developed cultural differences and internal political divisions are likely to make US-Russia cooperation harder and their disagreements more intense. In a world of growing interstate conflict, the involvement of large populations mobilized by media in support of exclusive and nationalist agendas promises to play a destabilizing role, pushing governments away from negotiation and the search for compromise. The lifting of sanctions, launching a new program of cooperation, or beginning the Helsinki Process 2 will have to wait until the world demonstrates a new, more positive dynamics and sees the arrival of a new, more responsible international leadership.

The second scenario assumes that the United States will seek to contain Russia through further economic sanctions and military buildup, while the Kremlin will escalate its global demands and seek to increase its capacity to apply pressure. In this case, Moscow may engage in an ultimately unsustainable arms race and competition for power with its strongest adversary. Necessary domestic reforms will be postponed, eventually exhausting Russia's competitive edge and power advantages.

This scenario is supported by the deepening contradiction between Russia's stagnating economy and the Russian elite's support for

Moscow's international assertiveness. The country's economic weakness is well-documented. In response to the collapse of energy prices in 2015, Western economic sanctions, and the absence of domestic reforms, the economy is underperforming. GDP growth was negative during 2015–16 and grew by less than 1.5 percent in 2017. Instead of becoming part of a vibrant non-Western alternative system, Russia is stagnating and experiencing economic difficulties. By 2017, Russian living standards had been in decline for four consecutive years, while the state has continued to allocate large sums of money for defense and limit expenditure on education and healthcare. The defense budget during the same year stood at 5.3 percent of GDP.[5]

The Kremlin's contemporary foreign policy, then, does not rest on solid economic foundations, yet there are powerful voices within the establishment in favor of continuing it. Against the warnings of those cautioning against Russia becoming excessively involved in Ukraine and Syria, some argue that the Kremlin should continue with its "victorious" foreign policy in defiance of the West's sanctions and attempts to contain Russia. A number of experts believe that it is due to this policy that "Russia has been able to turn from a power with an imposed inferiority complex into a power-victor."[6] This view assumes that the US-centered world order is rapidly unravelling and that Russia should do everything in its power to speed up the process while securing for itself an appropriate global status. Because the American international order is falling apart on its own, it may only need an additional push to be replaced by a different, Russia-favored system modelled after the Congress of Vienna.

Others argue that the combination of internal economic stagnation, continued assertiveness in defiance of Western sanctions, and the rising costs of maintaining its military security will work against Russia's long-term engagement in rivalry with America. Many in

Washington view contemporary Russian foreign policy as excessively risky and potentially unsustainable.[7] Trump's preparations to withdraw from or not renew major nuclear agreements may generate more pressure on Russia to increase its defense expenditure thus further undermining the country's economic and political stability.

This scenario of Russia's overstretch is possible but not very likely. As was argued in earlier chapters, Russia has learned its painful Cold War lesson and wants to avoid engaging in symmetrical competition with a stronger adversary at any cost. In the absence of a vibrant economy, it has instead relied on asymmetrical forms of geopolitical activism from Ukraine to the Middle East in order to demonstrate its global relevance and great power status. The Kremlin has been also careful to avoid excessive military spending. Its planned defense spending in the 2018–20 federal budget was reduced to correspond with the country's economic slowdown.[8]

The more likely than not scenario is that of a continued asymmetric rivalry with elements of limited cooperation. The two countries will maintain a modest positive engagement, while mobilizing their respective capabilities for competing with each other in various settings. Russia will eschew confrontation with America in the areas where it remains weak, such as the economy. However, in keeping with Putin's asymmetric judo tactics, the Kremlin will remain assertive in areas that are strategically important and do not require exorbitant spending. In the meantime, US domestic politics will continue to be highly volatile and uncertain, creating new potential opportunities for Russia. US domestic instability may also translate into an even less predictable US foreign policy.

If the United States refrains from pursuing further actions perceived by Russia as depriving it of great power status, then the Kremlin will not risk taking highly destabilizing steps such as the military occupation of

Ukraine or other parts of Eurasia, or targeting American and European military infrastructure, or engaging in major cyber attacks. However, if the West continues to challenge Russia's status by favoring containment and political confrontation over engagement, then there is good reason to expect that Putin will not hesitate to fight back to protect Russia's interests. Engaging Russia in a joint effort to stabilize the situation globally as well as in various regions is therefore important, yet the US and the wider West may not have the will for it, preferring instead to continue with the policy of containment.

In the meantime, Russia will continue to attempt to contain the power of the United States globally and especially in Asian, Middle Eastern, and East European settings. The Kremlin will continue to think in terms of leverage against US geopolitical encroachment by maintaining ties with anti-American leaders across the world and developing relations with China and other non-Western nations. It will also continue to develop relations within the SCO and greater Eurasia, pressing for a new global balance of power and new international rules, and it will form ad hoc coalitions with European nations while gradually reforming its own economy. On this scenario, America's communications with Russia in the foreseeable future will have a limited positive agenda and will largely be devoted to preventing a possible global confrontation or a wider regional destabilization resulting from clashes between their proxies.

This negative agenda should not be underestimated. Russia and America must reverse the dangerous trend in their relations by committing to mutual non-interference and the prevention of new conflicts. An explicit acknowledgment from both sides of the importance of mutual non-interference in internal politics, coordination of military actions in various regions, and steps toward conventional and nuclear arms control would help to develop the level of trust required for future positive developments. In the meantime, experts on both sides should commit to forming a constructive perspective on US-Russia relations and developing a roadmap toward their normalization. The two sides' perception of each other as (potential) foes only creates an environment which encourages confrontation, while reducing the opportunities for dialogue and cooperation.

Future solutions to the Russia-America conflict will have to be complex enough to account for the complexity of its root causes and the main actors' responsibilities. Both sides' concerns and responsibilities, and those of other contributing parties, must be fully addressed—ideally at an international conference that would result in a new set of legally binding obligations. But Russia and America currently remain too far apart in terms of their perceived interests, institutions, and, most importantly, level of mutual trust. Any expectation of an imminent robust settlement would therefore be excessively optimistic. Indeed, in the current security climate one can expect further crises between Russia and the West in various areas. For the foreseeable future, while the world continues to move away from US international dominance toward a new global power balance, the best we can hope for is sufficient cooperation between the main actors to prevent an escalation of disagreements between them. In the meantime, new rules for the international system are likely to emerge informally and through a process of continued global competition.

Selected Bibliography

Abdelal, Rawi and Igor Makarov, *The Fragmentation of the Global Economy and US-Russia Relations* (Cambridge: Working Group on the Future of US-Russia Relations, 2017).

Adamsky, Dmitry (Dima), "From Moscow with Coercion: Russian Deterrence Theory and Strategic Culture," *Journal of Strategic Studies* 41 (2018).

Bacevich, Andrew J., *America's War for the Greater Middle East: A Military History* (New York: Random House, 2016).

Bechev, Dimtar, *Rival Power: Russia in Southeast Europe* (New Haven: Yale University Press, 2017).

Blackwill, Robert D. and Jennifer M. Harris, *War by Other Means: Geoeconomics and Statecraft* (Cambridge MA: Harvard University Press, 2016).

Bremmer, Ian, *Us vs. Them: The Failure of Globalism* (New York: Portfolio, 2018).

Brzezinski, Zbigniew, "Premature Partnership," *Foreign Affairs* 73:2 (1994).

Brzezinski, Zbigniew, *The Grand Chessboard* (New York: Basic Books, 1997).

Charap, Samuel, "The Ghost of Hybrid Warfare," *Survival* 57:6 (2015).

Charap, Samuel and Timothy J. Colton, *Everyone Loses: The Ukraine Crisis and the Ruinous Contest for Post-Soviet Eurasia* (London: Routledge, 2017).

Cohen, Stephen, *Soviet Fates and Lost Alternatives: From Stalinism to the New Cold War* (New York: Columbia University Press, 2009).

Cohen, Stephen, *A War with Russia? From Putin and Ukraine to Trump and Russiagate* (New York: Hot Books, 2018).

Connolly, Richard, *Russia's Response to Sanctions* (Cambridge: Cambridge University Press, 2018).

Cooley, Alexander, *Great Games, Local Rules* (New York: Oxford University Press, 2011).

English, Robert, *Russia and the Idea of the West* (New York: Columbia University Press, 2000).

Feklyunina, Valentina, "Soft Power and Identity: Russia, Ukraine and the 'Russian World(s)'," *European Journal of International Relations* 22:4 (2015).

Forsberg, Tuomas and Graeme Herd, "Russia and NATO: From Window of Opportunities to Closed Doors," *Journal of Contemporary European Studies* 23:1 (2015).

Fridman, Ofer, *Russian Hybrid Warfare: Resurgence and Politicisation* (New York: Oxford University Press, 2018).

Gould-Davies, Nigel, "Sanctions on Russia Are Working," *Foreign Affairs*, August 22, 2018.

Grigas, Agnia, *The New Geopolitics of Natural Gas* (Cambridge MA: Harvard University Press, 2017).

Grygiel, Jakub J. and A. Wess Mitchell, *The Unquiet Frontier: Rising Rivals, Vulnerable Allies, and the Crisis of American Power* (Princeton: Princeton University Press, 2016).

Hahn, Gordon M., *Ukraine Over the Edge: Russia, the West and the New Cold War* (New York: McFarland, 2018).

Hill, William H., *No Place for Russia: European Security Institutions Since 1989* (New York: Columbia University Press, 2018).

Ikenberry, G. John, ed. *Power, Order, and Change in World Politics* (Cambridge: Cambridge University Press, 2014).

Ikenberry, G. John, Inderjeet Parmar, and Doug Stokes, "Ordering the World? Liberal Internationalism in Theory and Practice," *International Affairs* 94:1 (2018).

Jamieson, Kathleen Hall, *Cyberwar: How Russia Helped Elect Trump* (New York: Oxford University Press, 2018).

Kaczmarski, Marcin, "The Asymmetric Partnership? Russia's Turn to China," *International Politics* 53:3 (2016).

Kanet, Roger E., ed. *The Russian Challenge to the European Security Environment* (New York: Palgrave, 2017).

Kanet, Roger E., *The Routledge Handbook of Russian Security* (London: Routledge, 2019).

Karaganov, Sergei, ed. *K velikomu okeanu 5: ot povorota na Vostok k Bol'shoi Yevraziyi* (Moscow: Valdai Discussion Club, September 2017).

Karaganov, Sergei and Dmitri Suslov, "A New World Order: A View From Russia," *Russia in Global Affairs*, October 4, 2018.

Keating, Vincent Charles and Katarzyna Kaczmarska, "Conservative Soft Power: Liberal Soft Power Bias and the 'Hidden' Attraction of Russia," *Journal of International Relations and Development*, January 2017.

Kissinger, Henry, *World Order* (New York: Penguin Books, 2014).

Koffman, Michael, "Raiding and International Brigandry: Russia's Strategy for Great Power Competition," *War on the Rocks*, June 14, 2018.

Kuhrt, Natasha and Valentina Feklyunina, eds. *Assessing Russia's Power* (London: King's College, London and Newcastle University, 2017).

Lavrov, Sergei, "Istoricheskaya perspektiva vneshnei politiki Rossiyi," *Russia in Global Affairs*, March 3, 2016.

Larson, Deborah Welch and Alexei Shevchenko, *Quest for Status: Chinese and Russian Foreign Policy* (New Haven: Yale University Press, 2019).

Legvold, Robert, *Return to Cold War* (Cambridge: Polity, 2016).

Levine, Yasha, *Surveillance Valley: The Secret Military History of the Internet* (New York: Public Affairs, 2018).

Lieber, Robert J., *Retreat and Its Consequences: American Foreign Policy and the Problem of World Order* (Cambridge: Cambridge University Press, 2016).

Lieven, Anatol, *America Right or Wrong: An Anatomy of American Nationalism* (New York: Oxford University Press, 2004).

Lucas, Edward, *New Cold War* (New York: Palgrave, 2011).

Lukin, Alexander, *China and Russia: The New Rapprochement* (Cambridge: Polity, 2018).

McFaul, Michael, *From Cold War to Hot Peace* (New York: Houghton Mifflin, 2018).

Mead, Walter Russell, "The Jacksonian Revolt: American Populism and the Liberal Order," *Foreign Affairs*, January 20, 2017.

Monaghan, Andrew, *Power in Modern Russia* (Manchester: Manchester University Press, 2017).

Monteiro, Nuno, *Theory of Unipolar Politics* (Cambridge: Cambridge University Press, 2014).

Paul, T. V., ed. *Accommodating Rising Powers* (Cambridge: Cambridge University Press, 2016).

Porter, Patrick, "Why America's Grand Strategy Has Not Changed: Power, Habit, and the US Foreign Policy Establishment," *International Security* 42:4 (2018).

Posen, Barry R., "The Rise of Illiberal Hegemony: Trump's Surprising Grand Strategy," *Foreign Affairs*, March–April 2018.

Remington, Thomas, Chris Spirito, Elena Chernenko, Oleg Demidov, and Vitaly Kabernik, *Toward US-Russia Bilateral Cooperation in the Sphere of Cybersecurity* (Boston: Harvard University, Working Group on the Future of US-Russia Relations, May 2016).

Rumer, Eugene, Richard Sokolsky, and Paul Stronski, *US Policy Toward Central Asia 3.0* (Washington, DC: Carnegie Endowment for International Peace, 2016).

Russia: Military Power. Building a Military to Support Great Power Aspirations (Washington, DC: Defense Intelligence Agency, 2017).

Sakwa, Richard, *Frontline Ukraine* (London: Tauris, 2015).

Sakwa, Richard, *Russia Against the Rest: The Post-Cold War Crisis of World Order* (Cambridge: Cambridge University Press, 2017).

Sechser, T. S., "Goliath's Curse: Coercive Threats and Asymmetric Power," *International Organization* 64:4 (2010).

Slater, Matthew R., Michael Purcell, and Andrew M. Del Gaudio, eds. *Considering Russia: Emergence of a Near Peer Competitor* (Quantico, VA: Marine Corps University, 2017).

Soldatov, Andrei, "Reading the World: The Internet and Political Change in Russia," *Foreign Affairs*, April 6, 2016.

Stent, Angela, *The Limits of Partnership: US-Russian Relations in the Twenty-First Century* (Princeton: Princeton University Press, 2014).

Stuenkel, Oliver, *Post-Western World: How Emerging Powers are Remaking Global Order* (Cambridge: Polity, 2016).

Tertrais, Bruno, "Russia's Nuclear Policy: Worrying for the Wrong Reasons," *Survival* 60:2 (2018).

Toal, Gerard, *Near Abroad: Putin, the West and the Contest over Ukraine and the Caucasus* (New York: Oxford University Press, 2017).

Trenin, Dmitry, *Should We Fear Russia?* (Cambridge: Polity, 2016).

Trenin, Dmitry, *What Russia is Up to in the Middle East* (Cambridge: Polity, 2017).

Tsvetkova, Natalya, "Publichnaya diplomatiya SShA," *Mezhdunarodnyye protsessy* 13:3 (2017).

Tsygankov, Andrei P., *Russophobia* (New York: Palgrave, 2009).

Tsygankov, Andrei P., *Russia and the West from Alexander to Putin* (Cambridge: Cambridge University Press, 2012).

Tsygankov, Andrei P., "Vladimir Putin's Last Stand: The Sources of Russia's Ukraine Policy," *Post-Soviet Affairs* 31:4 (2015).

Tsygankov, Andrei P., ed. *The Routledge Handbook of Russian Foreign Policy* (London: Routledge, 2018).

Tsygankov, Andrei P., "The Sources of Russia's Fear of NATO," *Communist and Post-Communist Studies* 51:1 (2018).

Tsygankov, Andrei P., *Russia's Foreign Policy*, 5th edition (Lanham: Rowman & Littlefield, 2019).

Tsygankov, Andrei P., *The Dark Double: US Media, Russia, and the Politics of Values* (New York: Oxford University Press, 2019).

Valeriano, Brandon and Ryan Maness, *Russia's Coercive Diplomacy: Energy, Cyber, and Maritime Policy as New Sources of Power* (New York: Palgrave, 2015).

Ven Bruusgaard, Kristin, "Russian Strategic Deterrence," *Survival* 58:4 (2016).

Way, Lucan Ahmad and Adam Casey, "Russian Foreign Election Interventions Since 1991," PONARS Eurasia Policy Memo No. 520, March 2018.

Womack, Brantly, *Asymmetry and International Relationships* (Cambridge: Cambridge University Press, 2016).

Youngs, Richard, *Europe's Eastern Crisis: The Geopolitics of Asymmetry* (Cambridge: Cambridge University Press, 2017).

Ziegler, Charles, "International Dimensions of Electoral Processes: Russia, the USA, and the 2016 elections," *International Politics*, October 2017.

Notes

Chapter 1

1 For reviewing these relations as cycles, see Angela Stent, *The Limits of Partnership: US-Russian Relations in the Twenty-First Century* (Princeton: Princeton University Press, 2014).

2 See "Assessing Russian Activities and Intentions in Recent US Elections," January 6, 2017, www.dni.gov/files/documents/ICA_2017_01.pdf.

3 Michael McFaul, *From Cold War to Hot Peace: An American Ambassador in Putin's Russia* (New York: Houghton Mifflin, 2018).

4 Robert Legvold, *Return to Cold War* (Cambridge: Polity, 2016), 28.

5 Stephen Cohen, *Why Cold War Again? How America Lost Post-Soviet Russia* (New York: I. B. Tauris, 2019).

6 Sergei Karaganov and Dmitri Suslov, "A New World Order: A View From Russia," *Russia in Global Affairs*, October 4, 2018.

7 Ian Bremmer, *Us vs. Them: The Failure of Globalism* (New York: Portfolio, 2018).

8 Fareed Zakaria, *The Post-American World* (New York: W. W. Norton, 2012).

9 Oliver Stuenkel, *Post-Western World: How Emerging Powers Are Remaking Global Order* (Cambridge: Polity, 2016).

10 Dmitry Trenin, *Should We Fear Russia?* (Cambridge: Polity, 2016); Richard Sakwa, *Russia Against the Rest: The Post-Cold War Crisis of World Order* (Cambridge: Cambridge University Press, 2017).

11 For an introduction to Russia's thinking on the topic, see Ofer

Fridman, *Russian Hybrid Warfare: Resurgence and Politicisation* (New York: Oxford University Press, 2018).

12 Chapter 3 discusses Russia's objectives and asymmetric power. See also Andrei P. Tsygankov, *Russia's Foreign Policy*, 5th edition (Lanham: Rowman & Littlefield, 2019).

13 Dmitry Trenin, "Russia Will Stand Strong and Rely on Itself," May 28, 2018, www.raamoprusland.nl/dossiers/geopolitiek/971-russia-will-stand-strong-and-rely-on-itself.

14 Michael Koffman, "Raiding and International Brigandry: Russia's Strategy for Great Power Competition," *War on the Rocks*, June 14, 2018.

15 Henry Kissinger, *World Order* (New York: Penguin Books, 2014). In this book, international order and world order are used interchangeably. The next chapter returns to the problem of order in international relations.

16 Quoted at his first official press conference as the new foreign minister. Robert H. Donaldson and Joseph L. Nogee, *The Foreign Policy of Russia: Changing Systems, Enduring Interests* (Armonk: M. E. Sharpe, 1998), 119.

17 Stent, *The Limits of Partnership*, ix.

18 Scott Wilson, "Obama Dismisses Russia as 'Regional Power' Acting Out of Weakness," *Washington Post*, March 24, 2014. For further analysis of erroneous American expectations, see Seva Guntisky and Andrei P. Tsygankov, "The Wilsonian Bias in the Study of Russian Foreign Policy," *Problems of Post-Communism* 65:6 (2018).

19 "Concept of Foreign Policy of the Russian Federation," Russia's Foreign Ministry, December 1, 2016, www.mid.ru/en/foreign_policy/official_documents/-/asset_publisher/CptICkB6BZ29/content/id/2542248.

Chapter 2

1 Remarks by President Trump to the 73rd Session of the United Nations General Assembly, New York, September 25, 2018,

www.whitehouse.gov/briefings-statements/remarks-president-trump-73rd-session-united-nations-general-assembly-new-york-ny.

2 Robert Kagan, "'America First' Has Won," *New York Times*, September 26, 2018.

3 Kissinger, *World Order*, 9. For other perspectives on world order, see the selected bibliography. Some of the themes in this chapter are also discussed in Andrei P. Tsygankov, "The Present and the Future of International Relations," *Russia in Global Affairs* 1 (2019).

4 Robert Gilpin, *War and Change in World Politics* (Cambridge: Cambridge University Press, 1981).

5 For analyses of major changes in international systems, see Michael Cox, Tim Dunne, and Ken Booth, eds. *Empires, Systems, and States: Great Transformations in International Politics* (Cambridge: Cambridge University Press, 2001).

6 Kalevi Holsti, *Peace and War: Armed Conflicts and International Order, 1648–1989* (Cambridge: Cambridge University Press, 1991).

7 Kissinger, *World Order*, 60.

8 Hugh Seton-Watson, *The Russian Empire, 1800–1917* (Oxford: Oxford University Press, 1988), 177.

9 A. J. P. Taylor, *The Struggle for Mastery in Europe, 1848–1918* (Oxford: Oxford University Press, 1954), 61.

10 Andrei P. Tsygankov, *Russia and the West from Alexander to Putin* (Cambridge: Cambridge University Press, 2012), 89.

11 Ronald Grigor Suny, *The Soviet Experiment: Russia, USSR, and the Soviet Successor States* (Oxford: Oxford University Press, 1998), 343.

12 Vladlen N. Vinogradov, "The Personal Responsibility of Emperor Nicholas I," in Hugh Ragsdale, ed. *Imperial Russian Foreign Policy* (Cambridge: Cambridge University Press, 1993), 161–2.

13 Norman Rich, *Why the Crimean War? A Cautionary Tale* (Hanover: University Press of New England, 1985), 3.

14 Tsygankov, *Russia and the West*, 97–113.

15 Stephen Cohen, *Soviet Fates and Lost Alternatives: From Stalinism to the New Cold War* (New York: Columbia University Press, 2009), chapter 7.

16 For Russia's efforts to join the Western economy, see Andrei P. Tsygankov, *Russia's Foreign Policy*, 4th edition (Lanham: Rowman & Littlefield, 2016), 74–6.

17 Andrei Kozyrev, "Partnership or Cold Peace?," *Foreign Policy* 99 (1995), 13.

18 Marc C. Plattner, "Democracy Outwits the Pessimists," *Wall Street Journal*, October 12, 1988; Charles Krauthammer, "The Unipolar Moment," *Foreign Affairs* 70:1 (1991).

19 Tsygankov, *Russia's Foreign Policy*, 52. For more on the Russian perspective on the end of the Cold War, please see the selected bibliography.

20 Tatyana Shakleyina, ed. *Vneshnyaya politika i bezopasnost' sovremennoi Rossiyi*, Vol. 4 (Moscow: ROSSPEN, 2002), 51–90, 110–11.

21 Cited in Peter Baker and Susan Glasser, *Kremlin Rising: Vladimir Putin's Russia and the End of Revolution* (New York: Simon & Schuster, 2005), 286.

22 For good reviews of these issues, see Robert J. Lieber, *Retreat and Its Consequences: American Foreign Policy and the Problem of World Order* (Cambridge: Cambridge University Press, 2016).

23 G. John Ikenberry, Inderjeet Parmar, and Doug Stokes, "Introduction: Ordering the World? Liberal Internationalism in Theory and Practice," *International Affairs* 94:1 (2018).

24 Jeffrey M. Jones, "Confidence in US Institutions Still Below Historical Norms," *Gallup*, June 15, 2015, www.gallup.com/poll/183593/confidence-institutions-below-historical-norms.aspx.

25 "BRICS pomeryayetsya siloi s MVF," Editorial, *Nezavisimaya gazeta*, April 2, 2015.

26 "BRICS Establish $100bn Bank and Currency Pool to Cut Out Western Dominance," July 15, 2014, http://rt.com/business/173008-brics-bank-currency-pool.

27 "The Foreign Policy Concept of the Russian Federation," Kremlin.ru, February 18, 2013, www.mid.ru/bdomp/ns-osndoc.nsf/e2f289bea62097f9c325787a0034c255/c32577ca0017434944257b160051bf7f.

28 "Putin Blames West for Global Chaos," *Russia Today*, 27 September, 2012.

29 Fred Weir, "Chemical Weapons in Syria: How Russia Views the Debate," *Christian Science Monitor*, August 22, 2013.

30 Statement by the President on Ukraine, White House, February 28, 2014, www.whitehouse.gov/the-press-office/2014/02/28/state ment-president-ukraine.

31 Charles Clover, "Clinton Vows to Thwart New Soviet Union," *Financial Times*, December 7, 2012.

32 "Should the West be Afraid of Moscow's Plans for a Eurasian Union?" Expert panel, edited by Vlad Sobell, us-russia.org, July 12, 2013.

33 David M. Herszenhorn, "Russia Won't Renew Pact on Weapons with US," *New York Times*, October 12, 2012.

34 Luke Johnson, "Mitt Romney: Russia is 'Our Number One Geopolitical Foe'," *The Huffington Post*, March 26, 2012.

35 "Biden 'Opposes' Putin's 3rd Term," *Moscow Times*, March 11, 2011, https://themoscowtimes.com/news/biden-opposes-3rd-putin-term-5538.

36 "Moscow Dismisses Western Criticism of Gay Propaganda Law," *RIA Novosti*, August 7, 2013.

37 For background, see Cory Welt, "What the Snowden Affair Says About US-Russian Relations," *The Center for American Progress*, July 17, 2013.

38 Scott Shane, "A Homemade Style of Terror: Jihadists Push New Tactics," *New York Times*, May 5, 2013.

Chapter 3

1 Remarks by President Trump to the 73rd Session of the United Nations General Assembly, New York, September 25, 2018.

2 Cited in Robert L. Larsson, *Russia's Energy Policy: Security Dimensions and Russia's Reliability as an Energy Supplier* (Stockholm: Swedish Defence Research Agency, 2006), 58.

3 Vladimir Putin, "Poslaniye Federal'nomu Sobraniyu Rossiyskoy Federatsiyi," Kremlin.ru, March 2005.

4 Vladislav Surkov, "Suverenitet—eto politicheski sinonim konkurentnospo sobnosti," *Moscow News*, March 3, 2006.

5 Vladimir Putin, "Meeting of the Valdai International Discussion Club," Sochi, October 2013.

6 Vladimir Putin, "Poslaniye Prezidenta Federal'nomu Sobraniyu Rossiyskoy Federatsii," December 13, 2013, http://president.kremlin.ru.

7 Vladimir Putin, "Rossiya: Natsional'nyi vopros," *Nezavisimaya gazeta*, January 23, 2012.

8 *Kommersant*, December 19, 2012.

9 Address by President of the Russian Federation, Moscow, Kremlin, March 18, 2014.

10 Andrew Roth, "Trump 'Is Not My Bride': Putin Wades into Diplomatic Row with US," *Washington Post*, September 5, 2017.

11 Ibid.

12 Transcript of Trump and Putin's Joint Press Conference, *Time*, July 31, 2018, http://time.com/5339848/donald-trump-vladimir-putin-summit-transcript.

13 *Strategiya dlya Rossiyi: Tezisy rabochei gruppy Soveta po vneshnei i oboronnoi politike*, Moscow, May 2016, thesis 2.3.1.

14 Timofei Bordachev, "Pushki aprelya, ili vozvrashcheniye strategicheskoi frivol'nosli," July 3, 2017, www.globalaffairs.ru/number/Pushki-aprelya-ili-Vozvraschenie-strategicheskoi-frivolnosti-19210.

15 Boris Mezhuyev, "'Ostrov Rossiya' i rossiiyskaya politika identichnosti," April 5, 2017, www.globalaffairs.ru/number/Ostrov-Rossiya-i-rossiiskaya-politika-identichnosti-18657.

16 Andrei Kortunov, "'Neizbezhnost' strannogo mira," July 15, 2016, http://old.russiancouncil.ru/inner/?id_4=7930#top-content.

17 See, for example, Ruslan Ostashko, "Zakat epokhi globalizatsiyi," *Natsional'naya oborona* 10, 2017, http://oborona.ru/includes/periodics/geopolitics/2017/0126/140120429/detail.shtml.

18 Andrei Kortunov, "Rossiya proshchayetsya s Obamoi," December 5, 2016, http://ru.valdaiclub.com/a/highlights/rossiya-proshchaet sya-s-obamoy-poslanie.

19 Fyodor Lukyanov, "'Opasnost' 'bol'shoi sdelki'", February 9, 2017, www.gazeta.ru/comments/column/lukyanov/10516553.shtml.

20 For analysis of American nationalism, see Anatol Lieven, *America Right or Wrong: An Anatomy of American Nationalism* (New York: Oxford University Press, 2004).

21 Donald Trump, Inaugural Address, January 20, 2017, www.white house.gov/inaugural-address.

22 Ibid.

23 Jon Wolfsthal and Richard Burt, "America and Russia May Find Themselves in a Nuclear Arms Race Once Again," *The National Interest*, January 17, 2018.

24 Ibid.

25 Ryan Teague Beckwith, "Read Hillary Clinton and Donald Trump's Remarks at a Military Forum," September 7, 2016, http://time.com/4483355/commander-chief-forum-clinton-trump-intrepid.

26 Walter Russell Mead, "The Jacksonian Revolt: American Populism and the Liberal Order," *Foreign Affairs*, January 20, 2017.

27 Donald Trump, State of the Union Address, January 31, 2018, www.cnn.com/2018/01/30/politics/2018-state-of-the-union-transcript/index.html.

28 Shakleyina, *Vneshnyaya politika i bezopasnost' sovremennoi Rossiyi*, Vol. 4, pp. 110–11.

29 Vladimir Putin, Speech at the Munich Conference on Security Policy, Munich, February 10, 2007, www.kremlin.ru.

30 Vladimir Putin, Speech at a meeting with Russian ambassadors and permanent representatives in international organizations, Moscow, Kremlin.ru, July 9, 2012.

31 Vladimir Putin, Speech at the Valdai International Discussion Club, Kremlin.ru, September 19, 2013.

32 Vladimir Putin, Speech at the plenary meeting of the 70th session of the UN General Assembly, New York, Kremlin.ru, September 19, 2015.

33 Vladimir Putin, Annual Address to the Federal Assembly, Moscow, Kremlin.ru, December 12, 2012.

34 *Strategiya dlya Rossiyi*, thesis 3.7.

35 For analysis of why Trump's policy displayed continuity in foreign policy, see Patrick Porter, "Why America's Grand Strategy Has Not Changed: Power, Habit, and the US Foreign Policy Establishment," *International Security* 42:4 (2018), 9–46.

36 Transcript: Obama's remarks on Russia, NSA at the Hague on March 25, 2014, www.washingtonpost.com/world/national-security/tran script-obamas-remarks-on-russia-nsa-at-the-hague-on-march-25/2014/03/25/412950ca-b445-11e3-8cb6-284052554d74_story. html?utm_term=.14aedee22cdc. For analysis of US thinking about Russia, see Gunitsky and Tsygankov, "The Wilsonian Bias in the Study of Russian Foreign Policy."

37 Leonid Bershidsky, "No, Obama, Russia's Economy isn't 'in Tatters'," *Bloomberg*, February 26, 2015.

38 Alistair Bell and Tom Perry, "Obama Warns Russia's Putin of 'Quagmire' in Syria," *Reuters*, October 2, 2015.

39 Paul Saunders, "Donald Trump's Foreign Policy: Working with Russia from a Position of Strength," *Valdai Club*, March 2017.

40 James Masters and Ryan Browne, "Trump Defense Chief Mattis Tells NATO Members to Pay Up, CNN, February 15, 2017.

41 "Summary of the 2018 National Defense Strategy of the United States of America," 4–5, www.defense.gov/Portals/1/Documents/ pubs/2018-National-Defense-Strategy-Summary.pdf.

42 Jeffrey Tayler, "Russia is Finished," *The Atlantic Monthly*, May 2001.

43 Georgy Pankov, "Russia Lacks Public Optimism For an Economic Leap," *RIA Novosti*, February 6, 2007.

44 Andrei P. Tsygankov, "Vladimir Putin's Vision of Russia as a Normal Great Power," *Post-Soviet Affairs* 21:2 (2005).

45 Stephen G. Brooks, and William C. Wohlforth, "Power, Globaliza-tion, and the End of the Cold War," *International Security*, 25:3 (2000/01), fn. 41.

46 Nuno Monteiro, *Theory of Unipolar Politics* (Cambridge: Cambridge University Press, 2014), 78.

47 See, for example, J. Ikenberry, M. Mastanduno, and W. Wohlforth, eds. *International Relations Theory and the Consequences of Unipolarity* (Cambridge: Cambridge University Press, 2011).

48 Monteiro, *Theory of Unipolar Politics*, 48.

49 Bremmer, *Us vs. Them*.

50 Vladimir Putin, Annual Address to the Federal Assembly, Moscow, Kremlin.ru, December 12, 2012.

51 For further analyses of Russian military thinking, see especially Bettina Renz, *Russia's Military Revival* (Cambridge: Polity, 2018), and Fridman, *Russian Hybrid Warfare*.

52 Sergei Lavrov, Interview with Russian Minister of Foreign Affairs by the BBC Russian Service, April 23, 2009.

53 Sergei Lavrov, "Istoricheskaya perspektiva vneshnei politiki Rossiyi," *Russia in Global Affairs*, March 3, 2016.

54 Petr Pavel, "The Challenges Facing Nato Today," *Defense Review: The Central Journal of Hungarian Defense Forces* 145:1 (2017), 4.

55 Brantly Womack, *Asymmetry and International Relationships* (Cambridge: Cambridge University Press, 2016), p. 1.

56 Ibid., p. 23. For asymmetric power relations, see also T. S. Sechser, "Goliath's Curse: Coercive Threats and Asymmetric Power," *International Organization* 64 (2010).

57 David A. Baldwin, Review of Womack, *Asymmetry and International Relationships*, *H-Diplo, H-Net Reviews*, October 2016, www.h-net.org/reviews/showrev.php?id=47095.

58 Greg Simmons, "Media and Public Diplomacy," and Nikolai Petro, "Russian Orthodox Church," in Andrei P. Tsygankov, ed. *The Routledge Handbook of Russian Foreign Policy* (London: Routledge, 2018).

59 For bottom-up perspectives on Russian media, propaganda, and soft power, see Vincent Charles Keating and Katarzyna Kaczmarska, "Conservative Soft Power: Liberal Soft Power Bias and the 'Hidden' Attraction of Russia," *Journal of International Relations and Development*, January 2017.

60 Andrei P. Tsygankov, *The Strong State in Russia* (New York: Oxford University Press, 2015).

61 Vladimir Putin, Meeting with the Russian Federation Ambassadors, Moscow, Foreign Ministry, July 9, 2012.

62 John Hudson, "Russia Sought a Broad Reset With Trump, Secret Document Shows," Buzzfeed.com, September 12, 2017.

63 David Filipov and Anne Gearan, "Russia Condemns US Missile Strike on Syria, Suspends Key Air Agreement," *Washington Post*, April 7, 2017.

64 Fred Weir, "Does Trump Have a Foreign Policy? Mixed US Messages Leave Russia Wondering," *Christian Science Monitor*, April 12, 2017.

65 Vladimir Frolov, "Why Russia Won't Cave to Western Demands," *Moscow Times*, May 3, 2017.

66 "Full Transcript of Trump's Remarks on Russia," *New York Times*, November 11, 2017.

67 David E. Sanger and William J. Broad, "To Counter Russia, US Signals Nuclear Arms are Back in a Big Way," *New York Times*, February 5, 2018.

68 Andrew Desiderio, "Trump's Russia Ambassador: US-Russia Relations 'Done' if Kremlin Meddles in 2018 Elections," www.the dailybeast.com, January 9, 2018.

69 Henry Meyer, Laurence Arnold, and Olga Tanas, "All About the US Sanctions Aimed at Putin's Russia," *Bloomberg*, August 9, 2018.

70 Ilya Arkhipov and Henry Meyer, "Kremlin Sours on Trump After His Repeated Putin Snubs," *Bloomberg*, December 6, 2018.

71 Stepan Kravchenko and Henry Meyer, "Russia Vows Full Support for Maduro as US Sanctions Bite," *Bloomberg*, January 29, 2019.

72 Hal Brands, "The Five Lessons that Must Guide US Interactions with Vladimir Putin," *Washington Post*, September 22, 2017.

Chapter 4

1 Cited in Joseph Nye, *The Paradox of American Power* (Oxford: Oxford University Press, 2002), 33.

2 Kissinger, *World Order*, 95.

3 Dmitri Medvedev, Speech in Berlin, *Izvestiya*, June 6, 2008.

4 Robert Bridge, "Moscow Looking for European "Re-think" at Munich Security Conference," Russia Today, October 21, 2010.

5 Lilia Arakelyan, "EU-Russia Security Relations: Another Kind of Europe," in Roger E. Kanet, ed. *The Russian Challenge to the European Security Environment* (New York: Palgrave, 2017), 83.

6 Judy Dempsey, "Russia Wants to Formalize Relation With EU," *New York Times*, October 18, 2010.

7 William H. Hill, *No Place for Russia: European Security Institutions Since 1989* (New York: Columbia University Press, 2018).

8 Remarks by President Trump to the People of Poland, Warsaw, July 6, 2017, www.whitehouse.gov/briefings-statements/remarks-president-trump-people-poland.

9 Natalie Nougayrede, "Refugees Aren't the Problem. Europe's Identity Crisis Is," *Guardian*, October 31, 2015.

10 Kenan Malik, "The Failure of Multiculturalism: Community Versus Society in Europe," *Foreign Affairs*, March/April 2015.

11 Rawi Abdelal and Igor Makarov, *The Fragmentation of the Global Economy and US-Russia Relations* (Cambridge: Working Group on the Future of US-Russia Relations, Working Group Paper 8, 2017).

12 Sakwa, Russia *Against the Rest*.

13 For Russian perspectives on Europe, see Iver Neumann, *Russia and the Idea of Europe: A Study in Identity and International Relations*, 2nd edition (London: Routledge, 2016).

14 Vladimir Putin Answers Questions at Valdai International Discussion Club, Sochi, Russia, October 27, 2016, en.kremlin.ru/events/president/news/53151.

15 On Ukrainian identity divisions, see Olexiy Haran and Maksym Yakovlyev, eds. *Constructing a Political Nation: Changes in the Attitudes of Ukrainians During the War in the Donbas* (Kiev: Stylos Publishing, 2017).

16 Andrei P. Tsygankov and Matthew Tarver-Wahlquist, "Dueling Honors: Power, Identity and the Russia-Georgia Divide," *Foreign Policy Analysis* 5:4 (2009).

17 For Russia-NATO relations after the Cold War, see Tuomas Forsberg and Graeme Herd, "Russia and NATO: From Window

of Opportunities to Closed Doors," *Journal of Contemporary European Studies* 23:1 (2015); Andrei P. Tsygankov, "The Sources of Russia's Fear of NATO," *Communist and Post-Communist Studies* 51:1 (2018).

18 Sergei Yastrzhembsky, "Russophobia Still Rampant," *New York Times*, April 24, 2002.

19 Stephen Foye, "The EU's Enlargement; Russia Plays Bridesmaid," *Eurasia Daily Monitor*, May 3, 2004, www.jamestown.org.

20 "Georgia, Ukraine NATO Accession May Cause Geopolitical Shift—FM," *RIA Novosti*, June 2007.

21 Anatoly Tsyganok, "On the Consequences of Georgia's NATO Entry," Fondsk.ru, January 2, 2008, www.fondsk.ru/article.php?id= 1148.

22 For Russia's interventions in Georgia and Ukraine as shaped by Moscow's perception of geopolitical conflicts with the West, see Richard Sakwa, *Frontline Ukraine* (London: I. B. Tauris, 2015); Gerard Toal, *Near Abroad: Putin, the West and the Contest Over Ukraine and the Caucasus* (New York: Oxford University Press, 2017); Gordon M. Hahn, *Ukraine Over the Edge: Russia, the West and the New Cold War* (Jefferson: McFarland, 2018).

23 Tsygankov, "The Sources of Russia's Fear of NATO," 107–8.

24 For further analysis of post-Soviet Eurasia through the lens of Russia-West zero-sum competition, see Samuel Charap and Timothy J. Colton, *Everyone Loses: The Ukraine Crisis and the Ruinous Contest for Post-Soviet Eurasia* (London: Routledge, 2017).

25 Tuomas Forsberg and Hiski Haukkala, "The European Union," in Tsygankov, ed. *The Routledge Handbook of Russian Foreign Policy*.

26 Paul Stronski and Richard Sokolsky, "The Return of Global Russia," Carnegie Endowment for International Peace, December 14, 2017, http://carnegieendowment.org/2017/12/14/return-of-global-rus sia-analytical-framework-pub-75003.

27 Ibid. For a detailed review of Russia's Balkan priorities and actions, see Dimitar Bechev, *Rival Power: Russia in Southeast Europe* (New Haven: Yale University Press, 2017).

28 Lucan Ahmad Way and Adam Casey, "Russian Foreign Election Interventions Since 1991," PONARS Eurasia Policy Memo No. 520, March 2018.

29 Etymologically, "ukraina" is close to the Russian word "okraina," which means borderland.

30 Zbigniew Brzezinski, "Premature Partnership," *Foreign Affairs*, March/April 1994.

31 Richard Youngs, *Europe's Eastern Crisis: The Geopolitics of Asymmetry* (Cambridge: Cambridge University Press, 2017).

32 Such thinking was further confirmed by Putin's statement to the Security Council on July 22, 2014, and the Council's Secretary Nikolai Patrushev's interview in October 2014. Nikolai Patrushev, "Vtoraya kholodnaya," *Rossiyskaya Gazeta*, October 15, 2014, www.rg.ru/2014/10/15/patrushev.html.

33 Andrei P. Tsygankov, "Vladimir Putin's Last Stand: The Sources of Russia's Ukraine Policy," *Post-Soviet Affairs* 31:4 (2015).

34 Viktor Khamrayev, "Dlya Valdaiskogo kluba zakryli krymsky vopros," *Kommersant*, October 24, 2014.

35 Marlene Laruelle, *In the Name of the Nation: Nationalism and Politics in Contemporary Russia* (London: Palgrave, 2009), 114; Igor Zevelev, "Granitsy russkogo mira," *Russia in Global Affairs* 2 (2014), www.globalaffairs.ru/number/Granitcy-russkogo-mira--16582.

36 Cited in Andrei Illarionov, "The Russian Leadership's Preparations for War, 1999–2008," in Svante E. Cornell and Frederick Starr, eds. *The Guns of August 2008: Russia's War in Georgia* (New York: M. E. Sharpe, 2009), 229.

37 Vladimir Putin, "Samoopredeleniye russkogo naroda—eto poli-etnicheskaya tsivilizatsiya, skreplennaya russkim kul'turnym yadrom," *Nezavisimaya gazeta*, January 23, 2012.

38 Igor Torbakov, "'This is a Strife of Slavs Among Themselves': Understanding Russian-Ukrainian Relations as the Conflict of Contested Identities," in Klaus Bachmann and Igor Lyubachenko, eds. *The Maidan Uprising, Separatism and Foreign Intervention* (Frankfurt am Main: Peter Lang, 2014), 201.

39 Vladimir Putin, Press Conference, Kremlin.ru, March 4, 2014, http://eng.kremlin.ru/news/6763.

40 Lisa Gaufman, "Memory, Media, and Securitization: Russian Media Framing of the Ukrainian Crisis," *Journal of Soviet and Post-Soviet Politics and Society* 1:1 (2015).

41 Valentina Feklyunina, "Soft Power and Identity: Russia, Ukraine and the 'Russian World(s)'," *European Journal of International Relations* 22:4 (2015).

42 Andrei Soldatov, "Reading the World: The Internet and Political Change in Russia," *Foreign Affairs*, April 6, 2016, www.foreignaffairs.com/articles/russian-federation/2016–04–06/reading-world.

43 Michael T. Klare, "The United States and NATO are Preparing for a Major War With Russia," *Nation*, July 7, 2016.

44 Kathrin Hille and Roman Olearchyk, "White House Rejects Putin Plan for Ukraine Referendum," *Financial Times*, July 20, 2018.

45 Andrew Osborn, "Russia Seen Putting New Nuclear-Capable Missiles Along NATO Border by 2019," *Reuters*, June 23, 2016.

46 Michael Koffman, "Russian Hybrid Warfare and Other Dark Arts," *War on the Rocks*, March 11, 2016, http://warontherocks.com/2016/03/russian-hybrid-warfare-and-other-dark-arts; see also Bettina Renz and Hannah Smith, "Russia and Hybrid Warfare," available at www.helsinki.fi/aleksanteri/english/publications/presentations/papers/ap_1_2016.pdf.

47 Gaufman, "Memory, Media, and Securitization"; Andrei Soldatov and Irina Borogan, "Putin Trolls Facebook: Privacy and Moscow's New Data Laws," *Foreign Affairs*, November 3, 2015.

48 "More Ukrainians Hold Positive Views of Russia Than Negative, Poll Says," *Moscow Times*, October 10, 2018.

49 "Amid Church Rift, Kremlin Vows to 'Protect Interests' of Faithful in Ukraine," *RFE/RL*, October 12, 2018.

50 By early 2016 the conflict had claimed the lives of around 10,000 people, including over 3,000 civilians ("Death Toll in Ukraine Conflict Hits 9160, UN Says," *New York Times*, March 3, 2016, www.nytimes.com/2016/03/04/world/europe/ukraine-death-toll-

civilians.html). More than 800,000 people fled Ukraine, while the total number of refugees was over 2 million (www.euronews.com/ 2015/04/22/ukraine-crisis-has-created-more-than-2-million-refu gees-un-reports).

51 Tsygankov, "The Sources of Russia's Fear of NATO."

52 Nigel Gould-Davies, "Sanctions on Russia are Working," *Foreign Affairs*, August 22, 2018.

53 Sergei Kudelya, "Posle razmezhevaniya: kak dostich rossiysko-ukrainskogo soglasiya," *Russia in Global Affairs*, April 23, 2018, www.globalaffairs.ru/number/Posle-razmezhevaniya-19520.

Chapter 5

1 Paul Sonne and Missy Ryan, "Bolton: US Forces Will Stay in Syria Until Iran and its Proxies Depart," *Washington Post*, September 24, 2018.

2 David Ignatius, "How to Stanch Syria's Bloody Final Showdown," *Washington Post*, August 30, 2018.

3 Thomas Gibbons-Neff, "How a 4-Hour Battle Between Russian Mercenaries and US Commandos Unfolded in Syria," *New York Times*, May 24, 2018.

4 Philip Casula and Mark Katz, "The Middle East," in Tsygankov, ed. *The Routledge Handbook of Russian Foreign Policy*, 304–5.

5 For the destabilizing consequences of US military policies in the Middle East, see Andrew J. Bacevich, *America's War for the Greater Middle East: A Military History* (New York: Random House, 2016).

6 For an analysis of this strategy and challenges it poses for the US position in the region and globally, see Jakub J. Grygiel and A. Wess Mitchell, *The Unquiet Frontier: Rising Rivals, Vulnerable Allies, and the Crisis of American Power* (Princeton: Princeton University Press, 2016).

7 Loveday Morris, Ruth Eglash and Louisa Loveluck, "Israel Launches Massive Military Strike Against Iranian Targets in Syria," *Washington Post*, May 10, 2018.

8 Robert D. Crews, *For Prophet and Tsar: Islam and Empire in Russia and Central Asia* (Cambridge, MA: Harvard University Press, 2006).

9 For details see Andrei P. Tsygankov, "In the Shadow of Nikolai Danilevskii: Universalism, Particularism, and Russian Geopolitical Theory," *Europe-Asia Studies* 69:4 (2017).

10 Bruno Maçães, "Russia's New Energy Gamble," *The Cairo Review of Global Affairs*, Winter 2018, www.thecairoreview.com/essays/russias-new-energy-gamble. For Russia's views of the challenges in the Middle East, see Andrei P. Tsygankov, "La Russie et le Moyen-Orient: entre islamisme et occidentalisme," *Politique étrangère* 78:1 (2013); Casula and Katz, "the Middle East."

11 Yevgeni Primakov, *Russia and the Arabs: Behind the Scenes in the Middle East from the Cold War to the Present* (New York: Basic Books, 2009).

12 "Islam is Inseparable Part of Russia's Society and Culture—Putin," russiatoday.com, August 30, 2012.

13 Roland Dannreuther, "Russia and the Middle East: A Cold War Paradigm?," *Europe-Asia Studies* 64:3 (2012), 545; Irina Zvyagelskaya, *Beyond the "Arab Spring": Russia's Security Interests in the Middle East* (Paris: IFRI, 2012), 5.

14 For the relevance of Afghanistan in Russia's perception of the Middle East, see Dmitri Trenin, *What Russia is Up to in the Middle East* (London: Polity, 2017), chap. 1.

15 Edward Said, *Orientalism* (New York: Pantheon, 1978). Similarly ethnocentric assumptions have shaped the minds of Western scholars ever since Russia emerged as an independent power, and they remain strong today as critics of Russia frequently attack it for not embracing Western institutions and instead clinging to its own imperial and autocratic traditions. See Andrei P. Tsygankov, *Russophobia* (New York: Palgrave, 2009).

16 Gleb Bryanski, "Russia Says Action on Syria, Iran May Go Nuclear," *Reuters*, May 17, 2012.

17 Vladimir Putin, "Russia and the Changing World," *Moskovskiye novosti*, February 26, 2012.

18 Simon Tisdall, "Syria: Why Russia Changed Tack," *Guardian*, May 28, 2012.

19 James Brooke, "As Syria Unravels, Russia Tries to Bolster Future Position," *Voice of America*, December 4, 2012.

20 Transcript of the interview with the Minister of Foreign Affairs of Russia S. Lavrov on the *The Charlie Rose Show*, September 25, 2012, www.mid.ru.

21 Vladimir Kostin, "Russia Says West Reneging on Syria Deal," *Reuters*, August 15, 2012.

22 Fyodor Lukyanov, "Preventing Chaos in the Middle East," *Russia Beyond the Headlines*, www.rbth.ru, September 26, 2012.

23 Robert E. Worth, "Citing US Fears, Arab Allies Limit Syrian Rebel Aid," *New York Times,* October 6, 2012.

24 David E. Sanger, "Rebel Arms Flow is Said to Benefit Jihadists in Syria," *New York Times*, October 14, 2012.

25 Samuel Ramani, "Russia is Looking to Engage With the Taliban. Here's Why," *Washington Post*, January 15, 2018.

26 Joost Hiltermann, "Who Can Prevent a War Between Israel and Iran? Russia," *New York Times*, May 3, 2018.

27 Georgi Mirsky, "Tugoi uzel Blizhnego Vostoka," *Nezavisimaya gazeta*, February 17, 2012.

28 Cited in Julia Ioffe, "In Russia, Even Putin's Critics are OK With His Syria Policy," *The New Republic*, July 23, 2012.

29 For 9/11 conspiracies, see, for example, Alexander Dugin, ed. *Geopolitika terrora* (Moscow: "Arktogeya tsentr," 2002).

30 Victor Khamrayev, Alexander Savenko, and Irina Nagornykh, "Izborski klub predlozhit al'ternativu liberalizmu," *Kommersant*, September 10, 2012.

31 Zachary Laub and Jonathan Masters, "The Islamic State," Council on Foreign Relations, May 18, 2015, www.cfr.org/iraq/islamic-state/p14811.

32 Yelena Suponina, "Kak Yegipet opyat' stal luchshim drugom Rossiyi na Blizhnem Vostoke," *Nezavisimaya gazeta*, June 10, 2015; Anna Borshchevskaya, "Could Russia Flip Egypt?," *The National Interest*, June 21, 2018.

33 Simeon Kerr and Kathrin Hille, "Saudi Defence Minister to Meet Vladimir Putin for Talks on Syria," *Financial Times*, June 17, 2015; Will Kennedy, Elena Mazneva, and Wael Mahdi, "Russia-Saudi Plans for Super-OPEC Could Reshape Global Oil Order," *Bloomberg*, June 22, 2018.

34 Yeveniya Novikova, "Moskva i Tegeran soprotivlyayutsya sanktsiyam," *Nezavisimaya gazeta*, April 30, 2014.

35 Nikolay Kozhanov, "Understanding the Revitalization of Russian-Iranian Relations," Moscow Carnegie Center, May 5, 2015.

36 P. Bilgin and A. Bilgiç, "Turkey's 'New' Foreign Policy Toward Eurasia," *Eurasian Geography and Economics* 52:2 (2011).

37 Yury Barmin, "What's Behind the Saudi King's Historic Visit to Russia," *Moscow Times*, October 4, 2017.

38 Konstantin Truyevtsev, "Rossiya-Azerbaijan-Iran: kontury trekhstoronnei strategiyi," *Valdai Club*, November 2, 2017.

39 Andrei Kolesnikov, "Na poltona blizhe," *Kommersant*, May 12, 2015.

40 "Iran Nuclear Talks: 'Historic' Agreement Struck," BBC News, July 14, 2015, www.bbc.com/news/world-middle-east-33518524.

41 Amanda Taub, "Putin Has a Big Problem in Syria That No One is Talking About," vox.com, September 30, 2015, www.vox.com/2015/9/30/9426333/putin-syria-russia-problem.

42 Marianna Belenkaya, "After Two Years in Syria, What's Next for Russia?," *Al-Monitor*, October 5, 2017, www.al-monitor.com/pulse/originals/2017/10/russia-syria-campaign-two-years-cost-future-assad.html.

43 Dmitry Adamsky, "Putin's Game in Syria. Why a Withdrawal Does Not Mean a Pullout," *Foreign Affairs*, April 3, 2016.

44 Trenin, *What Russia is Up to in the Middle East*, 86.

45 Several observers found that the outcome of the Syria conflict was reminiscent of an informal partition. See Jonathan Spyer, "Putin's Endgame in Syria Has Arrived," foreignpolicy.com, May 24, 2018; Mark Langfan, "When Putin Drops Hints, the West Should Listen," *Israel National News*, June 13, 2018.

46 Holly Ellyatt, "Russian Military Threatens Action Against the US in Syria," CNBC, March 13, 2018, www.cnbc.com/2018/03/13/russia-military-threatens-action-against-the-us-in-syria.html.

47 "Russian Support Gave Assad Half of Syria: Study," *AFP*, May 15, 2018.

Chapter 6

1 Lyle J. Goldstein, "What Russia's Vostok-18 Exercise with China Means," *The National Interest*, September 5, 2018.

2 Wesley Morgan, "Russia's Military Dalliance With China," *Politico*, September 15, 2018.

3 Marcin Kacsmarski, "The Decreasing Asymmetry in Russian-Chinese Relations," *Finnish Institute of International Affairs*, February 28, 2018, www.fiia.fi/en/publication/the-decreasing-asymmetry-in-russia-china-relations.

4 For a summary of US thinking about China, see especially Graham Allison, *Destined for War: Can America and China Escape Thucydides's Trap?* (New York: Houghton Mifflin Harcourt, 2017).

5 For a discussion of US strategic options, see, for example, *Avoiding War: Containment, Competition, and Cooperation in US-China Relations* (Washington, DC: Brookings Institute, 2017); Aaron Friedberg, "It is America's Move in Its Competition with China," *War on the Rocks*, June 18, 2018, https://warontherocks.com/2018/06/it-is-americas-move-in-its-competition-with-china.

6 "China Must Prepare for US' Containment," *Global Times*, July 4, 2018, www.globaltimes.cn/content/1109537.shtml.

7 "China is Laying the Groundwork for a Post-American World Order," *Washington Post*, July 27, 2018.

8 Jane Pong, Cale Tilford, Joanna S. Kao, Ed Crooks, Robin Kwong, and Tom Hancock, "What's at Stake in US-China Trade War," *Financial Times*, July 19, 2018.

9 Eugene Rumer, Richard Sokolsky, and Paul Stronski, "US Policy Toward Central Asia 3.0," Carnegie Endowment for

International Peace, January 25, 2016, http://carnegieendowment. org/2016/01/25/u.s.-policy-toward-central-asia-3.0-pub-62556.

10 Stephen Blank, "Central Asia: Trump's Newfound Ally?," *Center for Global Policy*, January 17, 2018, www.cgpolicy.org/articles/central-asia-trumps-newfound-ally.

11 Leslie Gelb, and Dimitri Simes, "A New Anti-American Axis?," *New York Times*, July 6, 2013.

12 See especially "Narody mezhdu tsivilizatsiyami," and "Geopolitika dlya 'yevraziyskoi Atlantidy'," in Vadim Tsymburski, *Ostrov Rossiya* (Moscow: Rosspen, 2006).

13 Alexander Lukin and Vladimir Yakunin, "Eurasian Integration and the Development of Asiatic Russia," *Journal of Eurasia Studies* 9 (2018).

14 Ben Aris, "Russia Looks East for Business; Cool on US-led Asia Trade Group," *Business New Europe*, August 30, 2012.

15 For a critical Russian view of this perception, see Alexander Lukin, *China and Russia: The New Rapprochement* (London: Polity, 2018).

16 Dmitriy Trenin, "Zaglyadyvaya na pyat' let vpered," Moscow Carnegie Center, March 30, 2018.

17 Deborah Welch Larson and Alexei Shevchenko, *Quest for Status: Chinese and Russian Foreign Policy* (New Haven: Yale University Press, 2019).

18 Vladimir Putin, "An Asia-Pacific Growth Agenda," *Wall Street Journal*, September 6, 2012.

19 Ibid.

20 Russian experts have published a series of reports on their country's pivot to Asia. See, for example, *K velikomu okeanu 5: ot povorota na Vostok k Bol'shoi Yevraziyi* (Moscow: Valdai Discussion Club, September 2017).

21 Marcin Kaczmarski and Witold Rodkiewicz, "Russia's Greater Eurasia and China's New Silk Road: Adaptation Instead of Competition," *OSW Commentary*, July 27, 2016, www.osw.waw. pl/en/publikacje/osw-commentary/2016-07-21/russias-greater-eurasia-and-chinas-new-silk-road-adaptation.

22 For the importance of the communist legacy in Russia and China's identity construction, see especially Gilbert Rozman, *The Sino-Russian Challenge to the World Order* (Woodrow Wilson Center Press with Stanford University Press, 2014), and Jeanne L. Wilson, "Russia and China Respond to Soft Power," *Politics* 35:3–4 (2015).

23 Aglaya Snetkov and Marc Lanteigne, "'The Loud Dissenter and its Cautious Partner'—Russia, China, Global Governance and Humanitarian Intervention," *International Relations of the Asia-Pacific* 15 (2015).

24 That China views US hegemony as the biggest threat was also evident in Beijing's refusal to formally condemn Russia's intervention in Georgia in August 2008 or its annexation of Crimea in March 2014.

25 Mikhail Korostikov, "Kitai ne risknul svyazyvatsya s rublem," *Kommersant,* 27 December, 2018.

26 E. Wishnick, *Russia, China, and the United States in Central Asia,* Carlisle (PA), Strategic Studies Institute, US Army War College, February 2009, 41.

27 Marcin Kaczmarski, "The Asymmetric Partnership? Russia's Turn to China," *International Politics* 53:3 (2016), 2.

28 Ibid., 12.

29 Edward Schatz, "How Western Disengagement Enabled Uzbekistan's 'Spring' and How to Keep it Going," PONARS Policy Memo No. 531, June 2018.

30 Alexander Cooley, *Great Games, Local Rules* (Oxford: Oxford University Press, 2011).

31 The expression "pivotal" states is that of Zbigniew Brzezinski; see his *The Grand Chessboard* (New York: Basic Books, 1997).

32 For an analysis of Central Asian political systems and their strategies for survival, see John Heathershaw and Edward Schatz, eds. *Paradox of Power: The Logics of State Weakness in Eurasia* (Pittsburg: University of Pittsburg Press, 2017); and Alexander Cooley and John Heathershaw, *Dictators Without Borders: Power and Money in Central Asia* (New Haven: Yale University Press, 2017).

33 Kathleen Collins, "The Logic of Clan Politics: Evidence from the Central Asian Trajectories," *World Politics* 56 (2004).

34 Emil Kavalski, ed. *Stable Outside, Fragile Inside? Post-Soviet Statehood in Central Asia* (Abingdon: Routledge, 2010).

35 Yevgenii Minchenko, Andrei Kazantsev, Kirill Petrov, and Nikolai Murashkin, *Otsenka politicheskikh riskov* (Moscow: Minchenko Consulting, February 2015), 8.

36 World Bank, *Growth, Poverty, and Inequality* (Washington, DC: The World Bank, 2005).

37 Mariya Y. Omelicheva, "Central Asia," in Tsygankov, ed. *The Routledge Handbook of Russian Foreign Policy*. This negative economic development led some analysts to conclude that Central Asia remains peripheral to Russia's Asia pivot. See Arkady Dubnov, "Reflecting on a Quarter Century of Russia's Relations With Central Asia," Moscow Carnegie Center, April 19, 2018.

38 Sébastien Peyrouse, "Discussing China: Sinophilia and Sinophobia in Central Asia," *Journal of Eurasian Studies* 7 (2016), 16.

39 Ibid., 21–2.

40 On China's view of regionalism and its relations with its neighbors, see Zhang Feng, "Regionalization in the Tianxia?," in E. Kavalski, ed. *China and the Global Politics of Regionalization* (Farnham: Ashgate, 2009); and Marcin Kaczmarski, *"Silk globalization": China's Vision of International Order* (Warsaw: Centre for Eastern Studies, 2016).

41 Viktoriya Panfilova, "Bakiyev pozval amerikanskikh sovetnikov," *Nezavisimaya gazeta,* October 4, 2005.

42 F. William Engdahl, "China Lays Down Gauntlet in Energy War," *Asia Times,* December 21, 2005.

43 In November 2005, Russia and Uzbekistan even signed a new military alliance agreement. Roger McDermott, "Putin Pledges to Back Up Karimov in a Crisis," *Eurasia Daily Monitor,* November 16, 2005.

44 "Moscow Accuses 'Outside Extremists'," *RFE/RL Newsline,* May 16, 2005, www.rferl.org.

45 Chris Buckley, "China 'Honors' Uzbek Crackdown," *International Herald Tribune,* May 27, 2005.

46 "US Asked Russia to Send Troops to Kyrgyzstan at Height of Rioting," *Interfax*, September 6, 2010.

47 M. K. Bhadrakumar, "US, Russia Fail to Grip Kyrgyz Helm," *Asia Times*, June 26, 2010.

48 Ibid.

49 M. K. Bhadrakumar, "China Wary of US-Russia Nuclear Embrace," *Asia Times*, March 26, 2010.

50 Victoria Panfilova, "Karimov otkazal Vashingtonu," *Nezavisimaya gazeta*, September 2, 2015, www.ng.ru/cis/2015-09-02/7_karimov. html.

51 Schatz, "How Western Disengagement Enabled Uzbekistan's 'Spring'."

Chapter 7

1 Carol Morello and Anton Troianovski, "As U.N. Security Council Meets on Syria, Haley Accuses Russia of Lies and Coverups," *Washington Post*, April 13, 2018; Pamela Falk, "Haley Calls Out Russia, China for Skirting UN Sanctions Against North Korea," CBS News, September 17, 2018.

2 Joseph Nye, *Soft Power: The Means to Success in World Politics* (New York: Public Affairs, 2004).

3 For analyses of Freedom House's inherent neoconservative bias, see Diego Giannone, "Political and Ideological Aspects in the Measurement of Democracy: The Freedom House Case," *Democratization* 17:1 (2010), and Andrei P. Tsygankov and David Parker, "The Securitization of Democracy: Freedom House Ratings of Russia," *European Security* 24:1 (2015).

4 Kenneth A. Osgood, "Hearts and Minds: The Unconventional Cold War," *Journal of Cold War Studies* 4:2 (2002).

5 William Pfaff, "Redefining World Power," *Foreign Affairs*, January/ February 1991, 48.

6 Country Reports on Human Rights Practices—2007, US Department of State, March 11, 2008, www.state.gov/g/drl/rls/hrrpt/2007/ 100581.htm.

7 Ruth Deyermond, "Reset or Disconnected? Russian Media and Internet Freedom as a Site of Contestation in US-Russia Relations and US Domestic Politics," Paper presented at the International Studies Association annual meeting, April 1–4, 2012, San Diego.

8 "Hillary Clinton Declares International Information War," Russia Today, March 2, 2011, www.rt.com/news/information-war-media-us.

9 James Carden, "Uncle Sam Got a Shiny New Propaganda Bullhorn for Christmas: A New Partnership is Turning Radio Free Europe Into an Anti-Russia Propaganda Machine," *The Nation*, January 5, 2016.

10 "It's Worse Than You Thought: The 'Kremlin Troll Army' Exposed," Sputnik, March 28, 2015.

11 Natalya Tsvetkova, "Publichnaya diplomatiya SShA," *Mezhdunarodnyye protsessy* 13:3 (2015).

12 Ed Royce, "Countering Putin's Information Weapons of War," *Wall Street Journal*, April 15, 2015.

13 Mike Eckel, "US Congressional Press Office Strips RT of Credentials," *RFE/RL*, November 30, 2017, www.rferl.org/a/u-s-congress-rt-press-credentials-stripped/28886960.html.

14 "Hefty & Heftier: US Lawmakers Push Trump to Spend More on Russian 'Propaganda Fight'," RT, March 16, 2018, www.rt.com/usa/421527-lawmakers-ask-money-propaganda.

15 Legvold, *Return to Cold War*; Cohen, *Why Cold War Again?*

16 Tsygankov, *Russia's Foreign Policy*, 4th edn, chapter 3.

17 Andrei Kozyrev, "Rossiya v novom mire," *Mezhdunarodnaya zhizn'* 3–4 (1992), 93.

18 Vladimir Putin, "Rossiya na rubezhe tysyacheletiy," *Nezavisimaya gazeta*, December 31, 1999.

19 See Tsygankov, *Russophobia*.

20 Gary Hart, "Don't Lose Russia," *The National Interest*, March–April 2007.

21 Stephen Cohen, "New Cold War Between United States and Russia," *The Charlie Rose Show*, June 28, 2006, excerpt at Johnson's Russia List, July 2, 2006, No. 149.

22 Stephen F. Cohen, *The Failed Crusade: America and the Tragedy of Post-Communist Russia* (New York: Norton, 2001).

23 Ivan Katchanovski and Alicen R. Morley, "The Politics of US Television Coverage of Post-Communist Countries," *Problems of Post-Communism* 59:1 (2012); Nicolas Ross Smith, "The Re-emergence of a 'Mirror Image' in West-Russia Relations?," *International Politics* 55:5 (2018).

24 Andrei P. Tsygankov, *The Dark Double: US Media, Russia, and the Politics of Values* (Oxford: Oxford University Press, 2019), chapter 3.

25 Anne Applebaum, "War in Europe is Not a Hysterical Idea," *Washington Post*, August 29, 2014; Timothy Snyder, "Putin's New Nostalgia," *New York Review of Books*, November 10, 2014.

26 "Putin's Disinformation Matrix," *Wall Street Journal*, editorial, November 15, 2014.

27 Ann Applebaum and Edward Lucas, "Putin's News Network of Lies is Just the Start," Newsweek.com, August 11, 2015. See also David J. Kramer, "The West Should Take on the Putin P.R. machine," *Washington Post*, October 25, 2015.

28 Carden, "Uncle Sam Got a Shiny New Propaganda Bullhorn."

29 For analyses of the two-tier media system and its relations to the state, see J. A. Dunn, "Lottizzazione Russian Style: Russia's Two-tier Media System," *Europe-Asia Studies* 66:9 (2014).

30 See http://en.kremlin.ru/events/president/news/55882.

31 Daniel Kennedy, "Who's Afraid of Russia Today? Is RT (Formerly Russia Today) Really as Dangerous or as Effective as Its Critics Claim?," www.opendemocracy.net, December 5, 2014.

32 Ibid.

33 "It's Worse Than You Thought," Sputnik, March 28, 2015; Nicole Gaouette, "Sanctions-Strapped Russia Outguns the US in Information War. Moscow Drowns out Voice of America, and Facts Are a Casualty," *Bloomberg*, April 2, 2015.

34 Art Swift, "In US, Record 68% View Russia as Unfriendly or an Enemy," www.gallup.com, March 27, 2014.

35 See, for example, "Chuzhikh ne spasayem," *Nezavisimaya gazeta*, editorial, September 17, 2015.

36 "Amerikanskaya Stavka v igre protiv Kremlya," *Nezavisimaya gazeta*, editorial, June 4, 2014.

37 "Za mesto pod solntsem," *Nezavisimaya gazeta*, editorial, April 12, 2012.

38 Peter Rutland, "Trump, Putin, and the Future of US-Russian Relations," *Slavic Review*, August 2017.

39 For a detailed analysis of Russian coverage of Trump, see Laurence Bogoslaw, ed. *Russians on Trump: Press Coverage and Commentary* (Minneapolis: East View Press, 2018).

40 Vladimir Putin, Meeting with the Russian Federation Ambassadors, Moscow, Foreign Ministry, July 9, 2012.

41 Sirke Mäkinen, "In Search of the Status of an Educational Great Power? Analysis of Russia's Educational Diplomacy Discourse," *Problems of Post-Communism* 63:3 (2016).

42 Kathleen Hall Jamieson, *Cyberwar: How Russia Helped Elect Trump* (Oxford: Oxford University Press, 2018).

43 Some scholars relate this polarization to the country's belated democratization and the emergence of a divided Congress in the 1970s. See Robert Mickey, Steven Levitsky, and Lucan Ahmad Way, "Is America Still Safe for Democracy?," *Foreign Affairs*, April 17, 2017.

44 Legvold, *Return to Cold War*.

45 Stephen M. Walt, "The Collapse of the Liberal World Order," *Foreign Policy*, June 26, 2016.

Chapter 8

1 Hutchinson said she had not meant to suggest an American pre-emptive strike against Russia. See David E. Sanger, "'Take Out' Russian Missiles? US Envoy's Remark Spurs Anger, and Pullback," *New York Times*, October 2, 2018.

2 See, for example, George P. Shultz, William J. Perry, Henry A. Kissinger and Sam Nunn, "Toward a Nuclear-Free World," *Wall Street Journal*, January 15, 2008.

3 As cited in Wolfgang K. H. Panofsky, "Nuclear Insecurity," *Foreign Affairs*, September/October 2007.

4 *Rebuilding America's Defenses: Strategy, Forces and Resources for a New Century* (Washington, September 2000). For further analysis and background, see Tsygankov, *Russophobia*, chap. 6.

5 Drake Bennett, "Critical Mess," *The American Prospect*, July 3, 2003.

6 As quoted in William Endgahl, "V. Putin and the Geopolitics of the New Cold War," February 18, 2007, www.psj.ru/saver_guardian/detail.php?ID=7424.

7 On March 26, 2004, forty-nine US generals and admirals signed an Open Letter to the President (Endgahl, "V. Putin and the Geopolitics of the New Cold War").

8 Mark B. Schneider, "Russia's Nuclear Weapons Policy," *Real Clear Defense*, April 28, 2017, www.realcleardefense.com/articles/2017/04/28/russian_nuclear_weapons_policy_111261.html.

9 Matthew J. Belvedere, "Trump Asks Why US Can't Use Nukes," August 3, 2016, www.cnbc.com/2016/08/03/trump-asks-why-us-cant-use-nukes-msnbcs-joe-scarborough-reports.html.

10 David E. Sanger and William J. Broad, "To Counter Russia, US Signals Nuclear Arms are Back in a Big Way," *New York Times*, February 5, 2018.

11 Helene Cooper, "Pence Advances Plan to Create a Space Force," *New York Times*, August 8, 2018.

12 For a review of Russia's position, see Bruno Tertrais, "Russia's Nuclear Policy: Worrying for the Wrong Reasons," *Survival* 60:2 (2018).

13 National Security Strategy, May 2010, 39, www.whitehouse.gov/sites/default/files/rss_viewer/national_security_strategy.pdf.

14 Tsvetkova, "Publichnaya diplomatiya SShA."

15 Deyermond, "Reset or Disconnected?," 5; Tsvetkova, "Publichnaya diplomatiya SShA," 124.

16 Cited in Julien Nocetti, "Cyber Power," in Tsygankov, ed. *The Routledge Handbook of Russian Foreign Policy*, 192.

17 For details see the chapter on values and information rivalry.

18 David E. Sanger, "Pentagon Puts Cyberwarriors on the Offensive, Increasing the Risk of Conflict," *New York Times*, June 18, 2018.

19 Ibid.

20 National Cyber Strategy of the United States of America, White House, September 2018, www.whitehouse.gov/wp-content/up loads/2018/09/National-Cyber-Strategy.pdf.

21 Kenneth T. Walsh, "Trump-Putin Cyber Deal Blasted. Republicans Criticize Proposed Cyber Security Deal," USNews.com, July 10, 2017.

22 Yelena Chernenko, "Kak sorvalis' rossiysko-amerikanskiye perego-vory po kiberbezopasnosti," *Kommersant*, March 3, 2018.

23 Dustin Volz, "Trump, Seeking to Relax Rules on US Cyberattacks, Reverses Obama Directive," *Wall Street Journal*, August 15, 2018.

24 "Putin Suggests New Missile Shield Site," *Associated Press*, June 8, 2007.

25 "Putin Compares Missile Defense to Cuban Missile Crisis," *RFE/RL Newsline*, October 29, 2007.

26 Sergei L. Loiko, "Russia Reacts Coolly to Obama's Nuclear Proposals," *Los Angeles Times*, June 19, 2013.

27 Bryan Bender, "Leaked Document: Putin Lobbied Trump on Arms Control," *Politico*, August 7, 2018, www.politico.com/story/2018/08/07/putin-trump-arms-control-russia-724718.

28 Kristin Ven Bruusgaard, "Russian Strategic Deterrence," *Survival* 58:4 (2016), 9–10.

29 See especially Dmitry (Dima) Adamsky, "From Moscow With Coercion: Russian Deterrence Theory and Strategic Culture," *Journal of Strategic Studies* 41 (2018).

30 Ibid., 45.

31 See http://m.rg.ru/2015/12/31/nac-bezopasnost-site-dok.html for details of Russia-NATO interaction; see also Tsygankov, "The Sources of Russia's Fear of NATO."

32 Maxim Starchak, "Severoatlanticheski razlad," *Kommersant-Vlast'*, May 30, 2016.

33 Pavel Baev, "The Nuclear Dimension of Russia's Military Power," in Natasha Kuhrt and Valentina Feklyunina, eds. *Assessing Russia's Power: A Report* (King's College, London, and Newcastle University, 2017), 14–15.

34 Evgeny Buzhinsky and Alexander Khramchikhin, "Russia Will Not Lose From the Denunciation of the INF Treaty," *Valdai Discussion Club*, June 28, 2017.

35 Steven Pifer, "Arms Control, Security Cooperation and US-Russian Relations," Valdai Paper No. 78, November 17, 2017, http://val daiclub.com/a/valdai-papers/arms-control-security-cooperation-and-u-s-russian.

36 Vladimir Mukhin, "Rossiya razmestit v Karibskom more voyen-nuyu bazu," *Nezavisimaya gazeta*, December 11, 2018.

37 Interview with Sergey Karaganov, "Russian Foreign Policy: 'We Are Smarter, Stronger and More Determined'," *Spiegel*, July 16, 2016, www.spiegel.de/international/world/interview-with-putin-for eign-policy-advisor-sergey-karaganov-a-1102629.html.

38 Vladimir Isachenkov, "Putin Boasts of New Missile's Capability," *Associated Press*, January 31, 2006.

39 "Russia to Re-equip its New Mobile ICBMs With Multiple Warheads," *RIA Novosti*, December 15, 2007.

40 Vladimir Putin, Presidential Address to the Federal Assembly, March 1, 2018, http://en.kremlin.ru/events/president/news/56957.

41 Amanda Macias, "China and Russia are 'Aggressively Pursuing' Hypersonic Weapons, and the US Can't Defend Against Them, Top Nuclear Commander Says," CNBC, August 8, 2018, www.cnbc.com/2018/08/08/us-nuclear-commander-russia-and-china-are-not-our-friends.html.

42 Eugene Rumer, "A Farewell to Arms … Control," Carnegie Endowment for International Peace, April 17, 2018.

43 Nocetti, "Cyber Power," 190–1.

44 For the text of the US-China cyber agreement, see https://fas.org/sgp/crs/row/IN10376.pdf.

45 Cory Bennett, "Russia, China Unite With Major Cyber Pact," *The Hill*, May 8, 2015.

46 Nocetti, "Cyber Power"; Brandon Valeriano, Benjamin Jensen, and Ryan C. Maness, *Cyber Strategy: The Evolving Character of Power and Coercion* (New York: Oxford University Press, 2018).

47 Andrei Tsygankov, "Russia's (Limited) Information War on the West," *Public Diplomacy*, June 5, 2017; Charles Ziegler, "International Dimensions of Electoral Processes: Russia, the USA, and the 2016 Elections," *International Politics*, October 2017.

48 John Hudson, "Russia Sought a Broad Reset with Trump, Secret Document Shows," Buzzfeed.com, September 12, 2017.

49 Chernenko, "Kak sorvalis' rossiysko-amerikanskiye peregovory."

50 For assessments of Russia's cyber power and strategy, see Brandon Valeriano and Ryan Maness, *Russia's Coercive Diplomacy: Energy, Cyber, and Maritime Policy as New Sources of Power* (New York: Palgrave, 2015), and *Russia: Military Power. Building a Military to Support Great Power Aspirations* (Washington, DC: Defense Intelligence Agency, 2017).

51 Nocetti, "Cyber Power," 185.

52 For proposal to cooperate in the cyber area, see Thomas Remington, Chris Spirito, Elena Chernenko, Oleg Demidov, and Vitaly Kabernik, *Toward US-Russia Bilateral Cooperation in the Sphere of Cybersecurity* (Boston: Harvard University, Working Group on the Future of US-Russia Relations, Paper 7, May 2016).

53 Jon Wolsthal, "It's Not Too Late to Save the INF Treaty," *Foreign Policy*, December 7, 2018.

54 Mikhail Gorbachev and George P. Shultz, "We Participated in INF Negotiations. Abandoning it Threatens Our Very Existence," *Washington Post*, December 5, 2018.

55 For analysis of Russia as a "near peer competitor" including in military areas, see Matthew R. Slater, Michael Purcell, and Andrew M. Del Gaudio, eds. *Considering Russia: Emergence of a Near Peer Competitor* (Quantico, VA: Marine Corps University, 2017).

Chapter 9

1 Brzezinski, *The Grand Chessboard*.

2 F. William Engdahl, "The Emerging Russian Giant," *Asia Times Online*, October 24 and 25, 2006.

3 Michael T. Klare, *Blood and Oil: The Dangers and Consequences of America's Growing Petroleum Dependency* (New York: Holt, 2004), 59.

4 Ariel Cohen, "US Interest and Central Asia Energy Security," *The Heritage Tribune*, November 26, 2006, www.heritage.org/Research/RussiaandEurasia/bg1984.cfm.

5 Yukos's negotiations with ExxonMobil and ChevronTexaco took place in July 2003 following Khodorkovsky's meeting with Vice-President Dick Cheney (Engdahl, "The Emerging Russian Giant.").

6 Walter Russell Mead, "Trump's Path to Mount Rushmore," *The American Interest*, November 27, 2016.

7 Agnia Grigas, *The New Geopolitics of Natural Gas* (Cambridge MA: Harvard University Press, 2017), 4–5.

8 For a scholarly justification of this approach, see, for example, Robert D. Blackwill and Jennifer M. Harris, *War by Other Means: Geoeconomics and Statecraft* (Cambridge MA: Harvard University Press, 2016).

9 For details, see chapter 6 of Tsygankov, *Russophobia*.

10 A. Arbatov, M. Belova, and V. Feygin, "Russian Hydrocarbons and World Markets," *Russia in Global Affairs* 1 (2006).

11 The quotation is from the Foreign Ministry report "A Review of the Russian Federation's Foreign Policy" ("Obzor vneshnei politiki Rossiyskoi federatsiyi"), March 27, 2007, at www.mid.ru. Russia's foreign policy documents have embraced the notion of multipolarity since the late 1990s.

12 Vladimir Putin, "Poslaniye Prezidenta Federal'nomu Sobraniyu Rossiyskoy Federatsii," *Mezhdunarodnaya zhizn'* 5 (2002), 4–5.

13 Robert L. Larsson, *Russia's Energy Policy: Security Dimensions and Russia's Reliability as an Energy Supplier* (Stockholm, 2006), 58.

14 Richard Sakwa, *Putin and the Oligarch: The Khodorkovsky-Yukos Affair* (London: I. B. Tauris, 2014).

15 For analyses of Russia's energy strategy, see Stylianos A. Sotiriou, *Russian Energy Strategy in the European Union, the Former Soviet Union Region, and China* (Lanham: Lexington, 2015); Tracey German, "Russian's Energy Power," in Kuhrt and Feklyunina, eds. *Assessing Russia's Power*.

16 Will Kennedy, Elena Mazneva, and Wael Mahdi, "Russia-Saudi Plans for Super-OPEC Could Reshape Global Oil Order," *Bloomberg*, June 22, 2018.

17 Mikhail A. Molchanov, "The Eurasian Economic Union," in Tsygankov, ed. *The Routledge Handbook of Russian Foreign Policy*.

18 "US Punishes Key Putin Allies Over Worldwide 'Malign Activity'," BBC News, April 6, 2018, www.bbc.com/news/world-us-canada-43672190.

19 Tatiana Mitrova, "Western Sanctions on Russia's Oil and Gas Sector: A Damage Assessment," Carnegie Moscow Center, July 25, 2018, https://carnegie.ru/commentary/76909.

20 Ibid. Some experts estimate that even the short-term cost of US sanctions may be as high as $150 billion. See Ben Aris, "What's the Cost of US Sanctions on Russia?," Intellinews.com, April 17, 2018.

21 Richard Connolly, "The Empire Strikes Back: Economic Statecraft and the Securitization of Political Economy in Russia," *Europe-Asia Studies* 68:4 (2016), 9.

22 Jacob Poushter, "Russians Say Their Government Did Not Try to Influence US Presidential Election," Pew Research Center, August 21, 2018, www.pewglobal.org/2018/08/21/russians-say-their-gov ernment-did-not-try-to-influence-u-s-presidential-election.

23 Chris Miller, "The Surprising Success of Putinomics," *Foreign Affairs*, February 7, 2018.

24 Richard Connolly, *Russia's Response to Sanctions: How Western Economic Statecraft is Reshaping Political Economy in Russia* (Cambridge: Cambridge University Press, 2018).

25 Masha Hedberg, "The Target Strikes Back: Explaining Counter-sanctions and Russia's Strategy of Differentiated Retaliation," *Post-Soviet Affairs* 33:1 (2018), 36.

26 Tom DiChristopher and Sam Meredith, "OPEC and Allies Agree to Cut Oil Production by 1.2 Million Barrels Per Day," CNBC.com, December 7, 2018.

27 Fred Weir, "After Four Years of Western Sanctions, Russia Digs in for Long Haul," *Christian Science Monitor*, May 18, 2018.

28 For Russia's view of sanctions, see Ivan N. Timofeyev, *Sanktsiyi protiv Rossiyi: napravleniya eskalatsiyi i politika protivodeystviya* (Moscow: Russian Council on International Affairs, 2018).

29 Emily Goldberg, "Medvedev: US Sanctions Against Russian Banks Would be 'Declaration of Economic War'," *Politico*, August 10, 2018.

30 Connolly, *Russia's Response to Sanctions*.

31 Edward Fishman, "The Senate Just Passed a Monumental New Russia Sanctions Bill—Here's What's In It," *The Atlantic Council*, June 14, 2017, www.atlanticcouncil.org/blogs/ukrainealert/the-sen ate-just-passed-a-monumental-new-russia-sanctions-bill-here-s-what-s-in-it.

32 Mitrova, "Western Sanctions on Russia's Oil and Gas Sector."

33 Wolfgang Ischinger, "Why Europeans Oppose the Russia Sanctions Bill," *Wall Street Journal*, July 17, 2017.

34 Ibid.

35 Boris Barkanov, "Natural Gas," in Tsygankov, ed. *The Routledge Handbook of Russian Foreign Policy*, 143.

36 Vladimir Soldatkin and Oksana Kobzeva, "Russia Offers to Sell Gas to Saudi Arabia from Yamal LNG," *Reuters*, December 8, 2017.

37 Fred Weir, "Russia Woos a Europe Feuding With US Over Tariffs, Iran," *Christian Science Monitor*, May 31, 2018.

38 Yuri Barsukov, "'Turetski potok' proydet cherez Bolgariyu," *Kommersant*, May 30, 2018.

39 For background on the South Stream's initial failure and Russia's gas strategy in southeast Europe, see Dimitar Bechev, *Rival Power: Russia in Southeast Europe* (New Haven: Yale University Press, 2017), 200–10.

40 Bojan Pancevski and Emre Peker, "US Opposition to Pipeline Hangs Over Meeting Between Putin and Merkel," *Wall Street Journal*, August 18, 2018.

41 "US Warns of Sanctions Risk for Firms Invested in Russian Pipeline," *Reuters*, July 11, 2018, www.reuters.com/article/us-nato-summit-nordstream/u-s-warns-of-sanctions-risk-for-firms-inves ted-in-russian-pipeline-idUSKBN1K12X6.

42 Pavel Tarasenko, Dmitri Butrin, and Anna Osetrova, "SShA pereshli ot slov k sanktsiyam," *Kommersant*, August 6, 2018, www.kommer sant.ru/doc/3707074.

43 Thomas Wonder, "Why Russian Domestic Politics Makes US Sanctions Less Effective," *War on the Rocks*, December 7, 2018.

44 Lindsay Mackenzie, "The US Sanction on Russia Muddle," Intellinews.com, June 23, 2018.

45 Avantika Chilkoti, "US Sanctions Give Russian Economy an Unintended Boost," *Wall Street Journal*, October 16, 2018.

46 Nikos Tsafos, "A US Gas War With Russia? The Realities of the Global Energy Market," *Foreign Affairs*, May 16, 2016.

Chapter 10

1 Barry R. Posen, "The Rise of Illiberal Hegemony: Trump's Surprising Grand Strategy," *Foreign Affairs*, March/April 2018, www.foreign affairs.com/articles/2018–02–13/rise-illiberal-hegemony.

2 *Strategiya dlya Rossiyi: Tezisy rabochei gruppy Soveta po vneshnei i oboronnoi politike*, Moscow, May 2016, thesis 3.7.

3 Leonid Bershidsky, "The Maria Butina Case is Not About Spying," *Bloomberg*, December 14, 2018.

4 Geoffrey Roberts, "Trump Didn't Betray America. He Wants to Restore the Old US-Russia Alliance," *Fortune*, July 19, 2018, http:// fortune.com/2018/07/19/trump-didnt-betray-america-he-wants-to-restore-the-old-u-s-russia-alliance.

5 Anatoliy Komrakov, "Byudzhet strany vse bol'she pokhodit na predvoyennyi," *Nezavisimaya gazeta*, November 15, 2017.

6 Sergei Karaganov, "Rossiyi predstoyit vyigrat' mir," *Natsional'nyi bankovskiy zhurnal*, March 22, 2017, http://nbj.ru/publs/aktual-naja-tema/2017/03/22/rossii-predstoit-vyigrat-mir/index.html.

7 Marlene Laruelle, "Isolation and Reconquista: Russia's Toolkit as a Constrained Great Power," *Russia Matters*, December 12, 2018.

8 Richard Connolly and Mathieu Boulegue, "Russia's Military: More Bark Than Bite," *The National Interest*, May 23, 2018.

Index